Move Along, Please

Land's End to John O'Groats by Bus

Mark Mason

rh
BOOKS

Published by Random House Books 2013

2 4 6 8 10 9 7 5 3 1

Copyright © Mark Mason 2013

Mark Mason has asserted his right under the Copyright, Designs
and Patents Act, 1988, to be identified as the author of this work

First published in Great Britain in 2013 by
Random House Books
Random House, 20 Vauxhall Bridge Road
London SW1V 2SA

www.randomhouse.co.uk

Addresses for companies within The Random House Group Limited can be found at:
www.randomhouse.co.uk/offices.htm

The Random House Group Limited Reg. No. 954009

A CIP catalogue record for this book
is available from the British Library

ISBN 9781847947109

The Random House Group Limited supports the Forest Stewardship
Council® (FSC®), the leading international forest-certification organisation.
All our titles that are printed on Greenpeace-approved FSC®-certified paper
carry the FSC® logo. Our paper procurement policy can be found at:
www.randomhouse.co.uk/environment

Typeset in Fournier MT by SX Composing DTP Ltd.

Printed and bound by CPI Group (UK) Ltd, Croydon, CR0 4YY

FINISH

John O'Groats
Wick *Stayed over*
Dunbeath
Helmsdale
Dornoch

Inverness
Grantown
Aviemore

SCOTLAND

Perth

Glasgow   Edinburgh

North
Sea

Stayed over
Visited on route
Other main city

Cumnock
Thornhill
Dumfries   Gretna
Carlisle   Newcastle
Penrith
Keswick
Kendal
Kirkby Lonsdale
Settle   Ilkley
Skipton   Leeds
Wakefield
Manchester   Barnsley
Sheffield
Liverpool   Chesterfield
Nottingham
Burton-upon-Trent   Derby
Lichfield
Birmingham
WALES   ENGLAND
Worcester
Upton-on-Severn   Cambridge
Gloucester   Tewkesbury
Dursley
Cardiff   Oxford
Bristol
Wells   London
Taunton
Tiverton   Southampton
Exeter
Wadebridge
Bodmin
Truro   St Austell
Land's
End   Penzance
START

0   25   50   75   100 miles
0   50   100   150 kilometres

Introduction

Sometimes you want to be freed from speed. Sometimes slow is the way to go.

I'm standing here at Land's End, thinking of the different ways I could get to John O'Groats. If I flew there I could do it by tonight. If I drove, on those big, fast motorways, it'd probably take until sometime tomorrow. But then I wouldn't see anything, would I? Well, that's not quite true – in the first case I'd see the inside of a plane and some clouds, and in the second a load of identical motorway service stations and the odd sheep. In neither case, though, would I see what I'm trying to see: Britain. My home country. The land I've lived in for every one of my 41 years, yet which still – it's struck me lately – remains largely unexplored. That's why I'm deliberately taking the slowest method of transport I can think of. I'm engaging in anti-travel, a rejection of everything we always strive for. I want the method of travelling that takes the *longest* time possible. I want the one that slows me down. I want, in other words, the bus. Or rather the buses. The local buses, that is – the ones that wind through housing estates and the countryside and everything in between. Not those coaches that gobble up stretches of the M1 like so much spaghetti. Local buses are how people usually go down to the shops. I'm going to use them to travel the entire length of the country.

Because for once I want to explore that country. You don't,

normally, do you? Not your home country, not in the way you explore other countries. When you're abroad you set out to discover the terrain; the journey is exciting. At home you take it all for granted. You see bits of your native land, but only in passing as you go somewhere for work, or to visit Aunt Margaret or your friends who've just moved to Winchester. You do sometimes have holidays in this country but they tend to be to the seaside, which somehow isn't a real place. You don't go on holiday to Bristol. Or Preston. Or Newcastle.

And yet these places are full of surprises and full of history. Preston, for example: it gave us the word 'teetotal'. In 1833 a member of its Temperance Society, who had a stutter, announced that he would be 'reet down out-and-out t-t-total for ever and ever'. Over in Newcastle, a prominent city-centre landmark is Grey's Monument, a huge column topped by a statue of the 2nd Earl of that name – yes, the one who gave his name to the tea. His father the 1st Earl, meanwhile, was the man who introduced marching in step to the British Army. This sort of stuff is there to be discovered all over the country. At Hagley, south of Stourbridge, is the bridge on which the toy one in Hornby train sets is modelled.[1] Chislehurst in the London borough of Bromley has the telephone code 467 because it was once home to Emperor Napoleon III of France (the numbers corresponding to 'IMPerial' on the dial). When Harry Houdini appeared at the Glasgow Empire he accidentally locked himself in the toilet and had to bang on the door for staff to let him out.

Don't get me wrong, I have travelled around Britain – quite

---

1. Good old Frank Hornby. Not only did he invent the train set, he also came up with Meccano. Talk about a British hero.

a lot, actually. The big moves have been as follows: born in the Midlands, went to university in Manchester, lived in London for my twenties and half my thirties, and now reside in a village in Suffolk. Plus there have been all the little moves, the holidays, day-trips and friend-visiting. I could tell you things about plenty of places I've been to, and indeed about places I haven't. Westward Ho!, for instance: it's the only place in the country that has an exclamation mark in its name. And it was named after the novel, not the other way round.

But what I've never done is set out to cover the whole country in a single trip.

Ownership, I guess that's what this is all about. By drawing a line across Britain I'll draw a line under my relationship with it. It's the sort of adventure you come to relish in your forties: a very modest one, the sort that gives you an excuse to go to Halfords and buy a new rucksack. A new road atlas, too: what thrills traverse the spine at just the mention of that simple word 'map'.[2] I think it's in the national DNA, you know: the first-ever jigsaw, invented by an Englishman (John Spilsbury, 1767), was a map of the world.

If you're going to do a single trip, it has to be Land's End to John O'Groats. Maybe it's because we're an island that the journey has such a hold on the collective imagination. It goes from one natural, immutable border to another, from sea to shining sea. (All right, this is Britain – murky, greyish sea.) You don't get German people travelling from one end of their country to the other. There's an arbitrary border with Austria to the south, another with Denmark to the north, and in either case why wouldn't you just cross on over and keep going?

---

2. Among the reasons I settled on this book's title were its initials.

Perhaps to avoid bringing up some rather unfortunate history I should leave that point there.

Also in the rucksack will be what I've christened the Library. Plenty of people have done journeys around Britain before, and their accounts of those journeys will form my reading for the trip. (Some of them in eBook form, to prevent this being a weightlifting contest as well as an odyssey.) First up is H. V. Morton's 1927 classic *In Search of England*. Morton feels like a bosom buddy, having had the same sort of inspiration as me for his trip, though admittedly in rather more dramatic circumstances. Travelling in the Middle East, he became gravely ill, and believed he was going to die. 'I remembered home . . . I solemnly cursed every moment I had spent wandering foolishly about the world, and I swore that if ever I saw Dover Cliffs again I would never leave them.' Other stars of the Library include J. B. Priestley's *English Journey*, Daniel Defoe's *Tour thro' the Whole Island of Great Britain*, and just about everything George Orwell ever wrote. It seems that people have always appreciated the novelty to be found on their own doorstep. In 1880 Robert Louis Stevenson said of Cornish people that he could 'make nothing of them at all . . . Not even a Red Indian seems more foreign in my eyes. This is one of the lessons of travel – that some of the strangest races dwell next door to you at home.'

Also in the Library is Gertrude Leather. Not, as you might think from her name, a dominatrix specialising in the OAP market, but the Middlesex housewife who in 1954 decided to see how far she could get from her Twickenham home on public buses. By the next day she was at Land's End. Inspired by press interest in her jaunt, the next year Gertrude made the trip from Twickenham to John O'Groats and wrote a book about it, *Home with the Heather*. Already, having flicked through the first few pages, I see her as another kindred spirit: 'I saw a plane float off into the air as I passed [Heathrow, on the Hounslow to Slough bus] . . . the modern way of travelling, no doubt . . . but I was equally thrilled with the adventure of my own way of getting about. The faster you travel the less you see.' The picture of Gertrude on the back cover makes me like her even more. Well into her fifties, respectably dressed and with a dark blue headscarf tied in that 'nurses's hat' arrangement which lets a triangle of material hang down at the back, she nonetheless has an air of adventure about her as she waits at a bus stop. Physically she's not unlike Mary Whitehouse (without the awful glasses, thankfully), but you get the feeling she wouldn't have been averse to the odd bit of 'ripe' humour.

As well as their slowness buses appeal to me because of their ordinariness. I don't want this trip to be about that tedious creature the British Eccentric. There won't be any visits to the Nether Fiddling Handlebar Moustache Club, or the Civil War Re-enactment Society of Drabtown. I'm interested in the real Britain, the one of shops and pubs and streets and bus shelters. I want to see the sights, hear the sounds, smell the smells (well, some of them). This is going to be about the things you overhear, the little dramas of daily life, the things you see scrawled in the dust on the back of builders' vans. So buses will do me just fine. Very occasionally they're the venue for seismic events, as in 1958 when, on the top deck of one in Liverpool, a boy called Paul introduced his friend called John to his new friend called George. But mostly they're theatres of the everyday, and of the strangeness which that can produce. Alan Bennett credits buses and the conversations he's overheard on them for some of his best lines. 'That fool of a tortoise is out again,' for instance. And: 'Of course it won't be any good to her now – as a foot, I mean.'

The pace of the trip also means I'll have time to root around in the country's history and learn more about its heroes and villains and other assorted players. I love the bizarre connections that crop up as you read about Britain's past. Brian Jones and A. A. Milne, for example. The house that proved to be the Rolling Stones guitarist's final home (he drowned in its swimming pool) had previously been owned by Milne, and was where he wrote the *Winnie the Pooh* stories inspired by his son's toys. Then there are the surprises people can spring. Enoch Powell, whose controversial speech on immigration cost him his job in 1968, later sold his house in Wolverhampton to a Caribbean couple. Britain is still confounding our expectations today: despite all the talk about environmental degradation, for instance, we've got twice as much woodland now as we did a century ago. And our native wit can still cut through waffle at 50 paces. When Starbucks introduced that policy of writing your name on the cup so you know which one's yours, as the person at the front was asked their name, someone at the back of a queue called out: 'Don't tell him, Pike!'

So here we go. It's time to move along. Awaiting me are the cities and towns and villages, the cafés and bars and hotels, of the one country in the world I really should have discovered but never have.

I

In which we contemplate the ocean, make an error in St Austell, and hear a schoolboy explain the difference between 'hyper' and 'high'

I'm glad this trip is starting at Land's End because it means the very first thing I'm going to do is turn my back on the sea and head in completely the opposite direction.

This probably isn't the wisest confession with which to begin a book about an Englishman discovering his home country – but I just don't like the sea. I know, I know. Seafaring nation, defined by being an island, Britannia rule the waves and all that. Unlike virtually all my compatriots, though, I see a trip to the seaside not as a treat but as something to be endured. I just don't *get* the sea. It's not that I suffer from seasickness, unlike the most famous English seafarer of them all, Lord Nelson (had it his whole life, the loser). The sea doesn't scare me in any way – which is just as well, since wherever you go in Britain you're never more than 72 miles from it[1] – it's just that it *bores* me. It's all the bloody same. Square mile after square mile of cold, grey water. The only time it gets interesting is if humans do something interesting in it – like Evelyn Waugh, so depressed during his time as a young teacher in North Wales that he tried to commit suicide by swimming out to sea.

---

1. That point being Church Flatts Farm, slightly south-east of the Derbyshire village of Coton in the Elms.

He got stung by a jellyfish and decided to turn round.

At least this bit of coastline, the bit I'm sitting on at nine o'clock on a bright Tuesday morning in September, has the decency to provide rocky cliffs rather than a beach. Beaches are, in my opinion, the very worst thing about trips to the sea. The first syllable of 'sandwich' is not meant to be taken literally. Cliffs, on the other hand, add a sense of drama, a touch of danger even, amplified this morning by a roaring wind. The name of this place fits – the land really does seem to end here. I've walked a couple of hundred yards away from the visitor centre, out of sight behind some rocks where the ground slopes towards the water. Somehow it feels right to be utterly alone. And actually, as I sit watching the waves, no more than 40 feet below me here, I find myself softening. For once I'm prepared to cut the sea some slack. It's an interesting shade of greeny-blue rather than the tedious grey it so often seems to favour, and two sets of waves are crashing and swirling against each other to form a circle of white foam. A little way out from the rocks, it's the size of a fairground carousel. It hypnotises me for a moment. It feels like a starting point.

I get to my feet and clamber along the path to First and Last House, the most westerly point on the British mainland. It's one of the handful of buildings that cluster together to form the visitor centre. I approach with a sense of dread. It's owned by a company called Heritage Attractions Limited, and if that doesn't sink your spirits I don't know what will. But actually things aren't as tackily commercial as I'd feared. A few people are milling about, their numbers slowly increasing as time passes. First and Last House itself is a very modest whitewashed stone affair, now offering souvenirs and ice-cream. A few yards inland is a huddle of similar buildings: more gifts on sale, two red phone boxes, an exhibition called 'The End to End Story' about the enterprise known, I now learn, as 'Lejog' (Land's End to John O'Groats), and the Arthur's Quest Experience, about the legendary king from round these parts. The recorded voice enticing you in belongs to none other than Brian Blessed. Impossible not to love a tourist attraction when it's got St Brian booming 'Experience the legend!' at you.[2]

Halfway between the main cluster and First and Last House is the famous signpost, telling you that John O'Groats is 874 miles away, the Scilly Isles 28 (I can just make them out, which according to local lore means it's going to rain – if you can't see them it already is raining), and New York 3,147. A board displays photos of notables standing at the post, among them Keith Chegwin, Chris Moyles and a couple of naked ramblers – the pixelation indicating that there was one of each gender. Near the post is a wall covered in small rectangular plaques, fixed here as part of ITV's 'Year of Promise 2000' where people made such vows as: 'I will protect our precious environment by recycling whenever possible,' 'We will raise money for cystic fibrosis,' 'I will talk and pray to God each and every day.' One person has, I feel, rather missed the point: 'I will take my family to Disneyland Paris next year.'

I stand trying to get a sense of meaning from this moment, from this place. At first there's a stubborn blank, a void where my feelings about my homeland should be. But then, just

---

2. Please can we have him as the 'Warning, vehicle reversing' voice on lorries?

behind me, a family of Brummies notice that the signpost is a private business and that you have to pay to have your photo taken next to it. The charge is £9.95. One of them, in the fruitiest of fruity Midlands tones, declares: 'That is dis*gusting*.'

Welcome to Britain.

The country's most westerly bus stop is in the car park, a grassy, uneven affair a hundred yards or so inland from the visitor centre. Just a normal stop; a moss-stained eight-foot concrete pole with a white plastic sign at the top showing the black silhouette of a bus. There's a wooden bench beside it. A timetable fixed halfway up the pole confirms that this is indeed the departure point of the 1A to Penzance, and that the next such departure will be at 10.35 a.m. I have quarter of an hour to wait, so I sit down on the bench and take out Daniel Defoe from my rucksack. Wrestlers down here, he tells me, were much more 'manly' than in other parts of the country, and specialised in the 'Cornish hug'. (Suffolk men, meanwhile, were known for 'their dexterity at the hand and foot, and throwing up the heels of their adversary'.)

10.35 arrives, and then 10.36. I stand up and look east along the single-lane road leading from . . . well, from the rest of Britain. Half a mile away it disappears over a dip. There's nothing else to see except fields, and the coastline stretching off to both left and right. I am suddenly afflicted by a strange paranoia that perhaps I've got this all wrong. There can't really be a bus – a proper, normal, local bus – from somewhere as mythical as Land's End, can there? But then, over the brow of the dip, a slice of dark blue metal with a big window in it appears. A yellow dot-matrix display showing the number '1' and the words 'Land's End' comes into view beneath it.

Finally, beneath that, there is a lower window with a driver visible behind it. This is it: my first bus. As if to confirm that all is indeed as it should be, another passenger joins me at the stop, a slim guy with grey hair who seems to be an employee on his way home from the visitor centre. This is all routine to him, and that helps it feel routine for me. This is an ordinary local bus, for ordinary local people.

The double-decker, which is a smart new one, loops around the car park and pulls up at the stop. I'm expecting all the passengers to get off, but only four of them do so (they look like hikers, though probably not Lejoggers). This leaves another four who are staying on, and you can tell from their lack of curiosity about the landmark that they're locals too. This still doesn't explain why they're not getting off. Only when I take another look at the timetable do I realise this is a circular service, calling at different places on the way back from those on the way out. Hence the change of number from 1 to 1A, which the driver displays on the dot-matrix before welcoming her two new charges. I let the other guy go first (he shows a pass), then step aboard myself.

'Penzance, please.'

'Single?' she asks, smiling.

'Yes, please.' Then, inspired by the other guy's pass: 'Unless – I'm going on beyond Penzance to . . .' Where *am* I going? 'To . . . further east. Is there any sort of . . .' Again, I don't know what I'm asking for. Impressive start, Mason. 'Any sort of travelcard, or anything like that?'

'How far east?'

'As far as I can get.'

She nods. 'You want the seven pounds sixty. That's valid all day, and it'll take you right into Devon.'

£7.60? When I was a kid bus fares were ten pence. I hand over a tenner. Gone are the little slots that you used to slide your coins into, and indeed the ridiculous rule that you had to have the right money. (Did buses in the old days *want* your business or not?) The driver gives me my change with another smile, then the pass. It's a little square of white paper on which the ticket machine has printed the legend 'Adult Day South West – issued at LanEnd'. I notice that the default message on the driver's ticket machine is 'Good day'. A touch Australian, perhaps, but still a welcome welcome. As I make my way to a seat halfway back on the left of the bus it begins to dawn on me that actually the pass is quite good value. In fact I even start to feel a slight sense of power. Two whole counties for £7.60. Two biggies, as well. We're not talking Rutland here.

We set off. The route is a B-road curling round the south coast, and though the map tells me there is an awful lot of nothing round here, it's a nothing hidden from view by hedges and the winding, dipping nature of the terrain. Fields are there to be seen, but only a couple at a time. They – like the hedges – are pleasingly lumpy and untidy, with huge overgrown clumps of purple gorse and heather everywhere. A horse ignores our approach, standing statue-still, looking out over its fence; when we're ten yards off it drops a shoulder and wheels off, like George Best rounding a defender.

The narrowness of the road means that cars coming the other way often don't have enough room to pass. We're a hulking great double-decker bus, so it's they who give way. This adds to my sense of power, as though I've clambered on to a well-meaning monster roaming the land. A monster, what's more, with huge windows. This is useful not only because they give a good view, but also because they turn the vehicle into a greenhouse on wheels. Outside, the wind is whipping the trees, but in here it's as though someone's set the central heating to 'comfortably toasty'. Fifteen minutes in and the world of Bus feels nice.

We reach Porthcurno, or rather part of it. Like everywhere in Britain, villages in this county can be incoherent places, lacking a centre and not existing in any definite geographical sense – some houses and a couple of pubs flung randomly across a few square miles. We don't file our landscape very well, we Brits. The part of Porthcurno we stop at today is the Telegraph Museum – the driver announces it, obviously because a passenger (whose 'thank you' reveals him to be French) has requested it. The museum proclaims itself to be 'the Home of the Victorian Internet'. Yes, this was where Britain's first physical links to the rest of the world began, the place where under-sea telegraph cables were laid. The first one was in 1870, linking us to India.[3] By the 1930s Porthcurno had 14 cables, and could receive and transmit two million words a day. Not much compared to Twitter's typical workload, but still a staggering figure. The link continues today – the fibre-optic cables that allow the internet to work enter Britain here. It seems funny that a spot as remote as this should be linked so solidly (albeit out of sight beneath the waves) to countries all round the globe. Could this be a subconscious reason, however small, for Britain's 'complicated' relationship with the rest of the world? After centuries of priding ourselves on

3. The authorities chose Porthcurno rather than the busy port of Falmouth to reduce the risk of damage to the cables from ships' anchors.

our isolation, are we disconcerted by physical ties? Barbara Castle was. When the Channel Tunnel was first proposed, the Labour politician wrote in her diary that she had a 'kind of earthly feeling that an island is an island and should not be violated. Certainly I am convinced that the building of a tunnel would do something profound to the national attitude.'

We continue down the road to Treen, which again doesn't quite seem to exist. A couple in their twenties get off, manhandling a large suitcase that's been hiding in the spacious luggage rack near the driver. Tucked into their other bags are roll-up mattresses. Going on holiday on a *bus*? Who do they think they are, Cliff Richard? Near St Buryan a man walking in the opposite direction presses himself into the hedge as we pass. His rucksack is state-of-the-art, the look on his face determined. A Lejogger, I'll warrant, with just a few thousand steps to go. St Buryan itself is a harsh little village; no surprise that this is where they filmed *Straw Dogs*, the movie in which visiting academic Dustin Hoffman is terrorised by the locals. I have, it must be admitted, been wondering about this: Cornwall's reputation for . . . how can we phrase it? . . . not exactly putting the 'Welcome' mat out.

'There is a strangeness about Cornwall,' wrote H. V. Morton in *In Search of England*. As recently as 1949 (over two decades later) a Cornish woman was seen wringing the neck of a black cock[4] as her husband lay dying, so the bird could accompany his soul and guarantee him admission to heaven. Morton said you felt the strangeness 'as soon as you cross Tor Ferry'. Just as Britain has a watery boundary cutting it off from other nations, so does Cornwall from the rest of Britain:

---

4. I'll let you do your own jokes there.

most of its border with Devon is formed by the River Tamar. For some of the Cornish, Britain counts among the 'other nations' of the rest of the world. Morton encounters one 'who told me that he was "going up to England" next week, and then corrected himself and said "Plymouth"'. The writer also comments on the accent: one woman 'sang her words prettily, as the Welsh do. Like the Welsh, these people possess a fine Celtic fluency, so that their lies are more convincing than a Saxon truth.'

The only trouble is, I haven't heard any of that. Okay, the bus had no more than a dozen passengers, but not one of them has uttered an 'ooh', much less an 'aah'. Admittedly there's a certain twang that proves you're not in Liverpool or Glasgow, but the phrase 'me lover' has been conspicuous by its absence. The helpful driver, come to think of it, has a neutral 'anywhere south-east of Watford' accent. I look about at the adverts on the bus (mainly for various NHS helplines) – no Cornish translations visible. I've been wondering about this since last night, when I read one of those glossy 'Welcome to Cornwall' magazines placed by some sort of tourist authority in my Penzance B&B room. It had a piece about moves to revive the Cornish language. There was one native speaker still alive in 1914, the article claimed somewhat desperately, and Cornish is still 'recognised as a language by the European Union and is being taught in local schools'. But, the magazine admitted, 'you probably won't hear Cornish spoken on the streets'. Or, it would seem, the buses.

So why the campaign? Why the existence not just of the Cornish Language Partnership, and the Cornish Language Board, but also the Cornish Language Council and the Cornish Language Fellowship? (Hard not to nurture a hope that they're at each other's throats, like the Judean People's Front and the People's Front of Judea.) The answer, I guess, is that we all feel the need to belong. And for some people – the sort of people who form councils and boards and partnerships – what they belong to is defined by what they don't belong to. It's not so much 'I'm Cornish' as 'I'm not English'.

Already, I know that this is what my trip is really all about. It's about belonging.

We travel on past Lamorna, which has a pub called the Wink. Centuries ago lots of pubs round here were called the Wink, that being the signal the landlord gave you to let you know smuggled goods were available for sale. You'd expect the county with Britain's longest coastline to be a haven for smugglers, and so it was. Foremost round this neck of the sea was the King of Prussia, the nickname given to John Carter, who in the late 1700s shifted more contraband gear into Prussia Cove than you could shake a customs form at. Carter's defenders point out his 'honesty': on one occasion when the authorities confiscated his cargo he broke into their stores and confiscated it back – but left everything else untouched. Bet he never hurt no women nor children, neither.

Gradually the villages pass by. At the turning for two, Paul and Mousehole, the road sign displays them as though they're the forename and surname of a dodgy kids' entertainer.[5] We also go through a place called Sheffield, though the pace

---

5. Mousehole is so called because of a cave near its harbour that looks like one. Being Britain, though, a literal explanation doesn't mean a literal pronunciation – locals call it 'Mouzle'. Later in the day I'll see a poster advertising a concert by the Mousehole Male Voice Choir, and won't be able to rid my brain of the thought of them all squeaking their parts.

we are moving at matches that of another village near here: Drift. Dotted around, waving exotically, are Cornish palm trees. Now that I see them the memories return of adverts for Torquay and the 'English Riviera' – but it still surprises me that a tree you associate with Cannes or the Caribbean is to be found here too. In truth it isn't; these aren't palms but a near-relation known in New Zealand, where they originate, as the 'cabbage tree'. That wouldn't sound so good in the ads, though.

More passengers get on as we reach the outskirts of . . . where is this? Christ, it's Penzance! The hour has shot by. I feel a sense of euphoria, as though with one bus trip (nearly) completed I could simply photocopy the ticket a few dozen times and say I'd done the whole trip. Only then does it occur to me that the more accurate image is that of a flick-book – having drawn one bus in the bottom left-hand corner of the first page, I've now got to do another one on the next page *slightly* higher up and *slightly* to the right. Only at the end of the book will I be able to flick through and watch my progress north-eastwards across Britain. This 'starting point' feeling applies literally as we pass through Newlyn (technically a separate town, but in reality part of Penzance): the sea level here is the one used as zero by the Ordnance Survey in all their maps of the country.

Two women get on, one relating the story of a recent trip with her husband to a theatre production of *Murder on the Orient Express*. 'It was good. But we didn't know any of the people in it. Kate O'Mara was supposed to be the famous person. But she was off ill.' Winding our way round the tiny streets near the harbour, we eventually reach the bus station at 11.37 a.m. It's a car park with half a dozen stands at one edge, all sharing the same roofed shelter. My first journey is complete: 58 minutes, 14.3 miles. I deliberately don't look at the single-page map of Britain in my road atlas – I don't want to feel daunted this early on. Instead I concentrate on page one, cross-referencing the area map with the 'Buses from this station' notice in the shelter, trying to pick a likely next destination. There's St Ives up on the north coast, or Falmouth down on the south. But they'd render me a human pinball, ricocheting from one side to the other of what Defoe calls 'this utmost angle of the nation'. No – I want to be a golf ball instead, driven right down the middle of the fairway. Which means just one destination: Truro. The number 18 to Truro leaves at 12.20 p.m. From what I've already seen of Penzance, 40 minutes should be just right for a last scoot round the town.

I take an immediate liking to the place. The sun has not just got his hat on but his white tie and tails too, and now I am walking these tiny winding streets which protect me from the Atlantic's mighty breath, it's a temperature that can actually warm me. We're talking Ambre Solaire weather. People are smiling, lolling, stopping to chat with friends. There's only one main street that's actually got any shops on it, which means it's got every shop on it. This is Market Jew Street,[6] sloping up from the bus station (near the quay) for several hundred yards. I climb past the hairdresser's Cut Loose, as well as Sports World, the Glass House Art Gallery, several charity shops, W. H. Smith and – my favourite – a 'shabby chic furniture and giftware' shop called Dick the Dog. No, make that joint-favourite: there's also a slimming place called

---

6. Nothing to do with religion – it's derived from the Cornish for 'Thursday Market', which is what they used to have here.

Absolutely Flabulous. They are 'Cornwall's No. 1 Vibration Training Centre'.

Right at the top, surveying the whole street and forming the town's focal point, is a fantastic three-storey Victorian stone building. Built to house the market, it is now a branch of Lloyds TSB. As if its architecture (four columns forming a portico, arches over the windows, white dome, the lot) wasn't enough to date this building, the date engraved on the front is as Victorian as you can get: MDCCCXXXVII – 1837, the year she took the throne. Probably Britain's most famous monarch, Victoria is certainly the one who reigned over the country when the country reigned over the world, so this building feels very much part of the nation. That question of belonging again – does Cornwall belong in Britain, in England even? Do I belong here?

I wander round on to Chapel Street, and past the Union Hotel, from whose balcony the first announcement of Nelson's death was made. The ship bearing the news to Falmouth (ignominiously named HMS *Pickle*) had been intercepted by a Penzance fishing boat, so this town got its exclusive. At the Dolphin Tavern, further down towards the quay, there was another first: Sir Walter Raleigh smoked England's first pipe here. Today two of his tobacco-enabled successors stand outside with cigarettes. One of them is looking disgruntled. 'You can go home to get it,' he mutters to his friend. 'I have to pay to get it.'

When I was staying in Penzance last night, the only thing of note on my short walk through the dark back streets from the train station to my B&B was a knitting circle; a dozen women of all ages sitting in the front room of an anonymous building, clicking needles and swapping chat like a cosier incarnation of the ancient Greek Fates who spin the thread of a person's life. At the time it had given me the impression that Penzance really would turn out to be a slightly strange place, but today's lunchtime sun burns that feeling away. The people here, I decide, are more British than they are anything else. Sometimes that's a bad thing, as with the young woman I pass talking on her mobile: 'Yes, asset management . . . that's what my CV is most engendered to.' Mostly, though, it helps me feel welcome and creates a sense of belonging.

Back up on Market Jew Street I pass a J. D. Wetherspoon pub. Its doors are open, and I see that the signs inside are in Cornish as well as English. I learn, for instance, that *privedhyow a-wartha* means 'toilets upstairs'. But those are the only Cornish signs I see in my time in Penzance. The glossy magazine's prediction about not hearing the language spoken on the street proves to be entirely correct. Most people have a bit of an accent, but no more than a bit. So it isn't the revival of a dead language that comes to mind as I look at the pub – it's the British genius for self-invention. 'J. D. Wetherspoon' sounds like a hearty old cove, the sort of bloke you'd trust when it comes to beer. But the chain was actually started in 1979 by a guy called Tim Martin, who took the surname from a schoolteacher who'd told him he'd never amount to anything. The initials come from J. D. 'Boss' Hogg of *The Dukes of Hazzard.*[7]

Not that Penzance feels *exactly* like everywhere else in Britain. There's definitely a chilled-out feeling here, beyond

---

7. Rather like Charles Kalms and Michael Mindel opening their Southend photographic shop in 1937 and realising they only had room for six letters on the store front. They looked in the phone book, chose 'Dixons', and never looked back.

that caused by the weather, as though Cornwall's remoteness has helped it to calm down, avoiding the rest of the country's fast-paced lunacy. No surprise that the county's police officers average a shade over one arrest each per year. And yet still those separatists want to turn that remoteness into something aggressive, want to pick out the angry pages from Cornwall's history book. Those about the Romans, for example, who never got much change from the locals down here, the Cornovii tribe (from where the modern name derives). Caesar and his mob left pretty much everyone west of Exeter to their own devices. There are also the pages about religion. When the Cornish responded badly to the Protestant Book of Common Prayer being forced on them in the sixteenth century, the English Crown sent its soldiers in, killing 10 per cent of the local population. God must be delighted by some of the things that are done in His name. But as ever for the real story you have to follow the money. Self-governance round here was based for a long time on the area's economic strength due to its tin mines. The metal gave its name to the local 'Stannary' parliament and courts (a stannary being a tin mine). These took precedence over national ones, and regulated the lives of the tin workers. Right up to the 1750s it was the mines that ruled, and England (or Britain) could go whistle. Ideally on a tin one.

So Cornish separatists have some history on their side. But that's what it is – history. The mines have long since closed, making the claims of some local politicians to have revived the Stannary Parliament (they've been trying since 1974) seem silly. It isn't a ruthless, uncaring national government that is making Penzance part of Britain; it's the shoppers going into Boots and O2 and Costa and all the other nationwide chains.

I've never really understood this cynicism we Brits display about chains, and the way they 'destroy local shops'. Apart from the fact that, on Market Jew Street at least, they clearly haven't, there's the question of why we think the chains have us in chains. It can't just be that some of them (such as Starbucks or McDonald's) are American; Tesco gets it in the neck too, and wonderful, beloved Woolworths was (surprising though this may be to many of its former customers) another Yank import. In fact Woolies was the perfect example – Brits would do everything to keep that icon going except actually shop in it.[8]

Passing a café I notice a framed red 'Keep Calm and Carry On' poster on its wall. Now there's the *ultimate* proof that Penzance is part of Britain. Forget your Book of Common Prayer, that slogan is now the nearest thing this country has to an organised religion. The gift shops here sell the five short words on every object we've come to expect: cards, mugs, tea-towels, the lot. It can only be a matter of time before the Queen has them tattooed on her forehead and uses them to sign off her Christmas message. The usual variants are also on offer today: 'Keep Calm and Drink Tea', 'Keep Calm and Support Man Utd', etc. I'm still waiting for an Indian restaurant to display a poster saying 'Keep Korma Curry On'. I myself possess two examples of the original slogan, and I can't help thinking that my experiences with both of them reveal something about Britishness. One is a 'Keep Calm and Carry On' mug; I once dropped it and lost my temper.

---

8. Perhaps E. M. Forster was right, in his 1920 essay 'Notes on the English Character', to include 'hypocrisy' among the nation's defining values. We talk a good fight about local stores, but we actually spend our money in the supermarkets.

Meanwhile the poster that hangs on my kitchen wall came free with a newspaper, right at the beginning of the phenomenon. When, within weeks, the slogan had become ubiquitous, I resented everyone else for getting in on the act. I was annoyed because a poster about the country uniting had united the country. What was that about 'belonging'?

Back at the station, the number 18 awaits. Very handy, that, to have a unique number by which you can recognise your bus. Makes life so easy. It's such an obvious idea you'd think that bus companies must always have been doing it. You'd be wrong. It was only in 1906 that they became numerical. Prior to that buses had been colour-coded depending on their destination, a system that proved as confusing as you might expect. In fact it wasn't even the bus operators who made the change. It was only when the Baedeker travel guide allocated its own unofficial numbers that London's Vanguard bus company cottoned on and followed suit, giving their Gospel Oak to Putney route a number. As this was the first officially numbered service, they very logically chose the number 4.

Unlike the bus from Land's End, my second bus is a single-decker, and rather than a completely blue colour scheme it also throws in some fetching pink touches, as if to appeal to both sexes.[9] My pass works its magic, putting me on the same cash-free footing as most of the dozen or so other passengers, who enjoy the privilege because they're either pensioners (as most were on the first bus) or students. The driver thanks us all in his northern accent. I take a seat on the right, just

---

9. The current convention, incidentally, is a modern invention – in the early 1900s it was blue for girls, pink for boys.

in front of a teenager reading a Japanese Manga book, just behind a twenty-something man in a designer tracksuit and trainers trying to feed and shush a tiny pushchair-encased baby to sleep.

Across the aisle sits a man in his fifties, his striped shirt worn outside white trousers, his sandals without socks. Stylishly long grey hair frames a lean and weathered face. He wears a silver signet ring, and overall has the air of a keyboard player from a massively successful but nevertheless artistically credible rock band of the 1970s. Which prompts the question: what is he doing on a bus? My curiosity will increase as he stays on for the entire hour and a half it takes to reach Truro. Any of his several Ferraris could have done the journey in a third of the time. Okay, maybe he looks the sort whose environmental credentials dictate public transport wherever possible. In which case why not get the train, which only takes 40 minutes? Maybe he's planning a new concept album inspired by bus journeys. I love this feeling; being intrigued by a fellow passenger, wondering about their life. Already I feel attuned to the pace of this project, as though my body clock has obligingly slowed itself to stay in sync with the buses, rather as the clocks on GPS satellites have to be run slower than those on earth to take account of relativity theory.

A roundabout just outside Penzance is sponsored by Dolphin Stairlifts (now *that's* a trick they should do at Orlando Seaworld), and then our brief time on the A30 is enlivened by an eccentric old man using a 1960s tractor to tow a wooden traveller's caravan in the other direction; the looks on the faces of the drivers queuing behind him for a mile and a half are a picture. Then it's back to B-roads and villages.

After one of these, Connor Downs, we crest a hill to see a valley stretching east towards the town of Camborne. It's the first geographical 'wow, I wasn't expecting that' moment of the day, the first time the narrow horizon has opened out. At last I get a sense of just how huge this island called Britain is. Everything seems huge – the valley itself, the fields it contains, the sky that covers them both. It feels like a response to the Atlantic I left behind a couple of hours ago. 'Okay, so you're big,' the sunlit fields seem to be saying. 'We can do "expanse" too, you know.'

In Camborne the bus pauses outside the library, where there stands a statue of the steam-engine pioneer Richard Trevithick. Tucked under his arm is one of his small-scale models. Camborne is obviously as proud of its son as he was of his engines. Pity we're not always as good to our heroes in their lifetime as we are once they're gone: Trevithick died in poverty in Kent, a long way from here, where he'd ended up working for an engineering company. It was left to his employer and colleagues to pay for his funeral, and for the night watchman to protect his grave from the bodysnatchers common in the early nineteenth century.

There is more hero-worship over towards Redruth: now that the change in the landscape has put distant hills on the agenda, you can see on top of one of them, miles away, a huge stone obelisk-ish monument. It'll be the first of many such hilltop constructions I encounter; I'd never really noticed before how this country likes to commemorate its great and good in this way. This one turns out to be[10] a memorial to

_____

10. I love the way modern technology, coupled with the pace of the trip, means there's time to do research as I go along.

Francis Basset, 1st Baron de Dunstanville and Basset, an eighteenth-century politician who rounded up a load of Cornish miners and marched them to the coast to help repel a would-be Franco-Spanish invasion. You've always been able to raise English cheers by slapping the French down, so it's no surprise that the monument was paid for by public subscription. Just one thing, though. If we *are* so anti-French, how come he was the Baron 'de' Dunstanville? Well, the title harks back to Reginald de Dunstanville, a big cheese round here in the twelfth century. That was halfway through the 300-year period in which the English actually spoke French.

What? Proper, true-blooded Englishmen, chatting away in the enemy's lingo? You'll be telling us they were playing boules next. Well, as ever, the notion of what a proper true-blooded Englishman is, and which bit of the gene pool he's swimming in, isn't quite as clear-cut as some people would like us to think. After William the Conqueror[11] sailed over from Normandy and beat us in 1066, there followed three centuries when life was conducted in 'Anglo-Norman', a sort of Franglais cross between the two languages. All right, the change didn't happen overnight, and it's doubtful that everyone used the new tongue, but certainly the upper classes and officialdom did. Which is why we've now got terms like 'heir apparent' and 'court martial', where the words are English but the order (adjective after noun) is French.

Anyway, moving on. Redruth is . . . erm, actually, no – before we move on, there's something I'd better 'fess up to. Something else that we owe to the French. (Look, don't shoot me – I'm only the messenger here.) No, not the very word

---

11. Otherwise known, rather pleasingly, as William the Bastard.

'Britain'. I was assuming you'd know about that, so I could avoid giving the French any more credit on these pages than I had to. You were, of course, already aware of Geoffrey of Monmouth coining the term 'Britannia major' ('Greater Britain') in 1136, to distinguish it from 'Britannia minor', the 'lesser' Britain over the water that we now call Brittany. Actually, the thing we owe to the French, the thing I reckon I really do have to cover here is . . . brace yourself . . . the bus.

Yes, I know. Like me you thought the bus was as British as steak-and-kidney pie or bad teeth. Perhaps you even knew about George Shillibeer, the Londoner who started Britain's first bus service in 1829 (as opposed to a coach where you needed to pre-book), offering free newspapers for his passengers to read. But here's the bad news: Shillibeer got the idea from Stanislas Baudry, who'd been running buses in Nantes for three years. He hadn't originally meant to – he'd laid on coaches as transport to some steam baths he ran outside the city. But people with no intention of visiting the baths started using them as a convenient and relatively inexpensive way to get across the city, so Baudry began to concentrate on their trade. He's not just responsible for the concept, but even the word 'bus' itself. By coincidence his carriages terminated near a shop run by a Monsieur Omnes, whose slogan was a pun on his name, *omnes omnibus* ('everything for everyone'). The shortened version, which obviously had connotations with public transport too, stuck. Perhaps we should talk about *l'homme sur le Clapham omnibus*.

Okay, that awkward little matter dealt with, we really can move on. Redruth is the journey's halfway point, where the bus empties of those on their way to shop and their places are taken by those who've secured the weekly booty and are now heading home. The driver also takes the chance to come back to the teenage girl sitting behind me, who got on a few stops ago and paid with a £20 note. Only now has he got the right change for her, which he hands over. She thanks him, then continues applying the make-up that has been occupying her for ten minutes and will do so for another ten. In Truro, I get the feeling, someone special awaits. Redruth, locals will tell you proudly, was home to Britain's first lift, installed in 1842 to save copper miners an hour's climb. It also had the first house in Britain to be lit by gas, the 1790s home of William Murdoch. He was such a pioneer in this new technology that he even had a portable version, a bladder held under his armpit from which he discharged the gas as though playing the bagpipes, burning a flame so that he and a companion could walk through the countryside at night. Brave companion.

The villages pass by. In Scorrier a man has precariously placed three bottles of wine on his car roof as he reaches for his keys – sensing the vibrations from the approaching bus he quickly has to grab them again. Near Chacewater we pass a scarecrow from whose outstretched arms flutters a Union Flag, making it look like a winner in the recent Olympics. There are signs to Perranporth, north of here on the coast, the town where the actor Robert Morley ran a theatre company in the 1930s. He hit on the crafty idea of getting local people to lend items of furniture to the productions, thereby both cutting costs and raising ticket revenues, as the people in question would want to come and see their sideboard have its moment of fame. This all worked spiffingly until the rehearsals for one particular play, when an actor lost his temper and smashed everything on stage to pieces.

For a while I occupy myself with the interior of the bus.

Again the adverts are mostly NHS messages aimed at older passengers, such as the one asking: 'Looser poo?' We really need a new word inventing here, the equivalent of 'pee' – something more informal than the correct medical term without being either childish or a swear word. Then, before I know it, we're entering the outskirts of Cornwall's only city. How have we got to Truro so quickly? A glance at my watch tells me we're on schedule, perhaps even a little behind. I'd been thinking that strange journeys seem slower, and that ones you're used to flash by. But actually it's the other way round, isn't it? The first time, when everything's new, there's so much to look at. It's the familiar trip that breeds boredom. We reach Truro College, where several students join us, and then, a short time later, a large modern building emblazoned 'The Knowledge Spa', which I take to be a crappily titled part of the college. Its title becomes even more crappy when I discover it's actually part of a hospital. To be precise, the NHS website informs me that: 'The Knowledge Spa is centre of excellence [*sic*] for the delivery of education and training at the Royal Cornwall Hospital.' Recent events hosted there include 'Pathways to Health'.

We pass a council sign advising 'two in a car, room on the tar' (forty on a bus, brownie points for us), and soon we're pulling into the city centre. Yes, it's bigger than Penzance, and it's got a Monsoon and a Waterstone's and a Jaeger, but I've been to towns that feel just as city-ish as this. The distinction's all a bit lost these days; the 'cities have a cathedral' rule has been dumped, and towns regularly compete for the honour of the C-word. Chelmsford got lucky when it came to marking the Queen's Diamond Jubilee in 2012. This seems fair enough, but then so did St Asaph in Wales. No, me neither.

The Denbighshire community has a cathedral, and so was known as a city in centuries past – but it's now a village (sorry, Powers That Be) of about 3,000 people. You can be bumped down the order, too, as Rochester discovered in 1998. It had enjoyed city status since 1211, but a council official filled in a government form incorrectly and that was that.

Anyway, cathedrals are all very well, but what matters to me at the moment is bus stations, so I'm pleased that Truro's is a step up from the one in Penzance. Essentially still a car park, it nonetheless boasts a central building which all the buses pull up to, like piglets suckling on their mother. It's not very large, but it is clean and modern with a stylish metal roof, the green tinge of which gives the impression of the old copper ones that went that colour when they oxidised (like the Statue of Liberty). Inside are racks of timetables and 'things to do in Truro' leaflets, and, more importantly from my point of view, one of those controller blokes you always see at bus stations wandering around with a clipboard.[12] This one's a bit scruffy, and avoids catching anyone's eye, but then I suppose with some of the people you get hanging around bus stations, you can't blame him.

Positioning myself in his sightline as he's pretending to examine an approaching bus, I ask which destination is the furthest east I can reach from here.

'Where are you trying to get to?'

'Nowhere specific. Just as far east as possible.' I show him my road atlas, tracing an imaginary continuation of the line from Land's End. 'Bodmin, perhaps?'

---

12. Impossible not to mentally label him 'Blakey', but out of respect I won't call him that here.

Blake— . . . Controller Man shakes his head. 'No, not direct. You'd have to change in St Austell.'

'Right.' The implication seems to be that St Austell is itself the answer to my question, but I decide to double-check. 'No direct buses to, say, Liskeard, then?' I pronounce it 'Liskard', praying this is correct (can't be 'Liskeered', can it?), because if it isn't then Controller Man is going to get even more irritated than he is already.

'No. Where is it you're trying to get to?'

I consider answering 'John O'Groats', but decide better of it. 'It's OK – St Austell's good.'

A check of the timetables confirms this. The number 27 is the bus I want. Only a 40-minute hop, this one, and there's a departure at 2.20 p.m., which is . . . oh, right now. The double-decker is already being boarded by six passengers, so I hasten to make myself the seventh. My pass works its magic again (I'm beginning to feel it could get me into the Pentagon), and we're off. The journey turns out to be a simple one – most of the villages lie on the single-lane A-road to St Austell. The first is called Probus, which seems pleasantly appropriate for my trip, though actually comes from a saint of that name. Probus is also a Rotary-style organisation (members are PROfessionals and in BUSiness) – fantastically there's a branch here, making it the Probus Club of Probus.

The silly place names continue: Sticker, Lower Sticker, London Apprentice. Also Indian Queens: a Portuguese princess spent a night here on her way from Falmouth to London, and the locals assumed from her dark complexion that she was Indian – typical British level of accuracy when it comes to classifying foreigners. Many of the fields we pass slope very steeply. Not quite Gloucestershire cheese-rolling territory, but still enough of an incline to make life awkward for the cows that have to graze here. The weird thing is, they all stand in line with the slope, bending both their right legs or both their left legs at the same time. Surely it's easier to eat the grass facing *into* the slope, bending both your front legs, or maybe even kneeling down? I once saw a cartoon postcard in a hilly area of Yorkshire, about local sheep deliberately bred with their left legs shorter than their right so they could stand up easily. Yet here are cows in Cornwall standing that way for real. Why? Whoever said there's nowt so queer as folk should look at animals.

In Hewas Water we pause in traffic beside a couple on their bikes. Facing in opposite directions, they're snogging before saying goodbye. When it's time to part they find their front wheels have become entangled, and it takes some effort to separate them. All the time road signs are tempting us northwards to Newquay,[13] but we keep resolutely on to St Austell. As we trundle, two quotes from women of roughly the same vintage keep going around my head. The first is Margaret Thatcher, with 'any man over the age of twenty-six who finds himself on a bus can count himself a failure in life'. The slight complication here is that there's no evidence Thatcher ever said it; it seems to have been the Duke of Westminster's wife instead. Either way, you'll forgive me if I reject the argument. Instead it's a quote from good old Gertrude Leather (my 'to John O'Groats by local bus' colleague from the Library) that keeps me warm inside. Like mine, hers is an odyssey with the emphasis very much on the first syllable, but one of her fellow

---

13. Venue for the first-ever wearing of a bikini in Britain. Maisie Dunn, 1946. She was on her honeymoon.

passengers is charmed by it. 'Your idea is grand,' he says. 'It's simple – it's so simple as to be almost idiotic! I like it!' Thanks for the 'almost', old chap. I have to say this trip feels like it could disprove William Hazlitt, who once wrote that we go on journeys 'chiefly to be free of all impediments and of all inconveniences; to leave ourselves behind, much more to get rid of others'. I'm finding exactly the opposite: the inconvenience of this journey is what it's all about. It feels like it's putting me in touch with myself, with others, with my country.

As if to underline Cornwall's enmity with England, St Austell is named after someone who lived most of his life in France. And as if to underline the madness of British officialdom it is a town with a larger population than the city of Truro. I like it because it has a computer repair shop called 'Bits and PCs'. It also has quite a few residents with northern accents, the first two I notice being a couple who get off the bus with me. They're not the first I've heard in the West Country, and they won't be the last. (My next driver, for instance.) Seems this is a popular place for northerners to move to. I'm surprised by that. I'm surprised they move anywhere. Perhaps I was too influenced by all the 'born in the North, die in the North' T-shirts I saw at university in Manchester. It was the early nineties, when the city's bands ruled the world. Though come to think of it, the most famous of those bands was Oasis, whose Gallagher brothers loved the North so much that as soon as they could afford it they both went to live in London.[14]

---

14. What's more, the leisure centre the band named themselves after was in Swindon.

St Austell is the first place that hasn't had a bus station as such, just a collection of stops dotted around the town centre. This makes choosing the next destination a bit difficult, but I find a helpful driver whose bus is idling away the minutes until its departure. He puts me in mind of George Orwell's statement, in the essay 'England Your England', that the country's defining quality is its gentleness: 'You notice it the instant you set foot on English soil. It is a land where the bus conductors are good-tempered and the policemen carry no revolvers.' All this guy's helpfulness, though, brings us to the conclusion that, route-wise, my luck has run out. Until now I've been following that imaginary straight line north-east from Land's End. Wherever I've wanted to go, a bus has been waiting to carry me, allowing me to eat up the distance like Pac-Man eating up dots. Blithely I assume that the next place on the line – Liskeard – will be conveniently on the bus menus too. And to be fair it is. It's just that from there I'll be forced too far to the south. That way madness lies. As indeed does Plymouth.

'Can I do Bodmin?' I ask. This is more north-ish, but still to the east.

'Oh, yeah,' says the driver, looking at my map. 'There's buses to Bodmin.'

'And then Launceston?' (I go for 'Lawnston', and will later cringe when I hear a local pronounce it 'Lanston'.)

'No, there's no bus there from Bodmin. If you want to do that you'll have to go via Wadebridge.'

At first I can't even see it on the map. That's because it's north-west of Bodmin. It's even north-west of *here*, for God's sake. I'm going to have to go back on myself. Sod it.

Things get even worse when the 529 to Bodmin arrives.

The fact that the single-decker has a green-and-yellow colour scheme is the clue: it's operated by Western Greyhound, as opposed to First Group, whose blue-and-pink chariots have brought me thus far. So my pass isn't valid. I'm going to have to stump up some more coin of the realm. Four pound coins and one fifty pence one, to be exact. Much of the next hour, it becomes clear within a few stops, is to be spent in the company of school kids on the way home. Instinctively I regret my choice of a seat at the back, dreading being penned in by screeching, bawling, and quite possibly armed teenagers. But they're delightful. When I lose my place on the map one of them advises me which village we're in (Bugle). During one discussion a slightly younger boy, perhaps 11 to his neighbours' 13, uses the word 'high' when he actually means 'hyper'. After he's made the mistake twice, one of the older boys gently corrects him.

'Oh,' he says. 'Don't they mean the same thing?'

'No. Hyper's a good thing, like when you're excited. But "high" is . . . you know, er . . .' The boy looks embarrassed, and lowers his voice. 'Drugs.'

Temporarily, the quality of the countryside dips slightly. Like most English villages the ones we pass through have their ugly areas; squat 1960s houses plonked on the outskirts as though the Lego set had run out of everything except grey. One bungalow has statues dotting its garden wall, alternately Alsatian dogs and parrots. It is one of the scariest things I've ever seen. Then we pass some sort of establishment (B&B . . . restaurant . . . hard to tell, which in itself is often a bad sign) called Auberge Asterisk, a name that would have suited an experimental San Francisco rock group 40 years ago but which seems very out of place in the middle of the Cornish countryside. For a moment this feels a very long way away from anywhere in England I've been to before, or would want to come again.

But then Bodmin arrives and my mood improves for several reasons. The next bus is climbing the hill out of the town centre just as we come down towards it, meaning I can get off and run across the road to hop on. It's the 555, and the cricket fan in me is pleased by the quintuple Nelson.[15] Another green-and-yellow single-decker, it carries me along the road to Wadebridge, a nice winding green-hedge-lined job which restores the countryside's briefly tarnished image. For stretches of the journey there's that particularly pleasing thing of the upper branches of the trees on either side of the road meeting each other in the middle, forming a tunnel in which sunlight and shadows dance together on the tarmac.

The bus passes a whole hillside covered in solar panels, like a futuristic crop in a sci-fi film. Plenty of the roofs we've passed today have been clad in them too, even the roofs of period properties. Somehow they've earned a bad name for themselves, panels, in the same way that wind turbines have. Blights on our chocolate-box landscape, comes the charge. But actually I find both beautiful. What is a wind turbine but an elegant twenty-first-century windmill? And do we really want to live in a chocolate box for the rest of eternity? Can't we daub a few new elements on the lid once in a while? Yes, in the sixteenth century we thatched our roofs,

---

15. The unlucky score of 111 is so called because the Admiral had one eye, one arm and one leg. He didn't, of course; he never lost a leg, or indeed an eye, though he was blinded in his right one.

and they looked great, still do. Now, though, we've got new technologies, new priorities. Part of me doesn't even care whether the environmental arguments add up – it's just nice to see something new happening.

Near Washaway we're joined, for the first time in the project, by a member of that tribe Jasper Carrott did a whole routine about: the Nutter on the Bus. This one is pleasant rather than threatening. Thirty-something, he's swarthy and unshaven, though in a handsome Mediterranean way rather than a horrible unclean one. He's wearing shorts, and carries an acoustic guitar in one hand and a rucksack containing a pot plant in the other. Roots poking out of the side show that the plant has parted company with its pot. He shows no sign of bothering anyone and sits down, then stands up again, then repeats the process a few times before settling on a half-sitting, half-standing pose, one knee on the seat. He smiles the whole time, muttering the odd indecipherable phrase to himself. He seems content in his detachment from reality, and in some sense I almost envy him.

It was on this road that Nevell Norway travelled home to Wadebridge on 8 February 1840. At exactly the same moment his brother Edmund was thousands of miles away, on a ship near St Helena, asleep. He dreamed that Nevell was being attacked, criminals dragging him from his horse and then trying to shoot him. After their pistol twice failed to go off they used it to club Nevell to death. The nightmare was so vivid that the next morning Edmund mentioned it to someone else on board. 'Don't worry about it,' came the reply. 'You West Country people are too superstitious.' Months later, when Edmund got home, he found that Nevell had indeed been murdered that day. His dream was accurate in every respect.

I've happily lost track of time by now, and only as the bus pulls into Wadebridge do I notice that it's gone 5 p.m. A check of the timetable reveals that the last bus east from here left three hours ago. Wadebridge, it dawns on me as I survey the one-and-a-half streets that constitute this town on the River Camel,[16] is where I'm spending the night. I'd been wondering whether I should do this anyway, but the fact the decision has been taken out of my hands makes it seem scary. I'd never even *heard* of Wadebridge before today. That's what this trip is all about, of course, but somehow I'd imagined that all the places I stopped in overnight would be familiar to me, if in name only. Not gonna happen, though. I'm to spend more than twelve hours of my life in a town I didn't know existed until today, simply because the bus timetable says so. A funny feeling develops in my stomach; that mixture of excitement and fear that can tip over into either.

The first thing to do is find a bed for the night. One good thing about a small town is that it doesn't take you long to work out where the places to stay are. In Wadebridge's case they're above the pubs, which suits both my wallet and my desire to carry on Britain's coaching tradition. I plump for the Bridge on Wool. This, one of two pubs on the main street running parallel to the river, is not much more than a century old, and so has high ceilings and a big central bar rather than curiously angled beams and doorways offering concussion to anyone over five foot eight. It also has a woman in charge who says that, yes, they have a single room available, only

---

16. Nothing exotic – it means 'crooked river' in Cornish. Just as Turkey has a winding river called the Meander, which is where we get the verb.

£35 for the night, what time would I like breakfast? She's the sort of woman (middle-aged, no-nonsense) who by calling you 'love' manages to imply that you're about 16. This could be annoying, but somehow it's actually very refreshing. All those councils that want to ban their employees from saying 'love' need their HR departments knocking together. This woman is a British archetype, and it's great that she and her ilk are still around: they make for a very warm welcome. If I had a horse to be stabled she would no doubt have someone sorting it fresh hay as a matter of urgency.

My room is at the top of the building, a bit featureless but clean and warm, and en-suite to boot. Putting on the bedside rather than the overhead light for a cosier atmosphere, I'm reminded of Beryl Bainbridge who had the opposite preference. In *English Journey*, her 1983 tribute to J. B. Priestley's 1934 classic of the same name, she takes her own lightbulb with her because 'all hotels have 40-watt bulbs, and my eyesight is failing'. (Bainbridge also reveals her own 'never been there' blindspot: Norfolk.) Both books are subtitled 'being a rambling but truthful account of what one man ['person' for Beryl] saw and heard and felt during a journey through England'. Not 'Britain' – virtually the whole of the Library is the same, from Morton's *In Search of England* (he did Scotland, Wales and Ireland, but as separate books) through Jack Hilton's *English Ribbon* to Henry James's *English Hours*. Orwell and Forster wrote about the English rather than the British, while G. K. Chesterton did *A Short History of England*, and sociologist Kate Fox's book is called *Watching the English*. It isn't just literature either: in *Skyfall*, when Bond takes a word-association test and hears 'country', he replies 'England'. Herbert Asquith's grave says he was

'Prime Minister of England'. Even the internet disses the B-word – there was once a '.gb' suffix, but the domain-name registrar insisted on using '.uk' instead. The Act of Union happened in 1707; no one ever seems to have taken Britain seriously, though, even before Alex Salmond had Sassenachs bristling with his twenty-first-century William Wallace routine. Churchill may have said that there was 'a forgotten, nay almost forbidden word, which means more to me than any other – that word is "England"'. But for centuries most Brits – in other words, the English ones – seem to have been bandying it about with relish.[17]

Spreading my largesse, I decide to have dinner in the other pub on the main street, the Swan. Given the county I'm in there is only one possible choice for my repast: it has to be a Cornish pasty, washed down with a pint of Tribute, the local pale ale. The pasty was originally made for tin miners to take underground and eat at midday, often with their initials carved into the crust. Some workers even made it a two-course affair, meat filling in one end and fruit in the other. The thick rim was for the miner to throw away at the end to appease the 'piskies', the mythical creatures who lived in the mines. Or, if you prefer your explanations rooted in real life rather than tourist brochures, something for his arsenic-stained fingers to hold on to while he safely ate the rest of the pasty.[18] To this day people can become quite het up about the

---

17. An exception is Al Murray, the Pub Landlord, who quietens hecklers with: 'This country is called Great Britain – it would be Amazing Britain if it wasn't for people like you bringing the average down.'
18. In 2011 the world's first-ever Cornish pasty museum opened in, as you'd expect, Mexico. There are strong links between that country and Cornwall, enormous numbers of miners having emigrated

subject. The comedian Rory McGrath, for example, holds a very strong opinion as to whether or not a proper Cornish pasty should contain carrots. I would look up which side he comes down on, if I could be bothered to give a toss, but regionalist food pedantry bores me. Not as much as regionalist food protectionism, mind you. As of 2011 the Cornish pasty has been awarded Protected Geographical Indication status. Supposedly so that consumers know what they're getting, the PGI racket is actually to stop most producers getting what a few producers are getting, namely rich. The Cornish pasty doesn't even have to be baked in Cornwall. It only has to be assembled there. Send a frozen but uncooked one to be baked at the other end of the M6 and everyone's happy, apparently. This sort of lunacy abounds. Stilton got its name from the village in Cambridgeshire, but because cheese manufacturers in Derbyshire, Leicestershire and Nottinghamshire have taken out a PGI, you're no longer allowed to make stilton in Stilton. The most ridiculous situation of all came in 2004, when the manufacturers of Newcastle Brown Ale decided to move their factory over the River Tyne into Gateshead. Because they'd taken out a PGI saying you could only make Newcastle Brown Ale in Newcastle, they would have been in contravention of their own rule, so they had to have it revoked.

As I enjoy the pasty, a woman at the next table reveals to a friend that she has recently started having milk delivered to support the local milkman, and that 'my kids didn't know how to open a bottle of milk – they *didn't know*'. Beyond

there in the early nineteenth century to sell their world-renowned expertise. They even introduced football to Mexico – the country's first team, Pachuca Athletic Club, was made up entirely of British miners. The town's clock still replicates the chimes of Big Ben.

them a young man sits with a female companion; from the way he watches her lips as she talks it is obvious that he is hers whenever she wants. I think it will happen, but not just yet. Once I've finished eating, my legs remind me of the fact that I've been sitting for most of the day and that they are keen to be stretched. I step out of the pub and back into Wadebridge.

At the end of the main street a large park straddles the river. Inside it, dog walkers make their way round an impressively sight-screened cricket field. I feel a little sorry for the pedestrian bridge joining the park's two halves. Not because it's not good – it is, a metal-and-wood suspension job – but because it was built by Anneka Rice as part of her TV programme *Challenge Anneka*. That might be a bit of a stigma for a bridge wherever it's situated, but especially in this part of the world where several others can claim Isambard Kingdom Brunel as their originator. There's the Clifton Suspension Bridge in Bristol, where bungee jumping was invented by the Dangerous Sports Club in 1979. (A century earlier a woman called Sarah Ann Henley accidentally did something similar, when after a lovers' tiff she threw herself off the bridge; her skirts billowed and acted as a parachute, so although badly injured she survived and lived until her eighties.) Then there's the whopper made of stone, spanning the River Tamar near Plymouth, the great man's name carved on it in four-foot-high letters. I came through it on the train down to Penzance yesterday, which prompted me to read up a bit about Brunel. I was reminded that this is another point scored by our neighbours across the Channel – Isambard was the son of a Frenchman. Marc Brunel fled the Reign of Terror after the French Revolution, but sent his young offspring back to the homeland to be educated. So the guy who's regularly up there in the 'greatest Englishman ever' lists was actually half-French. *Tant pis*.

On the other side of the river I turn left, heading towards the stone bridge at the far end of the town; not a Brunel one either, dating instead from 1468 and known as the Bridge on Wool (hence my temporary abode's name). The name reflects the trade that traditionally earned this area the most money.[19] The light's going now, bleeding the park and the houses at its far edge of colour, blending everything into dusky monochrome shades. Surely the players on the bowling green are going to make this their last end?

Further on I reach a small war memorial, just three small roughly shaped lumps of granite overlooked by a pole bearing the Union Flag.[20] Fixed to the granite are small metal plaques, one for each of the world wars and a smaller one, bearing just a single name, marked 'Iraq 2003'. War memorials always get me. Not in a simple way, though, not in an upstanding, 'finest hour' way. There's something compromised there, something I feel confused or perhaps guilty about. This evening the feeling is there again, especially since I've learned that it was just north of here, on the cliffs near Padstow, that Laurence Binyon wrote the poem 'For the Fallen' in 1914. It contains

---

19. Indeed a lot of the country earned money from wool, which is why the Speaker of the House of Lords sits on the Woolsack. There was much embarrassment in 1938 when it was found the sack actually contained horsehair. It was promptly restuffed with wool, which as a symbol of unity was taken from the sheep of several Commonwealth countries.

20. I'm calling it that to keep the pedants among you happy, despite the fact that since at least 1902 the Admiralty have been saying that 'Union Jack' is also officially acceptable.

the lines that are always quoted at Remembrance ceremonies: 'They shall not grow old, as we that are left grow old . . . At the going down of the sun and in the morning, We will remember them.' Going down is exactly what the sun's doing now, and as I remember the fallen, my thoughts again refuse to clarify. But every city, town and village on the rest of this trip will have a memorial – Britain's got 54,000 of them. At some point I'm going to have to confront the issue.

As darkness falls, my mood follows suit. Passing an illuminated room in a modern apartment development, I see two naked shop dummies standing either side of a full-sized drum kit. (Someone hoping to follow Truro boy Roger Taylor on the path to fame? The irony is that the Queen drummer's most famous part, 'We Will Rock You', doesn't exist – the record contains only hands clapping and feet stamping.) On another night the surreal *Rear Window* moment could be amusing, but somehow tonight it fosters a sense of disconnection. Heading back over the bridge to complete a lap of the town, I pass the Swan again. On the pavement outside is a toddler, pottering happily around while a fifty-something woman is held back from him by a couple in their thirties. All three adults have clearly been on the booze all day. The older woman begs for 'two seconds, just two seconds' with the boy. When this fails she begins to threaten.

Two minutes later I'm back in my room, trying not to think about the scene. Or about how far I've travelled today. But the road atlas is an itch in the mind, and I have to scratch. The large-scale section tells one version of the story: I've managed the whole width of the first page, and am even slightly into page two. The one-page map of Britain at the beginning of the book has a very different tale to relate. I'm amazed to see just how far down in the corner of Britain Wadebridge is. Based on the age-old idea of Britain looking like a man sitting on a pig, with the West Country as the animal's leg, I've got no further than the top of its trotter. The other image which occurs to me is of a mineshaft. Everything west of Bristol feels like a shaft down which yesterday's train shot me at terminal velocity. Now I'm having to haul myself back up it by short pieces of rope tied to the sides, each one a bus journey. I get slowly to one level, rest, then reach out for the next piece of rope.

Noel Edmonds, who lives in Devon (or certainly did – I don't care to monitor his life too closely), found commuting anywhere from the West Country so time-consuming that he got a helicopter licence so he could fly himself.[21] And that was just Devon – I'm trying to get out of Cornwall by *bus*. A whole day, 82.5 miles of journeying, and I still haven't managed it. Of his John O'Groats to Land's End charity walks, Ian Botham used to say that you travelled and travelled and travelled, and then realised you hadn't even reached the border with England. To a Cornish separatist, I'm in the same position right now. I'm tucked away down the mineshaft. Pasty or no pasty, it feels lonely down here.

I go to the window, pull back the curtain and gaze down at Wadebridge's Tuesday night. The other side of the street isn't that attractive (undistinguished 1980s buildings, flats over shops) and there aren't many people about. That word comes back to me again: belonging. I don't feel that I belong

---

21. A skill he also put to use, publicity-shy lamb that he is, ferrying pop stars up to Wembley Stadium for Live Aid. Elton John went mental when Edmonds flattened all the flowers in his Windsor garden.

here. I think of Jo and my son at home, about as far east of here as you can get without hitting the North Sea. I think about how long it will be before I'm with them again. Despite what I said earlier about Cornwall feeling British, I might as well be in Korea for all the sense of attachment the county's producing in me at the moment. Travel, like all the important things in life, is contradictory. It's thrilling and threatening at the same time. The urge to explore, the desire to get back home. Wanderlust and fear are twins, which explains a lot. The British Empire for a start.

And despite what I said earlier about my body clock having slowed this afternoon, I now find that it's quickened again, and I'm restless. I struggle not to struggle against my self-imposed straitjacket. Deep breaths. This is what you wanted, Mason. Give yourself up to a higher power, like Alcoholics Anonymous members do. They're told it doesn't have to be God. Fair enough: mine is called Bus. Then another thought comes to me, one I hope any *real* AA members will forgive me for: as long as I'm on this journey where all the driving is being done by other people, I can drink as much as I want.

So I go downstairs for a pint.

2

In which we waver over a fry-up, learn how a stand at
Liverpool FC's ground got its name, and experience fear and
loathing in Bristol

I reckon Churchill got it wrong. The word he meant to say,
the one that was forgotten, nay almost forbidden, the one
that meant more to him than any other, wasn't 'England'
but 'breakfast'. The Library is groaning with references to it.[1]
In 'England Your England' George Orwell lists the country's
signature components and first up, before we get to 'green fields'
or 'red pillar-boxes' is 'solid breakfasts'. Somerset Maugham
said that to eat well here you should have breakfast three times
a day, while John Mortimer listed the meal as one of our three
greatest exports (the others being Shakespeare and trial by
jury). He also accompanied his own breakfast every day with
a glass of champagne. Asked by a doctor how long he'd been
doing this, he replied: 'Ever since I could afford to.'[2]

---

1. Or perhaps 'squealing' instead: we're talking about the fried
   breakfast here, the meal with its origins in Collop Monday, the day
   before Shrove Tuesday. You had to use up all your meat before Lent,
   and as so many people kept pigs that meant sausages and bacon.
2. Nice line, John – but tell me, on any meaningful definition of the
   word 'alcoholic', how were you not in the same position as the
   dosser on the pavement with a can of White Lightning? These
   'darker' sides to our national treasures always fascinate me. A man
   who worked in advertising in the 1970s once told me about Arthur

But the quote that's uppermost in my mind early this Wednesday morning is from Julian Barnes: 'Britain – the land of embarrassment and breakfast.' I'm thinking back 24 hours, to my Penzance B&B, where the two were served together. A small room, and a dozen people packed together at a time of day when, let's be frank, no one's at their perkiest – it's a recipe for awkwardness. We all know that at home no one says a word to their partner over breakfast, yet put us in a provincial B&B and for some reason we feel the need to be a cross between Oscar Wilde and Noël Coward (i.e. witty, not ostentatiously gay; though feel free). It's simply not allowed to scoff your Full English in silence: the other people might think your marriage is in trouble if you sit there saying nothing. So it's 'Did you see this?' and 'What do you think to that?' and 'Have you heard the other?'

Thankfully of course I was on my own yesterday, so could enjoy listening to the others suffering. At one point Radio 2 played 'Mirror Man' by the Human League. The quiet start (just synthesiser and tambourine) did little to drown out the sound of one resident crunching his cornflakes.

'Ooh-ooh-ooh-*ooh*,' sang the backing singers.

Crunch.

'Ooh-ooh-ooh-*ooh*.'

Crunch.

'Aaaaah-*aaaaah*.'

At which point the woman at the next table could stand it no more. 'That accordianist yesterday was very good, wasn't he?' she said to her husband.

The question this morning is this: do I go for a second

Lowe. He used a word with the same number of letters as 'Lowe'.

fry-up in as many days? It's dawned on me that not only will the trip's method of transport theoretically allow unlimited consumption of alcohol, but also that its accommodation arrangements will grant access to considerable servings of fat and cholesterol. Given the lack of exercise involved, this isn't an ideal situation. Luckily that same lack of exercise means I'm not feeling very hungry this morning. Add to this that I'm keen to make progress today, and that the timetable for the 510 to Exeter offers a 7.55 a.m. or a 10.05 a.m. with nothing in between, and the decision is made for me. Nice Woman gave me a price for room only and one for 'with breakfast', so I leave the dosh for the former on the deserted bar, together with a note explaining my change of heart on the dead pig front.

To wake myself up on my way down to the bus stop I get a takeaway tea from the café over the road (appropriate in Cornwall, the only British county that actually grows the stuff). The sun's out again, though can't produce much warmth this early in the morning. Waiting at the stop are a duffel-coated man and an Oriental woman lost to texting. Both are obviously on their way to work: this is my first commuter bus of the trip.

After yesterday afternoon's route shenanigans, the 510 feels like an arrow – due east all the way to Exeter on a single bus. This is why it costs £7.50, but the Western Greyhound driver who sells it to me is so cheery I don't mind. You can't dislike a man whose copious belly, untucked shirt and straggly blond hair put you in mind of Mel Smith after a particularly lively weekend. (In a while, when the sun gets really bright, he'll augment the look with a pair of round, blue-tinted John Lennon sunglasses.) The bus is a single-decker, shorter than normal ones, more of a minibus with ambition. The woman standing at the front chatting to the driver is a fellow employee learning the route. Strange to think that this needs doing – you just assume bus routes are parts of the landscape, transportational ley lines that the vehicle could follow on its own. Someone I used to work with in Coventry was late one day because the driver had taken a wrong turning. Apparently the passengers were so stunned it was minutes before anyone complained.

We pass St Breward, where one of the farms feeds its cattle on beer. The fields to the right as we head for Launceston stretch away towards Bodmin Moor. There is no sign of the famous beast. In 1995 a skull was produced as evidence of its existence; this was later revealed to have come from a leopard-skin rug. In the middle of the moor is a hill called Brown Willy. I feel guilty for sniggering at this, and indeed wouldn't be mentioning it here were it not for the fact that an esteemed Radio 4 presenter did just the same a few weeks later when mentioning a campaign to have the hill (Cornwall's highest) renamed. As the suggested replacement was Bronn Wennili, Cornish for 'hill of swallows', perhaps the campaigners would just be replacing one problem with another.

A sign points towards Tintagel, a name that the Kray twins came to resent as Tintagel House in London was where the team that arrested them was based (they had too many grasses inside Scotland Yard itself). The building got its name because, like the nearby MI6 headquarters, it's on land owned by Prince Charles in his capacity as Duke of Cornwall. Also nearby are Chipshop (no, it doesn't have one, just as Booze in Yorkshire has no pub), Sweets and Westward Ho!, the latter notable not only for its exclamation mark but also for being the place where Rudyard Kipling went to school. His poem 'If' is usually voted Britain's favourite in polls and is generally considered a summary of everything fine and upstanding about we of the stiff upper lip – so much so that it's quoted above the players' entrance to the Centre Court at Wimbledon.[3]

My phone beeps with a text: Nice Woman is thanking me for my honesty and asks if I'd like a receipt, then there's a hillside just before Launceston whose different fields (wheat stubble, grass, ploughed soil) catch the sunlight in such a way that they look unreal, as though they're in a Hockney painting. In the town a model of a terrier sits atop a narrow nine-foot brick wall, then moves its head and reveals itself to be a real dog after all. How did it get there? In the centre of Launceston half a dozen more people join us, including a twenty-something couple who are obviously besotted with each other. There are ways of showing this that make you go 'urgh' and ways that make you go 'aah'; these are very much the latter. I feel my cynical old heart defrosting slightly. At 8.59 a.m., shortly after Launceston on the A30, there are two firsts for my trip. We overtake someone – it's dual carriageway here, and even a modest bus like ours can only display so much patience with a dawdling Nissan Micra – and then, finally, we leave a county. Yes, Cornwall has spat me out at last. The 'Welcome to Devon' sign makes me think (obviously) of Derbyshire. That's where the Duke of Devonshire has his ancestral home, Chatsworth House.

---

3. An Australian fan once sent Kipling a request for an autograph enclosing a dollar, explaining that he'd heard that was what the author charged per word. Kipling sent back the reply: 'Thanks.'

He and his ancestors only have the title because the clerk writing out the original grant accidentally put 'Devonshire' instead of 'Derbyshire'. So much of British history comes down to spelling mistakes.

In Okehampton the bus finally fills up, meaning that one passenger, a student in chronic need of a haircut, has to sit next to me. You could do mathematical treatises on the way passengers on public transport position themselves so as to delay the sharing of seats until the last possible moment. Virtually everything between here and Exeter is Dartmoor, and although its edges are cosy-looking (the wild stuff left for the middle), there's still that sense of an expanse of countryside. I look at my map of Britain, and in particular the bit in the north of England where it gets narrow as motorways and old mill towns and football-mad cities crowd in on each other. Better enjoy the countryside now while I can. It comes as no surprise to me that Devon is England's fourth-largest county, though I am amazed at Cornwall only being twelfth. Even Suffolk, which as a resident I'd always thought of as a minnow, is eighth. The biggest is of course . . . ah, but more of that when I reach it. Which, looking at the map, I know I surely will.

At just gone ten we hit Exeter. Its outskirts offer Yonk Asian Foods, a cobbler's called Cobblers, and, in Queens Crescent, one of those beautiful Georgian street signs where each letter is done individually in brown tiles. You see them all over the country, their wonkiness as attractive as their terracotta sheen.

Everything's more regulated these days: there are only two typefaces legally permitted on UK road signs, called 'Transport' and 'Motorway', the latter reserved for where you'd expect. They were designed in the 1950s by Jock

Kinneir and Margaret Calvert, after extensive research involving propping trial signs against trees in Hyde Park and driving towards them at set speeds. There was controversy at the time about their decision to use lower-case letters as well as capitals, but Jock and Margaret stuck to their argument that a word like BIRMINGHAM is difficult to read from a distance, whereas Birmingham gives you 'word shape' to work with. Margaret in particular is a fascinating character. You could argue that she did more to form the look of modern Britain than even the other famous twentieth-century Margaret. As well as designing the fonts she drew the pictures for the road signs, including the legendary 'men at work' one that looks like a bloke trying to put up an umbrella.[4] Much of the inspiration came from her own life: the cow in the 'farm animals' sign is Patience, one-time resident of a farm owned by Calvert's relatives, while the girl in the 'schoolchildren crossing' picture is Margaret herself. That's why the girl is leading the boy, rather than the other way round: Calvert didn't like the old-fashioned overtones of a previous sign showing a boy carrying a satchel.

Further towards the city centre we pass a statue of someone on horseback. It's one of those 'look at me' ones – larger-than-lifesize, plumage on the hat, everything. Whatever their aesthetic value, I always love the educational component of these statues. On this occasion I read the story of Redvers Buller, for it is he who is depicted. Buller was sent out to take charge in Natal when the Second Boer

---

4. Calvert regrets it, saying she wishes she'd made the shovel more shovel-like.

War kicked off in 1899, but a series of 'setbacks' (military code for 'cock-ups') saw him replaced within a couple of months. By then known to the troops as 'Reverse Buller', he nonetheless remained as second-in-command. More defeats followed, one at the Battle of Spion Kop, a hillside whose steepness resembled the new stand at Anfield, Liverpool FC's ground, hence the stand's name of the Kop. He may have been a non-stop military catastrophe, but people round here remained loyal to Buller, hence the fact they coughed up for a statue. It faces away from his hometown of Crediton, a fact which apparently annoyed residents there. There's no pleasing some people.

At just gone ten we finally alight. Exeter city centre is impressive – some good olde worlde buildings and, at one end of the main shopping street, a mammoth glass-fronted John Lewis just days away from opening. On a bench nearby sits a pre-interview teenager in his first suit, practising lines he reads from a pad open on his lap; despite constant sips of 7 Up his lips remain dry with terror. I pop into House of Fraser to buy a new pen (the original ran out on the second day – it's planning that would shame Redvers Buller), and as I pass the toilets a woman emerges and says to the world in general, 'Ah, that's better.'

Walking around Exeter, even just for 20 minutes or so, feels good. It's another gravitational centre, another marker along my route across Britain. All depends on your sense of scale, of course. There's a saying round here: 'That's Exter [*sic*], as the old woman said when she saw Kerton,' which means, 'I thought I'd done all my work, but it turns out I was wrong.' It comes from the story of the woman who saw Crediton ('Kerton') church and mistook it for Exeter Cathedral, not realising she had another eight miles to walk.[5] Meanwhile a friend of mine, now a journalist on a national broadsheet, thinks of Exeter as a stop-off rather than a destination, having put in the hard yards of his early career here. He got hold of 'a reasonable yarn, for a local paper' (his words), relating to a guy who left an Exeter pub one night, eight pints to the bad, and came across a minibus with its engine running but no driver in sight. So he did the obvious thing: he jumped in and drove off. All very good, until the paper ensured that no one would read the story by giving it the headline 'Man, 26, takes bus to get home'.

Back in the café at the bus station (the 11 a.m. to Tiverton still some moments away), I nurse a coffee and survey my fellow travellers. In the corner sits an example of that wonderful British archetype, the Little Old Lady. She conforms to the maximum height requirement (five feet, not an inch more), and despite the day's warmth is wearing an LOL coat, LOL scarf and LOL hat. By her table stands an LOL shopping trolley. It's only as I look more closely that I realise she's seventy, tops. Virtually the same age as my mother, yet neither she nor any of her friends would ever dress like this. Where do you *buy* clothes like that? The ripples of the Gap revolution have reached M&S, Debenhams, everywhere. There simply can't be shops that sell coats like that any more – there must be a laboratory where the Little Old Ladies themselves are made, then sent into the world fully togged up.

As she sips her tea (it was never going to be a latté, was it?), and as some builders bemoan Tottenham's back four, I

---

5. The city's name also featured in fifteenth-century slang for the rack, the torture implement introduced to England by a local bigwig – it became known as 'the Duke of Exeter's daughter'.

think about the road atlas that has just helped me decide on Tiverton as my next destination. Like any map it inspires an almost religious fervour in me, but now I can't help wondering if these documents aren't forces for bad as well as good. This is because I'm playing the 'if I'd been blindfolded and dumped here, would I be able to guess where I was?' game. Without considerable planning, a lot of time and quite possibly the help of the SAS this is a game you could never realistically carry out, but nevertheless it's fun to imagine. Take away the destination boards on the buses outside, the road signs, the names on the shopfronts and the odd local accent, and this could be anywhere in England. That old lady, these builders – they're Standard British Issue. It's only when you look at a map and realise how far away from home you are that loneliness can strike (as it did for me last night). The School of Us and Them causes so much trouble in life, and there are few things that paint as vivid a picture of Us and Them as a map.

Stagecoach, for the privilege of a timetabled 37 minutes aboard their blue double-decker, charge me £5.40, easily the worst-value fare of the trip so far. Among the other passengers are a Polish woman and her toddler daughter, the latter dressed entirely in pink and putting pink stickers in her pink sticker book. After a few minutes the hypnotic effect of this lulls her to sleep. A couple of minutes later the mother nods off too, parent and child slumped happily together as Exeter disappears. Accordingly they miss the poster for local drum 'n' bass club Wonkeylegs, whose logo is the silhouette of a giraffe.

We are heading due north now, before a change of bus in Tiverton will allow me a north-eastwards shift towards Taunton. Going the other way would lead towards Ilfracombe, which I used to visit during childhood family holidays in nearby Woolacombe. This is as far west, if my increasingly feeble memory is to be believed, as I have ever previously been within Britain. The trip up the coast was always the highlight of our holiday week, timed as it was to coincide with the appearance in Ilfracombe of that seismic cultural showpiece of the 1970s, the Radio 1 Roadshow. To think of how excited I used to get at the prospect of seeing Tony Blackburn in the flesh – it gives you hope for the notion that humans really can improve themselves.

Just inland from Ilfracombe is Barnstaple, bit-part player in the single most gripping political scandal of the twentieth century, the Jeremy Thorpe affair. The hitman hired to kill the Liberal leader's one-time boyfriend Norman Scott was so inept that instead of going to Barnstaple he went to Dunstable (just the 160 miles out, then). Further along the coast is Porlock, which has come to be literary slang for anyone who interrupts your creativity. This is because Samuel Taylor Coleridge, who lived nearby, was halfway through writing 'Kubla Khan' when 'a person on business from Porlock' called to see him. Afterwards Coleridge was unable to remember the rest of the poem, which had occurred to him in a dream. The same stretch of coast was also the landing spot for – if the story is true – Britain's most notable visitor of all time. It's where Jesus Christ is said to have come ashore on a trip with his uncle, Joseph of Arimathea; the event that inspired William Blake to ask if those feet, in ancient time, really did walk upon England's mountains green.

South of here, meanwhile, near Torquay, is where another famous person *nearly* came ashore. When the Brits captured

Napoleon in 1815 they put him aboard HMS *Bellerophon* and anchored it off the Devon coast while they decided what to do. According to *Picturesque Touring Areas in the British Isles*,[6] 'the extraordinary beauty of what could be seen of the country drew from the captive a word of praise'. The word in question was *beau*, and Monsieur Bonaparte became quite keen on the idea of settling in England. Boats full of sightseers came out to take a look at the captive, who came on deck to return the favour, but in the end the Admiralty refused him permission to land. Off to the South Atlantic island of St Helena it was. Just as well. If he had settled in the land of his old enemy, Napoleon would have found that Brits were using chamber pots with a small model of him moulded inside the bowl.

It's funny, as we saunter along the Tiverton road, to contemplate Napoleon living in this part of the world. The countryside here is less wild than it was in Cornwall; not overly pretty (thank God), just very, very English. The hills and hedges seem comforting, inviting, rather than wind-tossed bulwarks against a raging Atlantic. You expect a textbook Englishman to come walking round the corner, possibly (depending on your frame of reference) John Bull[7] or David Niven or Stephen Fry. Yet Napoleon wouldn't have

---

6. I've become slightly addicted to this 1920s guidebook, largely because it's terrible and uses phrases like 'bedecked in Nature's richest drapery'. But also because of its opinion that it's 'high time the notion of East Anglia as flat, treeless and uninteresting was dismissed as the baseless myth it is'. If it wasn't a myth I wouldn't have to go to the top floor of my house to get a mobile phone signal.

7. He first appeared in a satirical story of 1712. There was also a character called Nicholas Frog. He was Dutch rather than French. The French character was called Louis Baboon.

been that unusual; plenty of unlikely visitors have graced this green and pleasant land with their presence. Everyone thinks Albert Einstein fled straight from Nazi Germany to America in 1933, but his first few weeks were actually spent hiding in a small hut on heathland near Cromer in Norfolk. He was smuggled out of Hitler's grasp by the British MP Commander Oliver Locker-Lampson, with help from (who else?) the King of Belgium. While in the hut Einstein continued working on the theories that would later produce the atomic bomb. Then there was Alois Hitler, Adolf's half-brother, who a couple of decades earlier had set up home in Liverpool. His son William was born there in 1911. In 1933 William moved to Germany to take advantage of his uncle's newfound prominence.

Meanwhile John Steinbeck, the writer so American that the very mention of his surname conjures up the wind whistling across an open prairie, was a big fan of Somerset. Fascinated by the legend of King Arthur, he used to visit Bruton (there it is, on the same page of the map I'm on now, not far from Shepton Mallet), even renting a cottage there for nine months in 1959. The view towards Glastonbury was so beautiful it made him weep. He planted lettuces, shot the rabbits that tried to eat them, and called his fridge 'His Majesty's Voice' because like George VI it stuttered. Years later, as he lay dying, he and his wife agreed that their time in Somerset had been the best of their marriage.

I have 40 minutes to wait in Tiverton, which is about 39 too many. Very few of the shopfronts reflect the fact that it's no longer the 1980s, and very few of the shoppers' steps have a spring in them. The butcher tries to jolly everyone up with a board for jokes outside his establishment. Today's offering is: 'I went to the doctor's, I said "Doctor, I feel like a spoon," he said "Sit down and don't stir."' A woman, several heavy bags in each hand, stops, reads it and then shakes her head, not in amusement but in genuine dismay.

Next to the bus station is a small visitor centre, where I learn that Tiverton's MP from 1835 until 1865 was Lord Palmerston, who holds the distinction of being the last British Prime Minister to die in office. His final words were reputedly: 'Die? That's the last thing I shall do.' In reality they were: 'That's article ninety-eight – now go on to the next.' If that doesn't exemplify the Victorian work ethic then what does? Another very English sentence left the politician's lips when a Frenchman, trying to charm him, said: 'If I were not a Frenchman, I should wish to be an Englishman.' Palmerston replied: 'If I were not an Englishman, I should wish to be an Englishman.'[8]

Back into action on the 92 to Taunton, another short single-decker like the first bus this morning. I'm beginning to think of the different types of vehicle as being like different breeds of horse carrying a traveller across the country in coaching days. Stop in a town, stable your beast at an inn to let it rest, then set off on a new one. If the double-deckers are thoroughbreds, then these buses are ponies, small but sturdily dependable. The driver, fresh from pouring a bucket of oats and filling up the water trough, informs me that for £7 I can have a one-day pass that will carry me well over the border into Somerset. 'It would even get you as far as Bristol!' he adds, chuckling as though such a thing would be lunacy. I

---

8. More Anglo-French tension at Winston Churchill's funeral. As ordered by the great man himself, his coffin left London from Waterloo station, just to annoy General de Gaulle.

laugh, thanking him as I take my ticket. Best not tell him that's exactly where I *am* trying to get to by tonight.

On the way out of town, as we pass the impeccably manicured grounds of the public school Blundell's, a woman sitting behind me finishes a phone call with a long sequence of ''Bye's, each one successively higher-pitched so that the last one vanishes into a frequency only audible to dogs. Somewhere after the village of Uffculme we cross the border into Somerset (the third county of the day – I'm really motoring now), then we arrive at the town that is the only sizeable settlement between here and Taunton: Wellington. The name means a great deal to any true-blooded Englishman, particularly those who need boots that come well up their leg or like their beef encased in pâté and pastry. Wellies certainly were named after the hero in question, though it's unclear whether the dish was.[9] When Arthur Wellesley came to decide on his title, he chose this place because his family had historical connections here, though he himself had been brought up in Ireland.

From miles away, as the bus weaves towards the town, a huge obelisk is visible on a hill to the south – another of those high-up monuments. The hill was owned by the Duke of Wellington himself, and the monument was erected to commemorate his victory at Waterloo. But my overriding feeling as the obelisk gazes down on us is of sympathy for Wellington's son, the man who would inherit his title. 'Imagine what it will be,' he said, 'when the Duke of Wellington is announced and only I walk in the room.' It wasn't even as though his father was the uncomplicated English hero everyone thinks he was. They

---

9. One theory is that the cooked joint resembles the Duke's own boots, which were made of polished brown leather.

never are, but we do like a national myth. His nickname of the 'Iron Duke' was nothing to do with military strength – it was gained when he later became Prime Minister, and bars had to be put over the windows of his house to stop people smashing them in, on account of his not wanting to give them the vote. On Wellington High Street the bus pauses in traffic, right outside the Conservative Club. I can report, and this would no doubt please the Duke, that its elegant Georgian façade has been freshly painted a pleasing shade of (what else?) blue.

It's a pleasing high street generally, in fact. The stores are thriving, from newsagents to a rather chic optician's called Watson & Smith, and even a little cinema called the Wellesley.[10] That might have been another ego-boost for Wellington, but I can't help wondering how he'd have found modern Britain. Or how we'd find him. It's unthinkable that a military figure could become a leading politician these days. The nation just wouldn't feel comfortable about it, not in the way Americans did about Colin Powell. As A. A. Gill puts it: 'the reason the English . . . won't allow their soldiers to walk around in uniform . . . is because they know where it leads. Far better to do the business as brutally and efficiently as possible and then get back to whatever you were doing before, as fast as is decent.' There is definitely that contradiction in the English psyche: the relish with which we watch *The Dambusters*, and the laughter with which we read about would-be leader Roderick Spode in the Jeeves and Wooster novels. The poppies worn with pride each November, and the shudder down the spine when we see a policeman with a

---

10. What *is* this about the death of independent cinemas in Britain? I've seen them all over the place – here, Wadebridge, even Tiverton.

machine gun at Heathrow. It strikes me that pretty much all our favourite cultural touchstones, war-wise, come from two conflicts: the campaign against Napoleon, and World War II. In both cases we were threatened with an actual invasion of the British Isles, a threat to our own safety. Give us a less clear-cut conflict, though, and we waver – Iraq, Afghanistan, even World War I, the biggest of them all in terms of casualties but the one nobody really understands, not in the sense of being able to tell you *why* we were fighting it.

We pass a local newspaper billboard reading 'Tributes to footy stalwart'. These boards always fascinate me.[11] Every time you read one you just *know* Britain will never have a revolution: we're too busy paying tribute to footy stalwarts. The place names pass by – Hockholler, Rumwell – inducing in me a very calm, comfortable feeling. Not only because Britain is so resolutely untrendy, but also because I'm making steady progress. There's also a sense of unity as I see how they all fit together, these villages that feed the local towns of (in this case) Wellington and Taunton. The places join up, and so do the people. Very rarely do the Brits adopt that hideous concept of the 'gated community'. We may have a class system so rigid you could bounce boulders off it, but those classes aren't geographically separated. We all see each other, all the time. Right now, in the middle of this day in the middle of this week, I love my country.

'Welcome to Taunton' says the sign. 'Best large floral town in the South West'. These awards always provoke a titter

---

11. The best one ever has to be from Norwich: 'Daniel O'Donnell Ticket Stampede'.

from me. You mean there's a *small* floral town in the South West that's better? A village near mine in Suffolk has a sign boasting that it was Village of the Year in 1992. Instead of being impressed, I always think, 'What have you been doing wrong for the last twenty years then?'

Taunton used to be a potwalloper, you know. In other words, it was one of the two dozen or so boroughs in England where in order to get the vote you had to live in a house with a hearth large enough to contain and boil ('wallop') a cauldron ('pot'). Now the franchise is somewhat wider, of course, and even includes the man I encounter as I alight at the town's bus station, the man who is quite openly, and without the slightest irony, whistling 'The Frog Chorus' by Paul McCartney. Don't want to get all Duke of Wellington on you, but I can't help questioning whether this really counts as progress.

The station itself is a brutal post-war brick cube, designed (or rather not) with insufficient room for queues to form at the five stands. The result is that the queues intermingle like confused pythons, the buses that back them up against the building feeling like the prongs of giant snake-handlers. Managing to squeeze myself next to a timetable in the midst of this mêlée, I learn that in 10 minutes' time the number 29 leaves for Wells, which is halfway between here and Bristol. Given the day's ultimate aim, the prospect is irresistible so I breathe in and wait it out.

A woman in the queue behind me – or technically she might be in front, I'm not sure – greets a friend. After initial pleasantries, she asks: 'How's Dave?'

'Huh,' comes the other woman's begrudging grunt. Then, bursting with enthusiasm: 'Our rockery's coming on a treat!'

The single-decker arrives to rescue us from the crush. Soon

we're out on to the A361, the Somerset countryside floating past the windows. West Lyng rewards us with a 'Thank you for driving carefully through our village' sign, though these always remind me of a smoker I once knew who happily ignored 'Thank you for not smoking' notices. 'They're not directed at me,' he'd say. 'I haven't not smoked.' Ah, the Brits and their speeding. The first one to be done for it was Walter Arnold of Kent, in 1896. He'd clocked a heady 8 m.p.h.; the policeman who arrested him caught up with him on his bicycle. To the south, near the village of Curry Rivel,[12] is yet another hilltop obelisk. Known as the Cider Monument, this one was erected by William Pitt the Elder, on land which was left to him by Sir William Pynsent, a local bigwig who'd made his money from Somerset's famous drink. The bequest, which unsurprisingly left Pynsent's relatives a touch miffed, was in recognition of Pitt's successful campaign against the tax on cider. Excise men had been enforcing the tax by entering people's homes unannounced, a practice that led Pitt to coin the phrase 'an Englishman's home is his castle'. You wouldn't expect the taxman to be well-loved creatures in any country, but ours sometimes seem to have gone out of their way to attract loathing and contempt. In 1941, both the 1st Baron Stamp and his son Wilfred were killed when a German bomb hit their house in Kent. The tax authorities followed the legal convention that when this happens, the elder person is decreed to have died first. This had the side-effect that Wilfred now holds the record for the shortest-held peerage ever (becoming the 2nd Baron for a split second before passing the title to

---

12. There's also a Curry Mallet. Nothing to do with smashing chillies, unfortunately – both places are on the River Curry.

his younger brother), but this was actually done so that the family would have to pay not one but two sets of death duties to the Inland Revenue.

We turn left into a tiny lane that slopes steeply up towards the village of Ashcott. Halfway we meet another bus coming down the hill, but as it has just gone past a passing place it reverses upwards rather than making us reverse downwards. *Serious* clutch control. A man behind me on his mobile says: 'We have to get this boat into the water today.' I cringe at the latest management cliché, before realising that he really is talking about a boat. In Street, the town that merges with Glastonbury, a pensioner proudly shows his bus pass in its Union Flag holder.[13] Glastonbury itself has a baker called Burns the Bread, and an estate agent called The Real Ralph Bending. (Have there been fake ones?) There are also plenty of shops with names like Man, Myth and Magik, Conscious Clothing, Crystals and the like. Not my bag, I have to say, but the town's always done well out of its King Arthur/Holy Grail connections. I love the very British way we deal with our 'alternative' beliefs. There are one or two people who truly believe in it all, but no one gets sacrificed and the horses don't get scared. Our appetite for magic – sorry, magik – is catered for in an orderly fashion, with receipts given and VAT forms correctly filled in.

---

13. Pedants will be disappointed that I wasn't close enough to check whether it was the right way up, i.e. broad white diagonal to the left. There's more basis for that than for the 'Not the Union "Jack"' thing, though it is still only convention rather than explicit direction. There were red faces in Downing Street in 2009 when Gordon Brown and Chinese Premier Wen Jiabao signed a trade agreement in the presence of an upside-down flag.

An Indian man gets on with his toddler; only now do I realise how few non-white faces I've seen in the West Country. On the opposite pavement an old man sporting a greying goatee and a leather cowboy hat pilots his shop-mobility scooter, its basket overflowing with odds and sods. He is a considerate driver, and looks as though he genuinely needs the vehicle. Not always the case. You remember that move a few years ago to replace the term 'disabled' with the term 'differently abled'? I think we need a new term now, one that applies to a lot of the people you see driving mobility scooters: 'differently-bothered-about-getting-off-their-arses-and-walking'. In case you think this is overly cynical, I once saw someone driving a mobility scooter with a set of golf clubs on the back.

And so to England's smallest city. Wells Cathedral has been around since the days when this *was* the mark of a city, and was also the centre of a circle (radius 30 miles) within which cheese had to be made in order to be called Cheddar. (Food protectionism isn't that new after all.) It remains a great cathedral, despite Cromwell's troops having used it for target practice during the Civil War.[14] Just as beautiful is the building next door, the Bishop's Palace, home to the holder of said post these past 800 years. The whole complex, if I can use such an un-churchy word, would have been perfect for an episode of *Midsomer Murders*. John Nettles could have found at least three corpses here without straining credibility (not, it has to be said, that that is one of the programme's primary concerns). An information board reveals that the

---

14. You have to question the usefulness of this practice. If you can't hit a cathedral . . .

medieval bishops included Ralph of Shrewsbury. I do love the way English history throws up unexpected names. The first Archdeacon of Cornwall, for instance, was called Roland.[15] Slightly lower down the C of E ranks, the Dean of Wells from 1551 to 1553 was William Turner, a man who hated Catholics so much that he trained his dog to snatch the square caps off their heads.

I wander back through the market square that separates the cathedral from the town's main street. Plenty of tourists are milling about. I'm always torn on this. It's nice to know your homeland is worth a peek, but too many peekers at one time and it starts to feel like Theme Park England. Many of the tourists are American, at least two of the checked-shorts-and-large-camera variety. It's amazing how closely some nationalities insist on conforming to their stereotypes. An American woman once went up to an attendant at the Bodleian Library in Oxford and said: 'Gee, nice place you got here. Is it pre-war?' 'Madam,' came the reply, 'this is pre-America.'

Down on to the high street, where the world's worst charity mugger is operating. Someone offers to sign up, and he responds with: 'Really?!'

'Yes,' says the woman.

'Honestly?!'

The woman nods. Thankfully the chugger manages to pull himself together enough to get the form into her hand. Another incredulous question and she would have changed her mind.

I take a short break at Coffee#1. As I'll learn over the next couple of days, this is a local chain that has taken the

---

15. Not that the English have a monopoly on this sort of thing. King Herod's wife was called Doris.

68

Starbucks format and made it feel . . . well, local. My lack of exercise means that at half-past three in the afternoon I'm still not massively hungry, despite only having eaten a couple of apples all day. I go for the hat-trick, accompanying my coffee with a Golden Delicious. This establishment likes its fruit, I note, mixing different combinations of berries to make its smoothies. The one containing every sort is called the Halle Berry.

A very pleasant half-hour ensues, in which I read about the history of Wells. In 1787 a young woman of the town won the hearts of two brothers. The elder one, 'perceiving that she manifested a partiality for the younger', said that unless she married him he would hang himself. Giving in to the threat, the woman agreed. But within days Elder and his new wife 'found themselves so much deceived in each other that on Saturday last the husband actually sold his bride (with her own approbation) for a half a crown to his brother'. The handover took place at a pub 'where the purchase money contributed towards the expenses of a convivial evening'. And we're shocked by Jeremy Kyle.

More relationship trouble at the next table, where a fifty-something woman is telling a friend about her daughter's recent divorce. In all the time I'm there the other woman utters perhaps a dozen words, most of them 'Mmm', with an occasional 'Really?' The main problem, it seems, is the son-in-law's drinking. 'I told you we were worried about that, didn't I? Right back even before they got engaged. And then on the *honeymoon* . . . Well, we couldn't believe it. To go out and get *that* drunk. And he *knew* the next day was when they were supposed to be going swimming with dolphins.'

My next bus, I know before I even board it, is today's last.

It is the 376 to Bristol. After yesterday's backtracking, hitting my target feels good. I look again at the map of Britain in the road atlas. The climb out of the mineshaft is nearly complete, with the chink of daylight that is Bristol getting ever brighter, ever closer to my outstretched fingers. Okay, if I look too long at the rest of the country, at the long haul up through the Midlands and the North and Scotland, the task still seems daunting. (The sheer *length* of Scotland – it's like someone's hammered it out on an anvil.) So I concentrate on the chunk I've already done, and on the warm glow of achievement this produces. I'm beginning, I think, to get a feel for the way a day on the buses should pan out. Five journeys a day (which happened both today and yesterday) seems the right balance between dawdling and not getting to see anywhere. I've found the project's pace. Or maybe it's found me.

And what's this? Am I about to get my first be-wellied co-passenger of the trip? It would be nice to think so, given the town I went through earlier today, but tragically the builder (for that is what he looks like, rather than a farmer) learns from the driver that this bus isn't for Street – he needs a 376 in the other direction. As it is we depart with me sitting immediately behind two sixty-something ladies of an elegant persuasion. One has found a 'rather good deal' on some books for her young grandchildren. She hands *Saturday Night at the Dinosaur Stomp* to her friend, and examines *Henry's Pirate Surprise* herself. Soon both are silently engrossed. When they've finished the books they swap, and reading recommences.

I get a text which tells me that in Bristol a plan is going to come to fruition; this is exciting. I text the other person back to arrange final details. A sign at the front of the bus reads: 'Hands up if you know how to catch the bus! Just hold out your hand to let the driver know you want the bus to stop.' Very helpful and all that, but shouldn't the sign be at the stop rather than on the bus? It brings back a memory from childhood. When I was 12 my younger brother and I were deposited at a bus stop on the outskirts of Birmingham. We were going to spend the day with our city-dwelling cousins, me to go with Cousin of Approximately My Age to Edgbaston for my first ever Test match, Steve to do with Cousin of Approximately His Age whatever it is younger brothers who aren't interested in cricket do. I'm not sure why my mum didn't drive us into the city, since the car was always king for us sticks-dwellers. Perhaps it was an early wing-spreading experiment. We were told the numbers of the buses we could catch, and left to get on with it. So we sat on the wall near the stop, and waited. One of our possible buses approached – then carried straight on past. A few minutes later the same thing happened. Steve and I weren't sure why these correctly numbered buses weren't stopping to pick us up. We could see they weren't full. But in the days before mobile phones, when you were a kid in this sort of situation you just sat there and waited for things to become clear. On this occasion it took 40 minutes for clarity to arrive, in the form of a woman who joined us at the stop and, when a bus appeared, put out her hand to signal that she wanted it to stop. The ribbing we got from our bus-savvy cousins at the other end . . . To this day, whenever I see the words 'request stop' I think of Viv Richards hooking sixes at will.

Near Clutton, the village church of which is dedicated to

St Augustine of Hippo,[16] a woman in a wheelchair attempts to board. The bus performs a special suspension-lowering manoeuvre, but this still doesn't quite bring it down to pavement level, so the driver manually pulls out a special metal plate. It only takes 20 seconds or so, but still the woman – who, let us remind ourselves, has done absolutely nothing wrong – feels the need to utter that most British of words: 'Sorry'. Ah, the S-word. It was the title of a Ronnie Corbett sitcom. Jackie Mason has observed that 'if an Englishman gets run down by a truck, he apologises to the truck', while according to Will Self 'it is even rumoured that some Englishmen say sorry at the point of orgasm'. Perhaps we should replace the St George's cross with a huge red 'SORRY' emblazoned across a white background. What is this strain of timidity inside us? It's not just the actual apologies themselves – the attitude shows in our whole demeanour. Its latest expression is the phrase 'I'm not being funny'. You hear this all the time now. 'I'm not being funny, but you've given me the wrong change' . . . 'I'm not being funny, but this pizza's cold' . . . 'I'm not being funny, but your dog has just ripped my toddler's leg off and is carrying it down the street.'

This attitude isn't a new thing, at least not if Jack Hilton is to be believed. His book *English Ribbon*, about a walking holiday around the country, was published in 1950, and he suggests (while in Bristol, as it happens) that 'our complaint is one of calm absence of spirit. A kind of gutless ennui has overtaken us.' Okay, he's a chippy so-and-so, Jack – at one point he listens to someone criticising the unions, 'then just when I was going to give him a mouthful Mary pulled me

---

16. That being the ancient name for the Algerian city of Annaba. I know, I was hoping for a different explanation too.

away' – but I think he's got a point. And this was just after we'd won a world war. Then again even the man who led us in that war was eventually to succumb to ennui. That same year, 1950, Churchill held a press call for his seventy-fifth birthday, and when a photographer said he hoped to take the great man's picture when he turned a hundred, the old dog replied: 'I don't see why not, young man – you look reasonably fit and healthy.' Yet when he died in 1965 Churchill's last words were: 'Oh, I am bored with it all.' Are we giving up as a nation? When Kate Fox, author of *Watching the English*, spoke to an American about our acceptance of poor service in restaurants and shops, she received the reply: 'I get the impression that at some deep-down, fundamental level the English just don't really *expect* things to work properly.'

We're heading northwards now, through the final few villages before we're claimed by Bristol. A few years ago the lanes round here echoed to the roar of the young Jenson Button's car. He took his test in Trowbridge, failing the first time because he judged that a gap between an oncoming car and a row of parked ones could be taken at speed. He turned out to be correct in this instance, but that wasn't really the point. Meanwhile, to the west, lies Weston-super-Mare. You can't use the words 'lies' and 'Weston-super-Mare' without thinking of Jeffrey Archer. His life had a touch of the improbable right from the start – the Weston flat his family moved into when he was a child had just been vacated by a family called Cleese, with their young boy John.

As we reach the city today, rush hour has been turned up to eleven, so there's plenty of waiting in traffic. Beside the bus at one set of lights is an ultra-cool cyclist – racing bike worth more than my car, state-of-the-art helmet, luridly tinted wraparound shades, the works. Unfortunately he ruins the effect as we wait for a green light by putting his thumbs in the straps of his backpack, unwittingly giving an impression of 1980s comedian Bobby Ball. Several passengers get off at Temple Meads train station, one of them having spent the last few minutes painstakingly creating a roll-up of almost artistic precision. His lighter clicks into action the instant his foot hits the pavement.

There's no doubt now that this is the first properly big city of the trip. As we pass the Bellyful Caribbean Diner and Takeaway, I try to work out which language is being used by an Indian girl on the back seat engaged in a long phone call; my money, though not much of it, would be on Bengali. Actually that should be 'being half-used' – she's flitting between this language and English, sometimes several times in the same sentence. From the bits I can understand the call concerns a disputed tenancy agreement, though not the girl's own. There is plenty of attitude, and not a few 'innit's.

Bristol's bus station, which we reach at 5.47 p.m., feels bigger than all the others on the trip so far combined. It's a 19-stander underneath a 10-storey building near the ring road. In fact after the two days I've just spent, every road in the city centre seems to be part of the ring road: the mass of dual and triple carriageways, viewed in the light of Wadebridge and Tiverton, makes Bristol feel like Los Angeles. The big roundabout that I reach on turning right out of the station is negotiated by several pedestrian underpasses, at least two of which contain homeless people. I'm sure there were homeless people in the places I've visited so far, but they weren't so apparent – an unhappy badge of city-ness.

And so this is it: I am in the only city in Britain to share a name with one of Sarah Palin's children. The city's rhyming-slang connotations clearly haven't reached Sweden, homeland of the female golf caddy who one day told an unshaven Nick Faldo that he couldn't go out to play with bristols like that.[17] Having said that, pronunciation problems were the reason this city became Bristol in the first place. Before that it was Bristow, meaning 'bridge-place'. The locals had a habit of turning 'l's into 'w's (for instance they'd have said 'middow' instead of 'middle'), so when posher people heard the city's name they mistakenly assumed it was spelled 'Bristol'. They 'corrected' it back to something it had never been in the first place.

Where to stay? The roundabout by the bus station is adorned by two hotels, both chains I've heard of, neither of which have any rooms tonight. One of them recommends a backpacker hostel just round the corner. 'Thanks,' I say, adding the 'but no thanks' in my head. Ten minutes on a bench with the iPad reveals a wider lack of availability. No matter, that'll just be the websites not catching up with cancellations. There is a whole city to explore, and the evening sun to warm my steps – a likely-looking hostelry will surely present itself soon enough. An hour later, after a couple more increasingly fraught iPad (and indeed phone) sessions, it becomes clear that there really is no room at the inns. There's a film festival on (see what I mean about LA?), plus all the students are returning this week. More than one receptionist mentions the original hostel at the roundabout, so when I end up back there I reluctantly take a look. The property comprises a big old Victorian pub and some smaller, more modern buildings,

17. The fact that her name was Fanny gives this anecdote a 'Carry On' quotient of approaching 100 per cent.

arranged around a courtyard filled with backpacker-ish types drinking and smoking and chatting. There is also food available from a covered stall in the middle of the yard. I don't look too closely, but strongly suspect the presence of noodles.

Reception is at the back of the yard. Behind the counter are shelves offering the staples of backpacker life: batteries, toothpaste, bottles of water, etc. I ask the girl on duty (early twenties, nose-stud, posh accent) whether they have any availability tonight.

'I've got a bed in a three-bed dorm.'

Oh, Christ. 'No private rooms?'

She shakes her head. 'Sorry. I've had hotels calling all day to see if we can help out. There's a festiv—'

'Yes, a festival on. I know.'

'There's only one other person booked into the dorm.'

I want to repeat the old 'you can't be a little bit pregnant' line – you've either got a room to yourself or you haven't. But I'm too busy trying to guess how likely it is that any of the hotels that have been calling here have suddenly and miraculously had a room become free. The answer that keeps coming back is 'not very'. That sort of thing only happens in films.

While this thought process is going on (if a mounting sense of panic can be dignified with the term 'thought process'), the girl is looking at her computer screen and clicking her mouse. 'Oh, hang on.'

Don't tell me, a couple have just booked those two available beds in the dorm.

'Actually I *have* got a private room.'

I have the sense to pause and savour the moment. This too is the sort of thing that only happens in films. And now it has happened to me. It's a good job I do pause in this way because it stops me vaulting the counter and kissing the girl, which might have lost me the room as quickly as it appeared. Arrangements are made and £40 changes hands; £45 actually, as there's a £5 key deposit. I can't remember when, if ever, I last stayed in an establishment that charges a key deposit. *Actually* actually it's £46, because on getting to my room I discover that there aren't any towels, and have to go back down to reception to rent one.

Even so the place seems like the Ritz, and not just because the alternative was starting to look like a park bench. The room (which is under the eaves – if this were Paris I would by law be required to start work on a novel) is bare but clean, with a double bed, a duvet cover and a pillow case I have to put on for myself, a table and a wooden chair. The shower room is perfectly acceptable, and I realise the hostel has taken my prejudices and smashed them to bits. If this were a normal trip I would have planned everything weeks ago, and booked myself into exactly the sort of hotel I always book myself into. But tonight, not having definitely known until a couple of hours ago that Bristol was to be where I would be laying my hat, that option wasn't open. The buses have led me to a backpacker's hostel and out of my comfort zone. Where, I discover, things are perfectly comfortable.

I venture out into the night (as it now is) for some dinner. Inspiration for exactly what sort of dinner has come from 'The English People', a 1947 essay that's just one of the George Orwell pieces in the Library. Orwell comments on his compatriots' attitude to food: 'they will refuse even to sample a foreign dish, they regard such things as garlic and olive oil with disgust'. That might have been true then. It might even have been true in the 1970s, when radio presenter Mark Radcliffe's family went on holiday to Spain minus his grandmother, whose refusal took the form: 'Spain? All that curry . . .' But for a long time now our national dish, so opinion surveys and our own eyes and tastebuds tell us, has been chicken tikka masala (invented, depending on which version of the story you believe, in Glasgow, Newcastle or Birmingham). And the glorious tradition of the Chinese takeaway goes back even further, certainly far enough that, to my recollection, at least one in four of the Two Ronnies' jokes ended with the line 'You want another one half an hour later.'

Accordingly, I vow at this point that I will, as I journey across Britain, journey around the world in terms of cuisine, sampling some of our nation's great staples of dining out. I start with Italian. Not one of your corporate places (Pizza Express, Bella Italia, any of that malarkey), but a proper old Italian restaurant with red tablecloths and dripping candles and phallically suggestive pepper grinders. I find one called La Grotta, a nice little cave-like place[18] crouching opposite a large shopping centre. Wednesday night business is slow, the only other diners being a pair of what are seemingly first-daters. She (Mexican-looking, late forties) is far from glamorous, but is still batting well below her average: his long, grey hair is straggly bordering on wild, and if that's the smartest shirt he owns it must be the only shirt he owns. Conversation struggles.

A lovely spaghetti carbonara with salad, ciabatta and a large glass of the house red sets me back £20 including tip. As my fork twirls I think of Thomas Coryat, the Somerset man considered the first Briton to undertake the 'Grand Tour'

18. Hence the name. It means 'cave'. I like a straightforward approach.

of Europe. When he returned from Italy in 1608 he brought with him this newfangled invention. Until then we Brits had eaten only with knives and our fingers. (We hadn't even used plates until the fifteenth century. Before then food was served on 'trenchers', pieces of stale bread into which all the juices soaked, and which after the meal were given to animals or – get this for generosity – the poor.) Charles I championed the fork in the 1630s, and by the end of the century we were all using them.

Time for a second lap of the city, this one starting with the plan that has come to fruition. My 'stately' progress across Britain means that intercepting me is going to be as difficult as hitting the ball in those very early Atari tennis games, where the bat moved up and down the side of the screen like an arthritic centipede. So I've gathered a list of people I might be able to meet up with, people who've got something to say about Britain in its many and varied aspects. Tonight is the first of those, and the easiest to arrange: the person concerned works in Bristol, which I always knew I'd be heading through. It's simply been a case of establishing when. And so here, in the Llandoger Trow, a seventeenth-century pub said to be the inspiration for the Admiral Benbow in *Treasure Island*, I meet Adrian Cole.

Adrian's one of those blokes – I'm meeting more and more of them these days – who despite being almost exactly the same age as me, makes me feel inadequate. He's a *proper* 41-year-old, who knows things like how a diesel engine differs from a petrol one, and which home insurance policy you should have, and the correct names for power tools. He is also on a committee. It is this, rather than his practicality with engines and DIY, that explains why we're meeting up.

Adrian, you see, is the membership secretary of the Land's End–John O'Groats Association. Within seconds of meeting him you can see that the role's a perfect fit. He's happy to chat to anyone, revealing in his West Country accent (a native of Weston-super-Mare, he's always lived locally) a deep love of the activity known as Lejog. Although for some people, as he points out, it is of course Jogle. Pints secured, we find a table in the bow-window at the front of the pub. The room at the back has a blacked-over ceiling; it used to show pictures of scantily clad women, but a previous landlady got annoyed at the sailors ogling them rather than her.

We start by Adrian recounting how he got involved with the association.

'I joined as a normal member, after I completed my second Lejog trip in 2006. My first one was when I was fourteen. A cousin of mine had done it by bike, and introduced me to the lad he'd travelled with, George. He started talking about doing it again, and I said I was interested, so we organised a trial ride in Devon over a weekend. Then we decided to do it, a group of us. We started in November 1984, doing it in stages. We finished in August 1985.'

His parents didn't mind him going off like that?

'No, they were fine. I used to go off camping, doing stuff with the Scouts. I suppose it was a different world back then.'

How did it feel to complete the trip?

'Oh, it was fantastic. Really momentous. Your sense of achievement when you finish is great. You say, "Yeah, I've done it." Then you think, Oh, I've got to get home now . . .' It was the memory of his first trip that prompted Adrian's second, in 2005. By then he'd become a father. 'That sense of achievement, of doing a thousand-mile trip like that, was something I wanted my son to be able to share.'

And so Henry, at the age of just three, saddled up on his trailer bike, one of those that attach to the back of an adult bike by means of a metal bar. It only had a back wheel, but it did have proper pedals, so Henry really was making a contribution. 'Again, we did it in stages, spread over a few months. Land's End to home in a week, then three days to Shrewsbury. Shrewsbury to Gretna took another week. Finally – Henry was four by this point – I booked two weeks off work to do Gretna to John O'Groats. But I said to my boss, "Pencil me in for my third week, because I'm not coming home without finishing." I'm just *not* coming home without finishing. In the end we did it in the fortnight. So before my son started school he'd done Land's End to John O'Groats!'

Henry's 11 now. What does he remember of the trip?

'He remembers bits and pieces of it. We kept a diary as we were going along, and he picks that up once in a while. He always says that he cycled downhill but let me pedal the uphill bits! He was too young, I suppose, to understand the vastness of it. Well, not the vastness, but you know what I mean. We've got the pictures on the wall even now, just like on the fireplace there's a picture of me doing my trip when I was fourteen. And our local bike shop still has our photo on their wall. Henry's proud as punch about that.'

What about Adrian's wife? How did she feel about the enterprise?

'She came with us. She drove the back-up car. Henry and I would cycle five, ten, fifteen miles, whatever, then phone Sara, she'd come and meet us, then we'd cycle on again. Whenever we got fed up we'd chuck the bikes on the back of the car, ready to start again at the same place the next morning. That was handy on the Bodmin bypass, when the police had a word with us. "I don't think you should be cycling on here," says the copper. "We're going to John O'Groats," I reply, "which way do you think we should cycle?" I tell him my wife's never far away, if there's a problem with Henry we can be off in minutes. He says, "Well, you be careful."'

The back-up car didn't always provide quite as much back-up as it could have done. 'A couple of times Sara got lost. Near Warrington, the first time was. A nice woman we'd met went to find her for us. Then again near Haydock. That time we had to cycle back and find her.' In the end, and not entirely due to Sara getting lost, the car clocked up 4,000 miles so that Adrian and Henry could cycle 900.

As we talk I sense that a large part of Adrian's enjoyment of a trip is in the planning of it. Is that fair?

'Oh, definitely, yeah. For the trip with Henry I had the idea of getting six water bottles, so each morning we could fill them all up, keep them in the car and replace the one on the bike as the day wore on, so we weren't always looking for somewhere to fill up the same bottle again and again.'

At this point I feel like genuflecting towards him. That is genius of the first order. (Or is that just my own impracticality showing?) In the association's magazine that Adrian has very kindly brought along for me, I'll later read about the woman who walked Lejog after first ordering 'the maps I thought I would need from the Ramblers' Association library to be sent to various Post Offices around the country'. Maps, pre-planning *and* a library, all in the same sentence. Sounds like my sort of girl. The magazine, incidentally, is called *Quo Vadis*.

This means 'Where are you going?', to which members can surely only give one of two answers.

'I loved planning the Scotland part of the trip,' continues Adrian, 'working out which youth hostels we were going to stay in. I tried desperately to get us into one I'd stayed in when I was fourteen, but it was being renovated, so that was a disappointment. Then with another one, just outside Dumfries, I phoned them, the bloke said sorry, they were jam-packed, there was going to be a big ceilidh on then. I said, well, you're the bloke on the ground, could you recommend somewhere nearby? I told him what Henry and I were doing. He rang back half an hour later, said, "I've had a chat with my wife, our son's bedroom is in the attic and it's got a sloping ceiling and it's a room we're not allowed to let out – but you're welcome to stay there. We won't charge if you give the money to charity instead." When we were there we got invited to the ceilidh as well. We didn't stay very long, because we'd had a really long ride that day, but still . . .'

At the youth hostel in Pitlochry one of the wardens kept a snake. 'Not that the other wardens were very happy about it. Henry was handling this snake, he loved it, he said "Here you go, Dad, you have a go." I said, "No, you're all right, thanks."'

Another thing that's becoming clear is just how much Adrian appreciates the value of exploring your home turf. 'I've always thought that,' he says, 'right from being a kid. I always said I'd never go abroad until I'd seen this country. And I didn't – I was fourteen when I got to John O'Groats, and I didn't have a passport until I was fifteen, when I went to Italy for the first time. Britain's so small in one way, but then it's so big too. For instance, I've never been to your neck of the woods, Suffolk and round there. Once I cycled the coast of Wales, and it amazed me how the accent changed as you went along, how it got stronger and stronger. You can make a trip exciting no matter where it is.'

When Henry was just two, Adrian and Sara took him on a UK tour. 'We did Carlisle, then Scotland, Skye, then Ayr, back down the east coast to York, then Alfreton, then home.' As the names trip off his tongue they sound as exotic as Indonesian islands. 'While we were in Scotland we took in John O'Groats – you have to, don't you? – and then a couple of months later we were down in Devon, so we took the chance to take him to Land's End. So before he was even three he'd been to both places.' Adrian adjusts a beer mat. 'Though obviously that doesn't count as a proper Jogle trip.'

Not all of Henry's travels have been domestic, however. 'We've been to Holland with him, and France. Oh – and Venice. That was a surprise for Sara's fortieth. She thought we were going shopping up at the retail place near Swindon. Passing Bristol airport I pulled in, got the suitcase out of the boot and said to her, "Come on, are you coming then?" She didn't know a thing about it, hadn't a clue. It was a generic check-in desk, so she didn't even know then. I said to the girl on the desk, "Please don't tell her where we're going." Same with the people at the gate.' He chuckles. 'We had a great time. Henry loved riding on the gondola.'

Adrian's pushing at an open door here. The joy of travelling with your child, discovering new places together – it's one of the things I'm most looking forward to with my own son. As Diana Vreeland, the 1960s editor of *Vogue*, said: 'Draw maps on your kids' walls, so they don't grow up provincial.' We talk more about Henry, and I ask Adrian if his son has any idea yet of what he wants to do when he grows up.

'When he was very young he was going to be a superhero. Now he's not so sure.'

'True of us all, eh?'

Adrian nods. 'Yep.'

'Is that why we do it, do you reckon? Go on these trips? Is Lejog our way of being superheroes?'

Adrian considers it. 'Could be.'

We both stare silently at our pints for a moment, in that way middle-aged blokes do when they're contemplating fundamental truths. The word was 'superhero', you'll notice. Not 'superheroine'. I ask if Lejog tends to be a male pursuit.

'Yes, I think that'd be fair. The majority of our members are male. And the committee, which is a dozen or so people – only two of them are women.'

Adrian ended up on the committee when the outgoing membership secretary asked if he'd like to take over. 'Obviously the main part of the job is processing any new applications. We've got about one hundred and seventy members now. Of course, in a little while we can add one more to that – if you're interested?'

'I'd be honoured.'

'Great.' He makes a note to send me the application form. 'Then every autumn one of my jobs is producing a spreadsheet of every completed journey that year and emailing it to the committee, ready for our AGM in January where we make the award presentations. We have that in a hotel in Torquay.'

Ah, yes – the awards. I've been reading about these on the website. It took quite a while. The main one is the Griffin Trophy (the logo of original sponsors the Midland Bank), awarded to the person who raises the most money for charity. There's also the Committee Cup, for a 'wholly exceptional journey'. Then things get rather specific. There's the Brenroy Trophy, for which only cyclists are eligible, the winner being the one who raises the most money for charity but who doesn't qualify for the Griffin Trophy. There's the Cock o' the North Shield, for a journey on a small-capacity motorcycle (defined as less than 100cc). And the Alroyd Lees Cup, for the oldest motorist to have driven the trip ('age verification is required'). Perhaps my favourite is the Christian von Conzendorf-Mattner Trophy, for a journey 'in either or both directions by means of pre-1940 motorised transport'.

Adrian doesn't decide who gets which trophy. 'I feel that's a job for the committee. I make recommendations, but I wait for a concurrence to come back. When it's sorted I email the trophy guy with the details. The trophies themselves remain at the hotel, but the winners get a smaller trophy to keep.' The inventiveness of the award categories only mirrors the inventiveness of the trips themselves. Most people walk, cycle or drive, though even here there are surprises to be had: the fastest cyclist, for instance, is Gethin Butler, at 44 hours, 4 minutes and 9 seconds. The fastest runner, meanwhile, is Andy Rivett, with a foot-bashing time of 9 days, 2 hours. Other records include wheelchair (8 days, 10 hours, 9 minutes) and skateboard (21 days). The fastest time of any trip ever is 46 minutes, 44 seconds: 1985, J. P. Brady and M. D. Pugh, in a Phantom jet fighter. The association's record books also record that 'Henry Cole is the youngest person to complete an end to end under his own steam . . . Henry was presented with the Jack Adams Richard Elloway trophy at the 2007 presentation weekend.'

Adrian runs through some of the other unusual modes of transport. 'There's been unicycle, turbo-charged JCB, motorised supermarket trolley. Spacehopper, someone did. That was Eddie Sedgemore, one of our long-time members. He likes obscure ways of doing it. Scooter he's done, too. Not a motorised one – just a scooter you push along with your foot. We've got some Australian members who come across to do it, I think they're professional record-breakers. They're in the *Guinness Book of Records* for doing it the most times – twenty, it is now. A couple of times they've done it in a Land Rover on one tank of fuel.'

Wayne Booth from Lancaster did it on a motorbike without stopping. Literally: not one pause of the wheels. He fitted the bike with a 74-litre petrol tank, as well as a drinks dispenser and a 'liquid disposal system' (don't conjure with that image too much). He spent months planning a route that would avoid busy roundabouts and traffic lights. Even then a traffic jam on the M6 nearly brought him to a halt – but plucky little biker that he was, Booth kept moving.

I think my favourite story, though, has to be that of Malcolm Wylie. Adrian has just processed his membership application. 'It split the committee, actually, because the journey started in 1995 and was only completed in 2006. Anyway, his thing was, he did John O'Groats to Land's End walking the watershed.'

The what?

'I know – I'd never heard of it, either. Basically it means he had to find the route where any water to his left ran into the North Sea, and any water to his right ran into the Atlantic. He wasn't allowed to cross running water.'

'That's staggering.'

'Yeah. God knows how he worked out the route. He's

sent me the details, but it's so in-depth, there are wiggles and squiggles and everything – I don't understand half of it. I mean, Devon and Cornwall are split by the Tamar, so how did he cross that?' We shake our heads in mutual wonder. What a fantastically elemental way of doing the trip, using the very source of life as your guide.

A little nervously, I ask Adrian about the End to End Club. They're a separate organisation. He shakes his head sadly. 'No, they're completely different. It's our thirtieth anniversary in 2013, and there was some talk on the committee of inviting some of the End to End members to our celebrations. But some people didn't want to. It's so political. All that started before I joined, so I just keep out of it.' He shrugs. 'It's a pity, because it's a common cause.' You can't help but think of the Judean People's Front again. Later, in the booklet that Adrian gives me summarising the history of the Association's first 25 years, I'll read that there have even been mild tremors *within* their ranks at points. The notorious membership meeting of 1998, for example. There was at least one resignation, and threats of more. Eventually 'a visit to the pilchard works at Newlyn, organised by Cilla, calmed the nerves'.

Before Adrian and I part company we talk about his day job. Not to be polite, you understand. Having contacted him because of his role in the Association, I knew for sure he was the man I needed to talk to when he mentioned what that day job is: Adrian works for a bus company. Sometimes things are just meant to be. He now has an office job at First Group's regional base in Bristol, but before that he drove their buses.

'I started driving coaches, actually,' he says. 'That was straight from school, at eighteen. That's the youngest you can drive a Public Service Vehicle in this country.' See what I mean about him being a proper bloke? 'Then later I switched to buses.'

His sociability must have made the job a joy for him? 'Oh, yeah, it was great. You had your regulars, obviously. And it was amazing who you'd meet. One day I was driving, I knew there was a stop coming up but I couldn't see it because a dustbin lorry had parked next to it. So I got level with it, and edged round very slowly, and there was an old lady waiting there. She got on, and I said, "I knew you must be for me and not the binmen because who'd throw a nice lady like you out?" We got chatting, and it turned out she was on her way to the hospice to visit her husband. She was there again the next day, and she said, "You know, it really cheered me up when you said that yesterday." We carried on chatting again, and I found out she'd represented Great Britain at one of the early Olympics! Just this ordinary old lady. You can never guess what stories people have got in their past.'

Occasionally passengers present more of a challenge. 'There was one guy I picked up on the seafront in Weston-super-Mare. He'd obviously had a few sherberts in the afternoon. He wanted to go to Clevedon. We get there, and I'm looking in my mirror, seeing which stop he wants, but he's fallen asleep. We get to the main stop in Clevedon, and I go back to him, say, "This is you." Still fast asleep, I can't wake him. Same thing happens at the very last stop in Clevedon. So I carry on to Portishead, where I know I'm going to meet the next bus *back* to Clevedon coming the other way. I go to him again, tell him, "If you look sharp you can jump off here, cross the road and get the bus back." He finally gets up, effing and blinding, calling me all sorts of names as he gets off the bus. Charming, I think, after what I've done to try and help him. Anyway later, when *I'm* coming back the other way, I get to Portishead and he's still there, slumped and asleep again — he's missed the bus. And I know I'm the last one back to Clevedon. So I open the doors, call out, wake him up, and I say, "You know all those things you called me earlier? They're all true." Then I close the doors and drive off. Now he's stranded.' Adrian chuckles. 'The next day I felt bad. I went to my boss, said, "I think you might be getting a letter of complaint here." My boss listens to what happened, then he says, "Well done, I'd have done exactly the same."'

It's common for 'sleepers' still to be on the bus when it gets back to the depot. 'But you're not allowed to go and shake them to wake them up, because that could count as assault. I used to leave it to the fuellers and shunters — they'd go up and bang the back of the seat. That soon wakes them up.'

These days Adrian's content to drive a desk. He asks me how I've found the trip so far, and I reassure him that his bus company (like all the others) has done me proud. We mention the fact that, unlike the OAPs, I'm paying for my travel. 'The Wrinkly Pass, that's what I call it,' he says. 'Though my mother-in-law goes mad if she hears me saying that.' He also passes on an industry saying: 'A bus runs for those that wait, it doesn't wait for those that run.'

One of the perks of the job is getting to keep unclaimed lost property. 'I've got a coat at the moment that was left and never picked up. Umbrellas, of course, they're the thing — we get loads of them. Every few months we just put them out and let the drivers take them. But *one* of them we fill with those little round bits of paper you get in hole-punchers . . .'

*

Would you call your business PMT? Someone in Bristol has, as I discover on my continued wanderings once Adrian has left to get the last bus home. It's just one element of the pleasing hotch-potch that is Bristol's streetscape. There's everything from the modish Hotel du Vin to grunge-chic Angry Dave's, a clothing store that has teamed up with next-door hair salon Harry Blades on the steep but delightfully named Christmas Steps. I see the billboard ads for PMT – House of Rock before I see the place itself, and assume it's a new musical that crosses *The Vagina Monologues* with *Rock of Ages*. Actually it's an instrument shop, the initials standing for Professional Music Technology. You wonder how anyone could do this. But then you remember the inverse relationship between how much a British male knows about the best pick-up to use on a 1973 Gibson L-5S and how much knowledge he has of women's bodies.

Bristol feels like a big city, not just in size and scale but in ambition. The river is a huge part of it – you can almost smell the salt in the air, sense the connection to the outside world that once made this city Britain's second-biggest port after London. Ships returning from Africa threw the mahogany they'd used as ballast on to the quay; anyone could help themselves to it. As recently as the 1920s H. V. Morton saw ships coming 'right into Bristol town. They nestle down with their cheeks against the Tramway Centre and go to sleep till the bananas are unloaded.' None of that tonight, but the international flavour's still there in the people. A Spanish businessman has thick black hair reaching so far down his forehead it looks like replacement therapy that's gone too well. An American student in Buddy Holly glasses finishes her phone call then bursts into tears.

It's always been this way, of course. In 1770 there were 14,000 black people in England; many working as servants, it's true, but still a far from unnoticeable number even in a population of seven million. And for centuries getting invaded was our national pastime, to the extent that it still defines who those nationals are. Modern studies identify no fewer than 11 major sources in the English gene pool – they are (in order of their first toe-dip in that pool) Celtic, Anglo-Saxon, Norse, Jewish, French, African, Irish, Polish, West Indian, Asian and Eastern European. As Daniel Defoe wrote: 'From a mixture of all kinds began, that heterogeneous thing – an Englishman.'

Nevertheless, we abandoned being invaded in 1066, after William the Bastard came visiting.[19] That's according to most history books. Others claim that the last successful invasion of Britain was when William of Orange sailed over from Holland in 1688 to take the throne from James II, though the 1066 brigade say that doesn't count because William was invited in by James's enemies. Either way we've been clean of the habit for several hundred years. It's over 200 years since there was even an *un*successful invasion of Britain: 22 February 1797, to be exact, when 1,400 French soldiers landed near Fishguard on the coast of Wales, looking to overthrow George III. They lasted all of two days, at which point they saw some local women in their traditional Welsh costume, mistook them for Redcoat soldiers and promptly surrendered. Sometimes you think the French *want* us to laugh at them.

---

19. The man who actually commanded the Norman army, and personally cut off King Harold's head, was Eustache Fiennes. If you want to see what he looked like, take a gander at the Bayeux Tapestry. If you want to see what his descendants look like, take a gander at the actor Ralph Fiennes or the explorer Sir Ranulph Fiennes.

So the 'island fortress' mentality is now firmly entrenched. It's had huge consequences, not least in our relationship with the countries who are our nearest neighbours. There was Churchill in 1950: 'We are with Europe, but not of it . . . We dwell among our own people.' In 'England Your England' George Orwell refers to British soldiers in World War I: 'In four years on French soil they did not even acquire a liking for wine.' A touch harsh, that, George. Pretty tricky to hop out of the trench to attend a tasting session at a local vineyard. Orwell also opines that 'nearly every Englishman of working-class origin considers it effeminate to pronounce a foreign word correctly.' Curious that we should have this attitude, when so many English words come from other languages. 'Blighty' itself, for instance: it's derived from *vilayati*, the Hindu word for 'foreigner'. And next time you see a bungalow with a Union Jack[20] flying in its garden, remember that word is another Indian import, meaning 'home in the Bengali style'.

By now my steps have reached Queen Square, which is large and manicured and tree-dotted, lined on all four sides with elegant buildings from the eighteenth and nineteenth centuries. The same bus-induced appetite for exercise as last night is with me despite my laps of Bristol, so as well as doing the perimeter of the square I start along its gravel tracks. These form two crosses meeting in the centre, one conventional and one diagonal (a St George's and a St Andrew's, you might say). At that centre is a statue of William III, which is what the aforementioned William of Orange became after his successful invasion of 1688. One of the first of the many to defect to him from James II (the defections that stop it being

---

20. Pedants: I've decided enough is enough. Union Jack it is from now on.

counted as a proper 'Johnny Foreigner' invasion) was John Churchill, 1st Duke of Marlborough and ancestor of You Know Who. So even in Winston's DNA there was the odd gene that didn't see Britain *completely* as an island fortress.

The historian Arthur Bryant referred to the British as 'a nation of many strains', saying this 'may account for the paradox that a people famed for stolid, patient, practical common sense . . . has produced more adventurers, explorers and poets than probably any other in history'. Is that what drives us, this central contradiction? It would explain our inconsistent attitude to the rest of the world: proud of 'dwelling among our own people', we nevertheless spent three centuries going all over the world collecting *other* people and their countries as though they were cigarette cards. You can see why we got up so many people's noses. Cecil Rhodes, the collector of most of the African cigarette cards, said: 'Remember that you are an Englishman, and have consequently won first place in the lottery of life.' I often think of that when I'm struggling to get served in a newsagent's; to be an Englishman these days you have to spend your whole life trying to win first place in the National Lottery.

The most famous quote on the other side of the debate came from the American Duncan Spaeth, who said the reason the sun never set on the British Empire was that 'God would never trust an Englishman in the dark'.[21] But he was only repeating what plenty of others had said about us down the ages. In the 1500s alone you had the Dutch merchant Emanuel van Meteren saying the English were 'very suspicious, especially of foreigners, whom they despise', a German visitor declaring them 'extremely proud and overbearing –

---

21. See, other people use 'British' and 'English' interchangeably, too.

they care little for foreigners, but scoff and laugh at them', and someone from Italy labelling the English 'great lovers of themselves . . . when a handsome foreigner walks by they say "he looks like an Englishman".'

By the 1800s you had the French writer Stendhal calling us 'the most obtuse and barbarous people in the world'. And it's as I think about this that things get complicated. Because, yes, I entirely agree that the English were pretty barbarous, certainly back then as we tried to paint the entire globe pink. But when a *foreigner* calls us barbarous, my reaction is to get annoyed. The 'belonging' instinct kicks in, and instead of recognising the truth of what he's said, I start getting defensive about my home nation. It's not that I'm accusing him of hypocrisy – though it must be said the French weren't entirely stay-at-home types themselves at that time, and not completely unacquainted with a musket and a map. No, I'm just getting annoyed because someone else has had a go at my country. It's like Keith Richards on Mick Jagger. Keef has had an awful lot of uncomplimentary things to say about his band mate over the years, on everything from his willingness to accept a knighthood to the size of his old chap. But as soon as anyone else has a dig, ranks are drawn. I can diss him, says Richards – you can't. Cross him and you cross me.

I'd like to think that deep down, having parked the complications, my real attitude is that of Edith Cavell. God, what a heroine that woman was – and is. A British nurse working in German-occupied Belgium during World War I, she not only helped smuggle 200 Allied soldiers to safety, she also treated every injured soldier she could, Allied or German. When the Germans discovered this they sentenced her to death. She was executed by firing squad at dawn on 12

October 1915. Despite the fact that hardly anyone seems to have heard of her these days, Cavell's name lives on in streets, schools and hospitals all over the country, from Billericay to Hull, Crawley to Salford, Bishop's Stortford to Norwich – as well as in India, Canada, Argentina and elsewhere. It also lived on for a while in Edith Piaf, who was named after her. I think she'd like the internationalism of all this. The night before she died a chaplain was sent to give her Holy Communion. 'Patriotism is not enough,' she told him. 'I must have no hatred or bitterness towards anyone.'

As I head back to the hostel, that word 'hatred' is the one that stays in my mind. I have not been a total stranger to that emotion. Only now that middle age has come knocking do I really start to appreciate how harmful it is, not just to relationships between people but to the hater himself. Why does it keep bubbling up? Why is it not enough just to say, 'I'm not going to hate any more'? Why is it there, like your blood or your bones? Fear, that's why. Because we're all afraid – of other people, of the unknown, of life's inherent uncertainty – and hatred is fear with its gun drawn. As Ratty says in *The Wind in the Willows*: 'Beyond the Wild Wood comes the Wide World . . . I've never been there, and I'm never going, nor you either, if you've got any sense at all. Don't ever refer to it again, please.'

So we lurch from one extreme to the other; one century we're empiring it all over the globe, teaching other nations how to live and helping ourselves to their natural resources, the next we're hunkering down in our cottages resenting the immigrants who land in Britain. Bristol feels like a punctuation point on my journey, the start of multi-racial Britain. I think of my own mother, whose family moved to

England from Ireland when she was 10. They moved to a big city, Birmingham, which is the reason she met my dad (he worked there, having lived, as he still does, in a small village outside it), which is the reason I'm here.

It makes you feel very insignificant, pondering the fact that your own existence is just an accident of geography. The older I get the more I like that – feeling insignificant. Life seems easier to bear that way. Is that why travel appeals to us? Do we like the sense of being very, very small in a world that's very, very large? Perhaps it's why I'm loving sitting on these buses, cocooned in anonymity as their wheels roll slowly across Britain. It feels safe. A good place to watch from.

3

In which we learn of Edward II's unusual death, have a curry, and discover time travel in Worcester

You would think, Britain being as small as it is, and my love of maps being as strong as it is, that I would have heard of every decent-sized town in the land. Even though I haven't been to lots of them, their names would surely have passed beneath my gaze as I pored over a modern Ordnance Survey or an eighteenth-century print – or indeed listened to a news bulletin, or read a newspaper. But no, this morning's first destination, which is a town big enough to be the halfway stepping stone between here and Gloucester, has never impinged on my consciousness. Plenty of other places round here are familiar enough – Chipping Sodbury (its first word meaning 'market', as in the street name 'Cheapside'), Tetbury, Stroud, Cirencester . . . but Dursley? Never heard of it. Admittedly the name will ring a bell with those familiar with the Harry Potter books: the unpleasant Dursleys are Harry Potter's only living relatives. J. K. Rowling used the name because she was born near there, in a town called Yate. That's news too: after all that stuff about writing her first book in an Edinburgh café, I always assumed she was one of those Scottish people who are so posh they sound English.

The café at Bristol bus station is a Pumpkin. Who chooses the names of these chains? As an overly cheery breakfast-show presenter plays Madness, I sip my tea and keep an eye out for the 310A. A neighbouring stand hosts boisterous sixth-formers queuing noisily for the bus to Bath, while next to them unsmiling young office workers wait in glum silence. What a difference a couple of years make. All the stands have dot-matrix displays, and as the 121 to Weston-super-Mare scrolls through its itinerary it displays the names of neighbouring villages Churchill and Langford. I can't help but think of Winston and Bonnie sharing a drink.

The First Group blue-and-purple single-decker arrives, and soon we're heading north out of the city, past bars and shops, everything from Head to Toe (they do 'follicles' and 'life and soul empowerment') through to Atomic Burger and Abba Taxis. There's a Royal Oak, the pub name that derives from the Shropshire tree Charles II hid in as he fled from Cromwell's forces; this one has gone trendy, though, and its logo is an acorn. Things feel messy now, marking an end to the rural idyll that was all I'd observed before Bristol. This city has marked the point at which Britain gets dirtier, less cogent, sometimes surreal. There's an electrical contractor called David Fear, a gym called Risk, a sex shop called My Only Vice. Six huge orange cement-mixing lorries sit parked outside a tool-hire company, but as they're shinily brand new I can't quite take them seriously – they look like Dizzy from *Bob the Builder*. Similar credibility problems for the police station in the suburb of Filton; it's been converted from a terrace of four 1960s council houses.

Nonetheless I'm enjoying the ride. This morning, for the first time, the trip seems like a job, the thing I do every day, rather than something new and strange. And it's a job I like doing. I feel at one with the other commuters on the bus. A businessman, middle-aged and chunky, wears standard-issue black brogues and grey trousers but rebels with a silver earring and wrap-round Ray-Bans. The pink-coated woman in front of him combines a zebra-print iPhone with a leopard-print handbag. We pass a huge Rolls-Royce plant, then an Airbus factory with its own runway; a small plane comes in to land, crossing the road frighteningly low in front of us.

We're out of the city now. Thornbury is home to the alarmingly titled Hammer Out – Brain Tumours (a charity named for a West Ham fan who succumbed to one). Just before Kingswood a sign informs us that we're now in Gloucestershire. This county's greatest cricketing star, W. G. Grace, had his own take on British fair play: a coin with Queen Victoria on one side and Britannia on the other side – as it was tossed he would call 'woman'. There's lots of Cotswold stone on show now. It's pretty to look at, but ever since the holiday when my partner and I took our bikes to that region it always stirs painful memories in me. We were looking forward to some pleasant pedalling, quite possibly humming 'Housewife's Choice' as we went. We'd forgotten that 'wold' means hill.

As the bus circles Dursley, mopping up the last few villages, we collect a dozen or so old people who all know each other. They call the driver 'Driver', and while many people on the trip so far have said 'thank you' when getting off, this lot do it as they get on too. I like this very unmetropolitan touch. A friend of mine in London makes a point of thanking bus drivers; they never acknowledge him, and one even said, 'What for?' Politeness reached its zenith on a bus I once took in Leicestershire – as an old lady got off she tipped the driver.

This morning's group all comment on the absence of one regular member, who has, I hear several times, got a ''pointment.' There is much discussion of the increased cloudiness, though two of the group differ over whether it is actually *too* cold today. You can hear in their voices, and see in the angles of their bodies, that the disagreement is really about far more than temperature. Then silence as we wait for a gap in traffic that will let us join a main road – everyone's head swings in unison from left to right and back again, as if watching a tennis match in slow motion.

This has been the longest journey of the project so far – 34.1 miles, taking a little under two hours (total mileage now stands at 257.7). It's also been the journey that confirms I won't be going to Wales, the nearest I'll get to the principality being the sight of it across the River Severn just north of Bristol. It was a few minutes before I realised that the two huge white road bridges marked the end of England. It's another reminder how silly national boundaries are – the terrain of Wales visible to me looks exactly like that of England. Wales tends to get lumped in as part of its larger neighbour anyway, much more so than Scotland. The Welsh are also one of the only remaining groups you can safely insult. (Them and ginger people.) Very often they'll get their retaliation in first, making the sheep jokes before you can. Just occasionally there's a bit of bite to it. A Crystal Palace fan I know went to see his team play Cardiff City in the FA Cup. Leaving the train station he asked a policeman for directions to the ground. He got the response – and this was a policeman, remember – 'It's that way, you Cockney c***.'

Back in the Civil War, Cromwell's troops, when they weren't chasing monarchs up trees, got a bit lively across the border. At one point they tried to blow up Caerphilly Castle, but only succeeded in making its south-east tower tilt (it's still tilting, and at a steeper angle than the Leaning Tower of Pisa). These days Anglo-Welsh militarism is confined to the SAS doing their training in the Black Mountains that straddle the two countries. In one exercise they're sent on a fully laden 10-mile run, and told they can stop only when their hand touches the back of a waiting Land Rover; just as the first man is reaching out, the vehicle pulls away and drives another five miles.

Dylan Thomas said of his home country: 'The land of my fathers – and my fathers can have it.' The Welsh should shout about themselves a bit more, in view of what they've given us over the years. It's not just Tom Jones and a fancy name for cheese on toast. There's the equals sign (invented by Robert Recorde of Tenby, circa 1550). The Welshman Major Walter Clopton Wingfield invented lawn tennis, while that most English-sounding of all English homemakers, Laura Ashley, was actually a girl from the valleys. The nation that houses Britain's smallest city (St David's, which is even tinier than Wells) also named the world's tallest mountain: George Everest was the surveyor of what the Brits then called Peak XV, though with Welsh modesty he was reluctant to let his name be used, staying embarrassed about the honour until his dying day. Las Vegas was founded by Welsh Mormons and, as if to complete the circle, there's a tiny village in Wales called St Elvis. Nothing to do with the King, though – the saint was a sixth-century bishop. From Ireland, naturally.

Perhaps it's the famous Welsh lilt that's to blame. Perhaps you just can't sound militant in a Welsh accent. Gertrude Leather sits next to a Welshman on her bus from Birmingham to Stratford-upon-Avon. (This, the geographers among you will have noticed, is a southbound journey – having reached

John O'Groats she gives an account of her return trip.) 'There is soft I am,' he says, having realised he's made a mistake. 'From Wales you are!' replies Gertrude, and the two fall to chatting. It's hard to intimidate people when you speak like Yoda from *Star Wars*.

And so the day continues. For the first time it really feels like I know what I'm doing. Any journey takes a while to find its groove, its sense not just of direction but of timing, and now, on day three, this one has done just that. It serves up a series of destinations I've never been to before, though surely I must have crossed this Gloucestershire/Worcestershire terrain at some point. First up, Dursley proves a serviceable little place. Its stone-pillared market building dates from 1738, and fantastically, instead of being roped off and daubed with plaques explaining its history, takes the radical approach of still housing a market (batteries for my portable radio: £1.49). Then it's a mug of tea in a café where someone has left a copy of the *Western Daily Press*. The headline 'Jesus refers to his wife in text' makes me splutter, but relates to a fragment of ancient papyrus rather than Our Saviour possessing a Samsung. As I leave I hear only one sentence from the two women sitting near the door: 'She does like going to the toilet.'

Consulting the map I notice, just the other side of the M5, the town of Berkeley, which is linked aristocratically to this place: the Earl of Berkeley's heir apparent was always known as Viscount Dursley. The family's castle was where Edward II was murdered, so the story goes, by means of a red-hot poker inserted somewhere familiar to customs officers, though to prevent tell-tale marks the killers first put the poker into a deer horn, then the deer horn into . . . well, you get the idea

(Edward certainly did). The family's pack of foxhounds, the Berkeley Hunt, gave us (via a change of pronunciation) the word 'berk'; Berkley Hunt used to be rhyming slang for the much ruder word that that Welsh copper used to my friend.

The nerd in me likes the fact that my twelfth bus is a number 12. As we await our departure for Gloucester with the engine ticking over, the driver brags to a regular passenger that he doesn't drink. 'Not on this job – if I have three or four days off, I *might* have a bottle of beer.' Next to me a teenager's red bandana stretches from underneath his black trilby all the way down his tattooed neck. After a few stops I have to move seats because a female pensioner gets on sporting a pink candy floss hair-do of such extravagance that it literally blocks my view.

Soon we're out into countryside, skirting the western edges of the Cotswolds. It's not pretty-pretty here, not like the heart of Celebshire to the east, but then I quite like that. There's an exclusivity about the Chipping Norton/Bourton-on-the-Water/Moreton-in-Marsh set that can wind you up. It seems almost preening, though of course the reason Kate Moss et al. moved there was for privacy. Salman Rushdie's first weekend on the run after his little difficulty with *The Satanic Verses* was spent there, at a hotel in Broadway. The bloke in the next room was a tabloid journalist entertaining his mistress, completely unaware that he was a few feet away from the scoop every newspaper in the world was after.

As we are nearing Gloucester a lad across the aisle from me, his headphones vibrating tinnily, fails to hear his phone ringing. I make the internationally accepted thumb-and-little-finger-to-the-head gesture; he takes the call and smiles his thanks. Unlike Dr Foster I've never been to Gloucester, and so am astonished to discover that it is – and here I'm going to be as generous as I possibly can be – a shithole. Perhaps it's the famous building society that has always linked it in my mind with lovely Cheltenham, but Gloucester turns out to be a far from charming place in which to spend a lunch hour (by now it's midday). A group of 'eccentric' dog walkers have met up in the main shopping arcade; these people, the sort whose lives revolve entirely around their dogs, always attract each other, like all the plastic bags out on the ocean coming together in a huge island. Nearby, a piece of day-glo lime green card announces: 'Polite Notice: Do not loiter outside this shop'. Signs like this always wind me up – you can't make something polite just by putting 'polite' before it. Even the cathedral (a spectacular building in itself) looks messy, a notice telling us that when the restoration work is complete it'll be the first time in living memory the building has been free from scaffolding. All in all I can't help thinking that Daniel Defoe was doing Gloucester a favour when he called it 'tolerably built, but not fine'. I'm pleased to depart on Stagecoach's single-decker to Tewkesbury.

Or, as I soon learn the locals call it, 'Chucksbury'. Behind me sits a middle-aged woman with a male companion, their conversation soon revealing that they're newly attached after failed first marriages. 'We've just had two pasties in Gloucester,' she tells a friend on the phone. '*Four pounds sixty*. And they were bland. *Bland*. Still – you learn from these experiences, don't you?' Putting her phone away, she notices the building over the road.

'What's that – Railway House?'

'It's the headquarters of the council,' says her companion.

'Why does it say Railway House?'

'It used to be the headquarters of the railway.'

The wind's getting up now, and a light rain starts to fall on the cellophaned flowers tied to a telegraph pole on the A38. These sad little memorials must always act as unofficial speed cameras, though the message is compromised a bit here by the addition of an unopened bottle of cider. Tewkesbury, when we reach it, turns out to be a lovely little town that likes its antiques and artisanal cheeses. It doesn't feel the need for a bus station, just a couple of stops on the main street. The Hop Pole Inn boasts its connections with *The Pickwick Papers*, a plaque announcing that the title character stopped there on his way to Birmingham. There's hardly a town in the country that doesn't have a Dickens plaque, many of them announcing that the great man drank there himself. It's a miracle he ever wrote anything at all – the bloke must have been permanently pissed.

I pop into the Roses Theatre, because I want to see the place where Eric Morecambe died, then feel guilty when the woman behind the ticket desk asks if she can help. I toy with the idea of pretending I'm interested in a forthcoming show, but decide to own up. She smiles, and says yes, this was where he did his last show before collapsing backstage immediately afterwards. They've even named a meeting room after him.

In a charity shop – like most places Tewkesbury is breeding these as a hobby – I find a fantastic Mr Man book, and decide to post it to my son. (He's almost certainly got it already, but I am missing him.) I take it to the till. After the assistant has typed in various codes (charity shop tills increasingly resemble the flight deck of a space shuttle), she asks if I know it's three for 99 pence.

'It's OK,' I say. 'I only want this one. I'll pay the ninety-nine pence just for this.'

'Oh. If you're only having this one I'll have to charge you full price.' She looks inside the cover. 'One pound fifty, please.'

Confronted with madness like that you can either quietly emit steam from your ears, or laugh. I choose the latter. Only as I walk away do I realise what I should have done – chosen another two books, paid my 99 pence, then instantly given the two unwanted books back as a donation.

It's a small white-and-red single-decker north from here to Upton-on-Severn. We're pretty well following that river now (Britain's longest), so it's pleasing that we go through a village called Ripple. Passing a horse on a very narrow lane, the driver slows almost to a standstill; all is well until his airbrakes suddenly decide to release themselves with a huge hiss, and the horse's rider has to work hard to stay in control. She's clearly a seasoned operator, though – even the horse's ankles bear hi-vis straps. The journey marks a rare exception from the 'accents morphing unnoticeably' rule that has seemed to apply on most of the trip. The first half echoes to Tewkesbury accents (essentially a Vicky Pollard Bristolian leavened by a hint of Welsh) but as we near Upton I get a shock. The accent that dominates now is one I know only too well from my childhood. It would appear, dear reader, that we are entering that mythical kingdom, that region of lore, that land of legend known simply as 'the Midlands'.

I say 'mythical' because to the rest of the country the Midlands simply isn't there: southerners lump it in with the North, northerners lump it in with the South. It's only ever brought out of non-existence when a TV programme needs a comic character: Barry in *Auf Wiedersehen Pet*, Benny in *Crossroads*, that character Harry Enfield did who always bragged about being 'considerably richer than yow'. Among the few real-life Midlanders ever to become famous was Black Sabbath's Tony Iommi. Asked why he moved back to the region after several years in Los Angeles, he replied that he missed the sarcasm.[1] But then that's the thing about the Brummie accent: it makes *everything* you say sound sarcastic.

It's amazing, as I potter round Upton, to hear those 'interesting' vowel sounds. (They were a challenge to the voice-recognition phone system recently introduced by Birmingham City Council, especially when it came to 'five' and 'nine'). I never knew the Midlands stretched this far south. A woman on her mobile asks, 'Is Derek there at all?', as though just part of him might be. Upton is easily the most patriotic place I've visited so far – it's well over a month since the Queen's Jubilee/Olympics fever ended and the whole town is still bedecked with Union Jacks. A small local museum merits three minutes, mainly spent listening to the posh lady on the desk dealing with a utility provider by phone. 'The property is let, you see. My managing agent wrote to you several months ago to inform you of this. Have you that letter on file? Oh. Clearly something has gone awry . . .' Eventually she gets her way, as only a posh woman who refuses to believe in call-centre scripts can.

Opposite the stop where I go to await the 362 to Worcester is a funeral director's establishment, the window displaying a respectful mix of flowers, headstones and urns, all backed with sombre wooden panelling. Unfortunately someone has

---

1. Rod Stewart coped with homesickness in LA by going to stand outside whenever it rained.

left one of the panels open, allowing you to see through to a desk bearing a sliced white loaf in a plastic Morrisons bag. My mother texts to say that if I'm passing Daventry I could call in to see my aunt and uncle who live there. I imagine the line from Land's End to John O'Groats, and chuckle as I try to guess just how far to the east of it Northamptonshire is. At the stop over the road someone runs for a bus that's pulling away, and *just* manages to appear in the wing mirror in time. I once caught a London Routemaster at Hyde Park Corner, jumping on the back as it sped up, only for the guitar case slung from my shoulders and the small amplifier in my left hand to start dragging me back. I was young enough that what really worried me as I struggled to cling on wasn't that I might break my back, but that I might break my guitar. Those were the days.[2]

Finally the 362 arrives, a mere 18 minutes late. On my timescale that's not very much, but the driver is far from happy. A small, grizzled man with a grey beard, he scowls as we board, though as the three other passengers seem as unconcerned as me he needn't worry. The fare is just £2, the cheapest ride of the trip so far. I think about pointing this out to him, but on reflection decide to stay quiet. The sun's back out again, dipping towards the Malvern Hills a few miles to the west, forming hints of rainbows. The light throws a ghostly shadow of our bus off to the right which seems to race us, sometimes pulling a few yards ahead, sometimes slipping behind. All is peaceful as Worcester beckons. The terrain is flat apart from the hills, and even they are modest and discreet, just as you'd expect from something that

---

2. Both the guitar and I survived.

provides such exclusive water. I feel a sense of contentment, of satisfaction with a good day at the office, or rather the five offices on wheels that have carried me 56 miles; 56 crow miles, that is – the buses have carried me 90. But that's okay. That's what this is all about.

There is so much of historical note in Worcester. Its cathedral is the final resting place of King John (they opened the tomb once and found he'd been buried in a monk's habit to try and improve his slim chances of getting into heaven), and also houses a monument to the Countess of Salisbury, the woman who inspired the Order of the Garter when she accidentally dropped hers in front of Edward III. Worcester was where the government would have relocated to if the Nazis had invaded, where the current Queen's Coronation gloves were made, and where, in the 1820s, Mr Lea met Mr Perrins and tried to make a sauce; it was disgusting, and only when they found the barrel several months later in a cellar did they find it had matured into deliciousness.[3] Worcester was a favourite place of local boy Edward Elgar, and was where the English Civil War was finally won. I therefore feel a little bit shallow in confessing that the thing I'll best remember it for is seeing the least convincing tranny I have ever seen in my life.

You only get this in Britain. Other nations – from what I've seen, which admittedly isn't as much as some – put in a real effort. Yet this bloke, stick-thin and in his fifties, standing outside a gay pub in fishnets and a basque while he smokes and nurses a pint, has gone to almost no trouble whatsoever

---

3. Good that both names remain famous. I always feel sorry for Mr Taylor, edged out by Mr Waite and Mr Rose.

to hide his masculinity. The Anna Wintour wig is askew, the shoulders are hunched, and you could strike a match on the stubble covering his Adam's apple. It has to be a deliberate statement, a very British 'up yours' to the notion of trying. There's also something of the saucy seaside postcard about it, a one-person cross between the ravishing secretary and the feeble old man.

Worcester isn't as pretty as I'd imagined, much more a working city than one where tourists amble round cloisters. Roads lined with factories force their way well into the centre, and the shopping precinct which houses the bus station in its basement is distinctly 1980s. As we arrive, an empty vehicle nearby accidentally sets off its recorded 'This bus is under attack' announcement. The female voice has a strong Midlands accent, but it's East Midlands rather than the Brummie of everyone else in Worcester – we are asked to 'please darl narn-narn-narn'.

There's the same trouble as last night finding somewhere to stay. It has never occurred to me that you could struggle like this, when every town and city in the land is peppered with hotels, B&Bs and guesthouses. Tonight I stand outside one row of B&Bs, their boards wafting invitingly in the breeze, and call all six numbers from my mobile; not one has a vacancy. People obviously move around Britain much more than I'd thought. J. B. Priestley had a similar problem in *English Journey*, and that was 80 years ago. In Bristol he blames 'commercial travellers'.[4] Finally a slightly ropey establishment out near one of the city's train stations (and twenty minutes' walk from the city centre) agrees to give

---

4. Also Gertrude struggles in Windermere.

me shelter. The twin room is en-suite, though a handwritten notice advises that hot water may take a few minutes to appear. The telly isn't too fuzzy, the towels are clean. We can work with this.

Thoughts turn to curry. Perhaps it's because I've entered the Midlands, home of the balti (which is Urdu for 'bucket'), or perhaps the Lea & Perrins story fires my imagination as I walk past their old premises (now a Debenhams). Their original commission came from an Army officer who wanted them to recreate a sauce he'd eaten in India. Either way, tonight's British Culinary Staple, I decide, will be a Ruby. The light is fading as I traipse the streets, evaluating possible venues. A group of men in black tie pass me, joshing loudly about the function they're off to. Who are they fooling? None of us feels comfortable in that garb, which is ironic really, seeing as the whole reason it was invented was to level the sartorial playing field and make everyone look the same. Nowadays it's only the nobs who can carry it off.

The rituals of going for a curry are now so deeply ingrained in the British psyche that, just as Pavlov's dogs salivated at the sound of a bell, a few bars of Indian music can get us feeling hungry. (If I listen to *Sgt. Pepper* all the way through I'm famished.) As I step into tonight's restaurant, the first faint pangs of hunger are stirred by the strains of the sitar. Within seconds my stomach is rumbling along in time with the tabla. Another great Indian restaurant tradition, even in posh places like this one with signature dishes and uplighting, is that the menu *has* to be riddled with spelling mistakes. I once saw one that contained four different spellings of the word 'papadum'. Tonight's menu contents itself with 'a very hot dish, not for the faint heated'. (*Possibly* deliberately humorous, if you want to be kind to them.) Sadly a third custom – the photo of the owner with a C-list celebrity – is absent here. It's always endearing to see the pride on the owner's face as his 'you're going nowhere' grip encircles the shoulders of someone who was in *Emmerdale* fifteen years ago. The only properly famous person I've ever seen was Anthony Hopkins; the photo had been blown up so that it filled almost an entire wall. The owner was smiling so widely the glare from his teeth almost blinded you.

My lamb rogan josh and aloo brinjal are accompanied by the local newspaper. They have seen fit to end a story about someone who died after crashing his car with the sentence: 'He enjoyed spending time walking.' Other than the paper my main source of entertainment is the man at the next table, who is the answer to the question, 'What would Donald Sutherland look like if every meal he had ever eaten in his entire life had been a huge curry?' Out with two work colleagues, he is treating not just them but the whole restaurant to the collected wisdom of many years. This includes: 'Carte d'Or in France is beautiful. Carte d'Or over here is *shit*.'

As ever, the bill is accompanied by a tiny chocolate. As ever, that gives me a craving for more chocolate, which can only be satisfied by diving into the nearest convenience store for a Kit Kat.[5] And as ever, once I've had chocolate I have to have coffee, so because all the Costas and Starbucks are now closed (it's gone nine), I find myself in a chain pub asking if they do their hot drinks to take away. 'Sure,' says the bloke behind

---

5. Like many members of the Chocolate Bar Hall of Fame, it's been around far longer than you'd think, dating from 1935. Even the Twix is older than me (b. 1967).

the bar, a Londoner. He's lively and engaged, conducting the 'what size/do you want sugar/etc.' dealings with car-mechanic levels of self-confidence. I respond in kind, so much so that I'm in danger, as I sometimes do in such exchanges, of slipping into a Cockney accent myself. It's so nice to be served by someone with a bit of character. And therefore so shockingly disappointing to hear him say: 'Emma, could you refocus on remenuing the tables?'

Sipping the latté, I indulge in my now-customary evening constitutional. There's a very upmarket tattoo parlour called Faithful City. I still haven't entirely got my head round the fact that tattoos have become respectable. Prime Minister James Callaghan always wore long-sleeved shirts, so ashamed was he of the tat-covered arms he'd acquired in the Navy. Yet the current Prime Minister's wife talks openly about the dolphin on her right ankle. (Not everyone does it as stylishly as Sam Cam, though. A woman in Newcastle got the word 'Angel' tattooed across her back. Only when it was finished did she find they'd spelled it 'Angle'.) On my wanderings I also see a branch of the store known in this country as TK Maxx; in America it's actually TJ Maxx but they had to change it over here to avoid being confused with the Liverpool department store T. J. Hughes. A man pauses outside the shop to check a text message. He adopts a look of deep concentration, then says simply: 'Wanker.'

It's starting to feel like a jigsaw; Britain, I mean. The country is one enormous jigsaw puzzle, every bus journey another piece put into place, every day another chance to assess the picture. Only by joining the pieces up am I really getting to understand them all – today, for instance, came the shock of how far the Midlands sticks out at its bottom-left corner. In fact there's a very 'middle' feeling to everything now. I'm a middle-aged man approaching the middle of his country, and somehow, tonight, that makes me fall in love with Britain a little bit more. I feel at one with it, this nation that's had its youth, its time of running round the world and trying to prove itself. Your forties are a time for coming to terms with things, a time of acceptance, like water finding its level. You learn to stop worrying and love the bomb of life's essential absurdity. I'm starting to see Britain as a friend of about my age. Its Victorian imperialist urges all spent, it's content to kick back and watch China take over from America, certain in the knowledge that one day someone will take over from China. 'Young blood must have its course, lad, and every dog its day.'[6]

As my steps echo along a pedestrianised street now devoid of shoppers, a lifetime's view of Britain as passive, listless and faintly decrepit begins to change. Okay, it's true we don't make anything any more; that we're not vigorous or thrusting. But then in every life there comes a time for vigour and thrusting to stop. You can be passive because you're broken – or just because you're at peace. Britain's lack of animation, you could argue, is not because we've lost our way but because we've found it. This whole trip, it strikes me, is the perfect example of that. I'm floating slowly but determinedly across the country on a very unshowy form of transport. And it feels just fine.

I pass Foregate Street train station. It's fairly small, the entrance little more than a cubby hole beside the bridge

6. I've always loved those lines. Only tonight do I look them up and discover they're by Charles Kingsley, author of *Westward Ho!*

that carries the track over the road. And it's only now that a memory comes back to me: I *have* been to Worcester before. It's just that I never got any further than this station. I was 16, and had caught the train from Birmingham with a friend to see Warwickshire play cricket against Worcestershire. On the way it started to rain. Then it *really* started to rain. As the drops lashed against the carriage window I found myself feeling both glad and nervous. Glad because it meant the game would be called off, nervous because the reason I wanted it to be called off was that back at home, in the nearest town to the village where I lived, there was a Girl. If the cricket was called off I could go back and see her. I had reason to believe, or at least to hope, that if I asked her out the answer might be positive.

So when we got to Worcester, and saw the sheets of rain pounding against the pavement – the very bit of pavement I'm standing on now – and my friend said, 'This is pointless, isn't it?', I was only too eager to agree. We turned straight round and caught the next train back to Birmingham. For the whole journey I was in equal parts ecstatic at the prospect of seeing the Girl and terrified at the prospect of asking her out.

Tonight, the sight of this station, this stretch of pavement, picks me up and plonks me right back in that moment. God, the *intensity* of youth . . . I'm so glad I once had it in me to be like that, so glad I no longer do. Your nerves just couldn't take it. Experience intensity in your younger days, then let the memories of it swirl round when you get older, like very strong squash diluting in a glass of water. Visiting a place after a stretch of time can do this to you; fill you with feelings you had the last time you were there. Why the great mystery about time travel? We can all do it, whenever we want.

She said no, by the way. But only because she had a boyfriend. If it hadn't been for him, she said, the answer would have been yes. God, was I grateful to her for that.

The next morning is day four of the trip, and also the final working day of the week – the day whose name we owe to Britain's Anglo-Saxon heritage, specifically the goddess Frigg.[7] In the café above the bus station (the only bit of the shopping centre open at 8.30 a.m.) the regulars collect their regulars and banter with the staff. Cradling a tea, I check my emails, and learn that today is the day another plan will come to fruition. This will happen in the city at the other end of my first bus ride: Birmingham.

Downstairs, in the cavernous subterranean gloom of the bus station, the 9 a.m. incarnation of the 144 awaits. This route has been known by that number since 1928, which is a comforting fact as I step aboard and pay my £3.70. You can't help but imagine all the courting couples who held hands on the 144, then saw their children take the 144, then their grandchildren. There's a further sense of continuity as I chat to the First Group employee who's killing time with my driver (it's still several minutes before departure). He's fiercely proud of their buses: 'One of them's done a quarter of a million miles in seven years.' That's ten times round the world.

Traffic is heavy as we leave Worcester, meaning we're so late by half-past nine that a couple of pensioners get tricked. 'Really sorry,' says the driver as they show their off-peak passes, 'I'm actually the 9.20 running late. You'll have to wait

_____

7. I promise you.

117

for the next one.' They take it in good part. Soon we're in Droitwich, the town it's impossible to pronounce in anything other than a Midlands accent. I've always imagined it to be a dreary place, forgetting that there's a 'Spa' on the end of its name. Leamington, yes – Droitwich, no. But it turns out to be very pretty, a calming mix of Edwardian and Elizabethan buildings, lots of timber in the framing, plus a huge red-brick Victorian Gothic pile called Chateau Impney. Now a hotel, it was built in the style of Louis XIII by a local salt magnate because his wife was pining for her native Paris. He threw the equivalent of £17 million at it – but still she left him, ran off to North Wales for some reason, which is surely not an area noted for its resemblance to the French capital.

We pass a Harvester. Are they still asking if you've ever been to one before? I do hope so.[8] A woman is helped on with a toddler-filled buggy by her boyfriend; he then steps off and waits hopefully for a final wave, but as the bus pulls away she ignores him. Inspired by a pensioner couple who spring nimbly up the stairs, I decide it's time for me to break my upper-deck duck. The trip has been a downstairs-only affair so far, and while that might be where the party has tended to be, the view from on high is better. Certainly the playwright David Hare thinks so: he always rides upstairs for just that reason, though thinks this is a 'sign of growing old'. Simple pleasures, David, simple pleasures. Even bus shelters can be interesting from this angle nowadays: some cities have started putting adverts on the roofs. Previously there was nothing to be seen but broken umbrellas and prankster-purloined trainers.

---

8. A woman I know was once taken to one on a first date. First and only.

Both front seats have been taken, unfortunately – the right by a long-legged teenager, the left by his shopping-laden mother (she must have hit the aisles early). So I park myself on the seat behind her and watch Bromsgrove shimmer into view. An unlovely prospect, it has to be said. They may have made the gates of Buckingham Palace here, but little if any of the grandeur rubbed off. A barber's shop boasts that 'Men walk in, legends walk out', while another sign announces the 'Princess of Wales Hospital Minor Injuries Unit' (unfortunate juxtaposition). Hard to believe that this is the hometown of Trudie Styler, Sting's wife. Just as the memory returns to me of their interview about tantric sex we pass the turning for a place called Lickey End.

Gradually the top deck fills up. A 6'7" man squeezes himself around the stairwell and into a seat (all bar the odd kneecap, anyway). An old guy displays a comb-over of near-geometric excellence; a comb-forward-and-round-and-up, in fact. We're really into the heart of England now. Just over to the east (at four o'clock to Birmingham – Bromsgrove is seven) lies Meriden. The stone cross on its village green claims to be the *exact* centre of the country, defined as the point at which a 2D cutout would balance.[9] A little further east is Coventry, the city that gave the English language the phrase 'Peeping Tom' (he was the only one to sneak a peek at the naked Lady Godiva), and also gave me my first job. As I remember that year between school and university spent

---

9. This excludes England's offshore islands – that shifts the point to Fenny Drayton in Leicestershire. Britain, meanwhile, balances (islands included) at the North Lancashire village of Dunsop Bridge. The 100,000th public telephone was installed there in 1992 to mark the fact.

office-junioring for a firm of solicitors, I realise what last night gave the first intimation of: this bit of the project is a trip into my past. The same thing happens to J. B. Priestley in Bradford: he can't 'visit it in the same spirit in which I visit the other places. I am not merely returning to a city I know well, but to my childhood and youth.'

Birmingham, on the other hand, is virgin territory for him. Beryl's blindspot of Norfolk you can understand — but this, the country's second city, for a man of 39? How could Priestley never have seen, as I do at just gone ten on this increasingly dank morning, a sign that says 'Welcome to Birmingham'? For we are here, in the place that inspired the Two Towers in J. R. R. Tolkien's *Lord of the Rings*; the author grew up in Birmingham, and remembered two prominent brick towers near his home, one of them part of the local waterworks. The place that in the Domesday Book was valued at £1, only having enough land for six ploughs; now, like the rest of Britain, it is full of shops where you can buy things for £1. The place that gave us custard powder; Alfred Bird (like Messrs Lea and Perrins, a chemist by trade) invented it in 1837 because his wife was allergic to eggs and so couldn't eat normal custard. Nor could she eat bread made from yeast, so he invented baking powder too.[10] The place whose council, when Bill Clinton visited in 1998, painted the grass green — but failed to notice that his motorcade would go past a hair salon called Monica's.

We reach Longbridge, only to find that it doesn't exist

---

10. Meanwhile up in Cheshire, Bisto was invented by two men whose wives asked for an easier way of making gravy. It stands for 'Browns, Seasons and Thickens in One'.

any more. The suburb that was once essentially a huge car plant is now essentially a building site. The plant has been demolished, leaving acre upon sprawling acre laid out in front of us. Cement mixers and pallets of bricks and half-built concrete shells stretch off into the distance, with orange-jacketed men scurrying to build what is effectively a whole new town. Somewhere in there is the spot that would have been home to the British Leyland pickets who featured in every local news bulletin of my childhood. Pilfering there was so rife that if a worker's wife asked what colour they were going to paint the front room, she would get the reply: 'Depends what colour the new batch of Allegros are.' There were much warmer industrial relations a few blocks to the east of here in the area known as Bournville, built by Cadbury for the workers who churned out its chocolate bars. Though even that's very British: when Cadbury tried doing the same thing in Australia their employees said, in effect, 'Forget your football pitches and museums – if you can afford those you can afford to give us higher wages, so we'll just take the cash.'

It's been spotting for a while now, and in Selly Oak the spots become a downpour. Only now do I realise what the bottom decks of buses have that the top decks don't: windscreen wipers. Within minutes the view ahead has disappeared. It should be like in the early days of omnibuses – you should pay less to sit upstairs. (Though admittedly back then that was because there was no roof, so I'm not expecting a massive discount.) The side window is still usable, fortunately. We pass the Ali Baba Café, offering 'Sheesha pipe, Falafel, Panini, Baguettes' – talk about multicultural Britain. Then the floodlights of Edgbaston cricket ground, the destination that day my brother and I sat watching buses sail by. Another time, in weather not unlike today's, I came here to get the Warwickshire players' autographs as they arrived for pre-season training. As Anton Ferreira's frostbitten fingers reached for my pen he turned to a teammate and uttered the phrase that to this day reminds me of him: 'Fuck this for a game of marbles.'

Almost as if the bus knows it's returning me to my personal ground zero, it slows and slows, city-centre traffic ambushing it to a near-standstill. By the time we reach the Bull Ring shopping centre we're over 40 minutes late. I disembark at 11.24 a.m. That's OK – still half an hour to spare.

At midday I have someone to meet.

As we've already noted more than once on this trip, the map of Britain contains an awful lot of place names that leap out at you for one reason or another. Quite often that reason is rudeness, making a perusal of the map almost as much fun as looking up dirty words in the dictionary. Who, for instance, can remain unmoved by the fact that east of Kidderminster and south of Halesowen – in fact if my bus this morning had veered a few miles off course we'd have gone through it – is a village that rejoices in the name of Bell End? Whose lips can avoid an upward curl at the revelation that Britain has a Lusty Glaze, a Pant, a Pratt's Bottom and two Twatts? Even when the names aren't rude they're silly. Norfolk has a Great Snoring, Essex a Matching Tye. There's Wrangle in Lincolnshire, Sixpenny Handley in Dorset. In Staffordshire you can literally find yourself at Loggerheads, while Yorkshire boasts a Fryup. Don't think they're immune north of the border, either – Moray has a Maggieknockater (it's near Dufftown). I genuinely think it says something about the British refusal to take life too seriously that we allow these place names to persist. Occasionally you get lapses in the sense of humour (as with the attempts to rename Brown Willy in Cornwall), but by and large people are perfectly happy, when ordering something over the phone and getting to the stage where they have to give their address, to tell a complete stranger that the place in which they have chosen to live is called Ugley.[11] The Welsh actually go out of their way to attact attention: the legendary Llanfairpwllgwyngyllgogerychwyrndrobwllllantysiliogo-gogoch was a nineteenth-century publicity stunt to ensure the town had the longest train station name in Britain.

All good clean fun. Which I've been indulging in by reading Caroline Taggart's *The Book of English Place Names*. And what I'd never really twigged until now – at least not to the point of actually doing anything about it – is that those place names are a guide not just to the country as it is now, but also to how it used to be. Map-reading, in other words, isn't just geography, it's history. The different monikers our settlements now possess were given to them by different groups of people over different time periods. By and large, by the people who have invaded us. Like most people I know, I was processed through a series of memory tests that the English laughably call an education system, and so still, at the age of 41, don't really have any clear idea of who those invaders were and in which order they showed up. There were the Anglo-Saxons, I know that much: we Brits always use them as an excuse whenever we swear. And the Anglo-Saxons came after the Romans: everyone knows that. But how

---

11. Essex again. The Ugley Women's Institute did let the side down slightly by insisting on a change to the Women's Institute of Ugley.

many centuries after, or where the Vikings fit in, or the Jutes (it is Jutes, isn't it?) – I have no idea.

Caroline, I've realised, could be just the teacher I need. Fortunately she's out and about in these fair isles herself at the moment, researching another book on British history, this time told through its food. She's returning home to London after a research trip in the Midlands, and it so happens that her train timetable and my bus one allow for an early lunch in Birmingham. I'm going to be put straight about 2,000 years of warfare and conquest over a cup of tea and a sandwich.

In fact I think it was the tea that swung it. Caroline adores our national drink with an almost Tony-Benn-like zeal,[12] and so wasn't going to pass up the offer of a free cuppa. We've arranged to meet in Drucker's, a café at the top of the Bull Ring. This is the new Bull Ring, of course, the shiny, sensuously curving 2003 replacement for the large lump of concrete that had stood here since 1964. It's so big, and the city centre that surrounds it is on so many different levels, that you can easily lose track of which floor you're on and how many of the several hundred escalators you need to go up or down to get where you want to be. But eventually I locate Caroline, recognising the elegant bob of silver hair from the picture on her website. Enquiring whether the tea is up to scratch, I'm relieved to hear that it is. I remember Drucker's from my time in Coventry, an unassuming little gaff. Seeing the firm here, inhabiting one of the enormo-units perched atop a chasm of retail, is like hearing that someone you went to primary school with has just been elected Prime Minister.

---

12. He has a pint-sized mug, which he uses ten times a day.

Sitting down, I ask Caroline how the research has gone, and learn that there is something called the Coventry God cake. It has three sides, apparently, signifying the Father, the Son and the Holy Ghost. Not the first time I've heard the words 'Coventry' and 'God' in the same sentence, though normally there's an 'oh' in there as well. Soon Caroline and I are swapping facts: before becoming a writer she was an editor. As she puts it herself: 'I've been a freelance editor of general adult non-fiction for twenty years – no one plays Trivial Pursuit with me.'

So how did she get interested in place names?

'I remember going on holiday to Dorset years ago, and feeling as if every second village was a character in a P. G. Wodehouse novel. Shepton Montague, Hardington Mandeville, Bradford Peverell . . . There had been lots of scholarly books on place names, but I'm not a scholar – not an expert on anything. I just set out to write a "scratch the surface and see where it leads us" kind of book.' Scratching surfaces proved to be an apt metaphor. 'It was a bit like archaeology,' continues Caroline. 'There are all these different layers of our history, shown in all the different ways place names work. It goes all the way back to the Celts. It was very amusing to someone like me who was brought up partly in the London Borough of Bromley that one of the few remaining Celtic names in the capital is Penge. God knows why. Possibly because it's always been so awful that no one wanted to move there so no one ever bothered to change the name.'

That 'partly' is a clue to Caroline's complicated national identity. We'll get on to that later, but for now she zooms me through a potted history of the country whose map I've been looking at my whole life without ever really appreciating what it meant. Starting, as is only logical, with those Celts.

'They were the ones who were here even before the Romans invaded. "Pen" is the most common relic from those days – Penzance, for instance, and lots of Welsh names like Pen-y-ghent. It means "hill". Not that the people who came afterwards always knew that. There's a place in Lancashire called Pendle Hill. The "dle" bit is Old English for "hill", and was tacked on to Pen by people who didn't realise that it meant the same. Then even later, another group came along and added the second word. So we've ended up with a name that means "Hill Hill Hill".'

Then the invasions get underway. First up are those aforementioned representatives of the Emperor Claudius. 'That's why we have "-cesters" and "-chesters" everywhere – Leicester, Manchester, Chester itself. They come from "castra", which was the Roman word for a military camp.' We also get 'Albion' from this period, the old-fashioned word for Britain: *albus* is the Latin for 'white', the colour of the cliffs at Dover that were the first thing visitors saw in the days before EasyJet.

Already it feels reassuring having Caroline as a teacher. Her style of conversation is just as you'd expect from the author of *I Used to Know That: Stuff You Forgot from School*, her bestseller explaining everything from photosynthesis to the plot of *Jane Eyre*. Her explanations work around what *interests* us, the reasons these questions were studied in the first place, not around what some faceless examination board thinks is worthwhile. Caroline, I think, should be made Secretary of State for Education as soon as possible.

'The Romans were around until 410 AD,' she continues. 'Or

at least that's the date the history books usually give. Actually their empire had been in trouble for over a century by then, and the soldiers here were always being shipped off to deal with uprisings elsewhere. Eventually they were all gone, creating a vacuum.'

'Filled by the next wave of invaders?' I ask.

'Correct. The Anglo-Saxons. Made up of three groups from northern Europe, the Angles, the Saxons and the Jutes.' Ah, so that's where the Jutes come in. It seems unfair that they lost their billing, like Taylor losing out to Waite and Rose, but still, I let Caroline continue. 'Unlike the Romans, the early Anglo-Saxons were largely illiterate, so records from the time are pretty scarce. But we do know that the Saxons got the south and west of the country, the Angles got the north and east, and the Jutes got Kent and the Isle of Wight.'

That might explain it. Not going to keep yourself in the national consciousness if they're your only cards, are you? England's only one-syllable county and an island that will only become famous centuries later when Queen Victoria dies there and Jimi Hendrix plays its pop festival.

'This is the period that gave us the vast majority of our modern place names,' says Caroline. 'Any place ending "ham" or "ton" probably dates from Anglo-Saxon times. "Ton" meant farm, and "ham" meant homestead.'

Quick-witted soul that I am, I notice that this applies to the place we're sitting in right now. 'So Birmingham would have been . . . ?'

'The homestead of Beorma.'

I look over at Tie Rack, and wonder what Beorma would think.

'But the pronunciations used to be very different,' explains

Caroline. 'It was only in the sixteenth century that we started saying "ham" and "ton", part of what's known as the Great Vowel Shift.'

It's a good job Caroline isn't stuffily academic about all this: she understands when I snigger at the phrase. We collect ourselves and resume.

'Before that, "ham" was pronounced "hahm",' says Caroline, 'while "ton" was "toon".'

'So we sounded like a nation of Geordies?'

'You could say that.'

Americans, of course, are still struggling with the vagaries of our pronunciation. They say 'Birming-*ham*' as though it's their own city of that name in Alabama.[13] Even the most clued-up Anglophile Yank I know, a San Francisco writer who lived in Britain for a while, can't stop himself turning the last five letters of Edinburgh into 'burrow'. Top prize, though, goes to the Canadian who pronounced Loughborough as 'Looga-barooga'.

Invader Group Number Three, Caroline tells me, were the Vikings. They sailed over from Denmark and Norway in 865 AD. 'Alfred the Great, who was King of the Anglo-Saxons, negotiated with them. Essentially they drew a line from London to Chester. The Vikings got everything north-east of it; Alfred kept everything south-west of it. He was one of the first to call it "England" – "the land of the Angles".'

That word that meant more to Churchill than any other actually commemorates some people who invaded us. Being

---

13. We Brits, of course, always take immense trouble to pronounce places and other words correctly when we travel abroad.

a historian he'd have known that, of course. But plenty of those who invoke his name whenever immigration's under discussion probably don't.

It's now that you can really start to see our history being played out on the map. 'The Viking word for "homestead" was "-by",' says Caroline, 'so in the territory they controlled you start seeing words with that ending. Whitby, Derby, Ashby, as in Ashby-de-la-Zouch.' The last three words of that will get explained shortly. 'In the other part of the country those places would have been "hams".'

By this stage I'm beginning to feel a little bruised. Three massive invasions and I still haven't finished my cheese roll. It's therefore a relief when Caroline says there's only one more invasion to go. The last successful one ever mounted against this sceptred isle. Yes, it's 1066 time.

'After William the Conqueror came over from Normandy and beat King Harold . . .'

I interrupt Caroline. 'With an arrow in the eye? Or is that a myth?'

She smiles. 'Maybe, maybe not. Anyway, after he was crowned – on Christmas Day, incidentally – William gave lots of land to his noblemen. And, as noblemen like to do, they started adding their names to things. So all these places that had had perfectly sensible names – Shepton, Leighton, Milton – started sounding posher as the new landlords satisfied their egos. Now they're Shepton Mallet, Leighton Buzzard and Milton Keynes.'

So *that's* the reason for the Buzzard. I always wondered if it was something to do with birds. No: all down to Theobald de Busar. Just as Ashby's triple flourish is down to the de la Zouche family. There's also an Ashby Folville (the de

Folevilles) and a Mears Ashby (the de Mares). None of this continental frippery at Cold Ashby in Northamptonshire, though. It was just cold.[14]

William didn't just give land to the nobles. 'He also gave lots to the church,' says Caroline. 'They did the same "add something to the existing name" trick. That's why there's a village in Dorset called Toller Fratrum – the second word means "of the brothers" – in other words, monks. Meanwhile another village on the same river, the Toller, is called Toller Porcorum. That means "of the pigs" – probably because the monks ate pork.' I bet 'Toller Porcorum' has had to be spelled out to a few call centre operatives over the years. Religion also explains another of our most common place-name endings, 'minster': it comes from the fact monks used to 'minister' to the sick. Spelling mistakes again, you see. The entire history of the British Isles is one long list of spelling mistakes. And, adds Caroline, pronunciation problems. 'Ipswich, for instance, used to have a "Y" sound on the front, but the Normans couldn't get their tongues round "Yipswich" so they just dropped it.'

So there we are: a thousand years of getting invaded, the thousand years that essentially made us the Brits we are, summed up in four lots of place names. I am sure my teachers at school must have run me through the dates, but the fact I can't remember the experience tells you how much dates tell you. Explain to me why Man has got its -chester, though, and Leighton its Buzzard, and the invaders are lodged in my memory for good. Romans, Anglo-Saxons, Vikings,

---

14. More 'does what it says on the tin' naming at Hungerford in Berkshire – the land surrounding it could never grow crops.

Normans. A bit like the roll-call in Trumpton but with rather more firepower.

Just because Caroline's talented at the grand sweep of history, mind you, it doesn't mean she's immune to the charms of a good old-fashioned bit of daftness. One of her favourite British place names is Twenty, a village in Lincolnshire. 'In the nineteenth century a railway was being built between Bourne and Spalding. Although that stretch of country was just fenland, and hardly anyone lived there, it was decided they needed three stations along the line to transport farm produce. But what could they call the first one? There wasn't a village there to name it after. The surveyor looked at his Ordnance Survey map, found that that plot of land was number twenty, so used that as the station name. Over the years a village grew up around it.' Further down the line one of the other stations *did* have a village to take its name from. 'But the village was called Tongue End, and the railway company didn't fancy that. So the surveyor looked at his map again, found that there was a drainage ditch nearby called Counter Drain, and used that as the station name instead.'

We talk more about the absurdities of pronunciation. Bicester is 'Bister', Fowey 'Foy' and Zwill, for some reason, 'Yool'. In England's smallest county, Rutland, you'll find the Vale of Belvoir, pronounced 'Beaver'.[15] We compare Britain's strange place names to those in other countries. France's Châteauneuf-du-Pape means 'the Pope's new

---

15. Which adds piquancy to the fact that Rutland is the most fertile county in England (the average woman producing 2.81 children). Even better, the county's highest point is a place called Flitteris. Can be quite tricky to find, apparently.

castle' ('What did he do with the old one?' asks Caroline), while, to take just one letter of the alphabet, there is a town in Austria called Hard, one in Ukraine called Hat, a Heavy in Argentina and a Hilda in Peru. (As for rude names, there's a Bum in Sierra Leone, a Dildo in Canada and a Bollock in the Philippines.) We also talk 'shortest place names in England', Caroline revealing that there are 70-odd three-letter places (from Aby to Wye to Ely – and the latter genuinely does mean 'place with lots of eels'), but no two-letter places. To get over my disappointment at this, and seeing as we're visiting the Isles of Silly, I subject Caroline to a test I've devised.

'I'm going to give you five English place names. Four of them are genuine, one is fake, taken from a list of spoof names in Bill Bryson's *Notes from a Small Island*. You've got to spot the fake.'

The anticipation on Caroline's face reveals her as the quizzer she really is. 'Okay.'

'North Piddle. Catbrain. Thong. West Stuttering. Ogle.' I make sure to keep my voice down. There are two ladies at the next table who might get completely the wrong idea.

'Well, I'm almost certain there's an Ogle,' says Caroline. 'And I know there's a River Piddle, with a place on it called Piddletrenthide, so there could well be a North Piddle. What were the others again?'

'Catbrain, Thong and West Stuttering.'

Caroline recites them a couple of times; they sound like a surreal shipping forecast. 'Could there be a Catbrain? Really? Then again Thong . . . No, I'm going for Catbrain.'

'Afraid it's West Stuttering.'

'You're joking! There should be a place called West

Stuttering!' Thong, for the record, is in Kent. It's near – and I promise you this is true – a place called Shorne.[16]

We get on to the subject of identity, and of where we're from originally. 'When people ask me that,' says Caroline, 'I say, "How long have you got?" The short answer is that I was born in London to Scottish parents, lived most of my childhood in New Zealand, went to university in Sheffield, was confused for a long time, now think of myself as a Londoner but still change allegiance whenever it suits me. Particularly during the rugby season.'

Her accent, I have to say, had been intriguing me. Caroline definitely has a subtle trace of Kiwi in there, though now that she mentions Scotland I can hear that too.

'We moved to New Zealand when I was four,' she says. 'My dad worked for Unilever, and like all multinationals they sent promising young men all over the world. We moved back when I was fifteen, right at the end of the sixties. For a very long time I didn't know if anything I said was standard English, Kiwi or Scottish, because my parents spoke, and we were exposed to, a mixture of all three. Sometimes I still don't know. There are words I know I still say in a Scottish way, because the only people who said them were my parents. Like "Aberdonian".'

It's true. Caroline almost chews the third syllable, showing that it is an Aberdonian, rather than any other,

---

16. For a truly priceless collection of spoof names, I recommend Grayson Perry's wonderful 2004 *Map of an Englishman*. Drawn as a Tudor map, it has counties called Bitch, Cliché and Myth, villages including Cotton, Up-the-Duff, Fret, Gap-Year and Nice, and the sea areas Dementia and Withdrawal. The British Consul-General in New York liked it so much he hung it in his office.

Scottish accent – very different, for example, from 'refained' Edinburgh.

'It's completely daft,' she continues. 'I've spent four weeks of my life in Scotland, and haven't been to Aberdeen since my grandfather's funeral in 1972 – but I do feel an attachment to the city. I love granite, for instance. And I support the Scottish rugby team, woeful experience though that's been for the last few decades. Unless, as I say, I feel like changing allegiance. About fifteen years ago the All Blacks were over and did very well against England. I suddenly started talking about "us".'

Caroline finished her schooling in Bromley. Her father was later transferred back to New Zealand, then the Philippines. 'I'm the only person I know where, when I grew up, my parents left home. From the moment I graduated, "home" was where I lived – first in the London suburbs, then central London. I've been there nearly thirty years now. For most people, for a long time "home" is still where your parents live. I think that's something that probably changes only when you become a parent yourself, which I never did.'

I wonder. I still use the H-word, it dawns on me, for both my current home and my childhood homes. I always have, and three years of parenthood haven't changed it. Surely the only thing that could change it would be my parents moving?

There's only one part of Caroline's identity that she feels strongly about. 'It's almost hypocritical of me to call myself Scottish. And it's inaccurate to call myself English, unless I'm abroad when you call yourself "English" or "British" and it doesn't really matter. But I do very fiercely and firmly think of myself as a Londoner.' It's a regionalism that she notices in one or two other groups. 'Yorkshire people, for instance. And

Liverpudlians. Geordies and Glaswegians, too. My brother, like me, went to university in Sheffield, and on his architecture course they were shown pictures of various buildings from around the country. When there was one from Glasgow all the Glaswegians in the room cheered. You wouldn't expect that from many other groups, would you? I don't know why these places should feel like that. Are they places that have been deprived or put upon in some way? You can understand the Cornish, because they've been independent for a very long time. The others, though?'

Emotions take no account of geography, it seems. We mention that great Englishman who was born in Ireland, the Duke of Wellington. 'When people used to say he was Irish,' Caroline tells me, 'he would respond with "Just because you're born in a stable it doesn't make you a horse".' Bernard Manning used to deploy the same line when explaining why people with a different skin colour from him couldn't be British.

We move from Britain's history to its language. At one point, Caroline asks whether I share her preference for Chambers over other dictionaries. Feeling a touch nervous, and even though I know Chambers is the one that shows some humour ('*middle-aged*: between youth and old age, variously reckoned to suit the reckoner'), I admit to being what you might call 'anti-dictionary'. 'Not in a serious way,' I explain, 'just because I dislike language pedants.' Caroline's certainly not one of them, but you do get people whose 'love' of our language is nothing more than a love of slapping down people who write 'it's' instead of 'its'.[17] They always remind me of

17. As if that rule made any sense in the first place.

the husband in *Abigail's Party*. Stroking his *Collected Works of Shakespeare* he says: 'Part of our heritage.' Putting it back on the shelf he adds: 'Of course it's not something you can actually read.'

Caroline understands what I mean. 'There is a great debate between the English approach to the dictionary – coming "behind" the language, acting as a record of what's already happened – and that of the French Academy, who want to stay in front of the language, to tell you which words you're allowed to say.' They are the ridiculous body that tries to stop English words like *le weekend* entering the language. They've recently told people to use the specially invented *motdiese* (literally 'sharp word') instead of 'hashtag'. *Bonne chance* with that one. In our case, a refusal to define our language could be part of our refusal to define ourselves, a trait that was noted as early as 1742 by the Scottish philosopher David Hume: 'The English, of any people in the universe, have the least of a national character; unless this very singularity may pass for such.' Jeremy Paxman, in his book *The English*, calls it 'a mark of self-confidence: the English have not spent a great deal of time defining themselves because they haven't needed to'.

John Baskerville. I'd never heard of him. In fact I only just notice him today, as I leave the Bull Ring: there's a small plaque to him on the side of the building. This eighteenth-century Brummie was the 'King of Print', apparently. We are invited to 'open a book and face his legacy'. Further digging reveals that he *might* have been the reason for the name of the hound-haunted family (Arthur Conan Doyle lived in Birmingham for a while), but that he definitely *is* the reason for the name of the font: he designed it. Nearby some Japanese tourists have their photo taken next to the huge bronze sculpture of a bull that guards the shopping centre. It's very similar to the one at the bottom of Broadway in Manhattan.

I steer a course through the city centre roughly northwards, looking for likely destinations (there's no station here, so the stops are spread out as in St Austell). There have been some changes since the teenage Saturday afternoons I spent walking these streets, not least the streets themselves: they're nearly all pedestrianised. One thing hasn't changed, though: I'm on my own. I never really got the hang of friendship at school (that trip to Worcester was an exception, and given my enthusiasm to get out of it I suppose you can see why). Part of you embraces solitude, part of you worries about it – and then 25 years later you find yourself back in the same place having come to understand your own nature, having made an accommodation with it.

I exchange a text or two with my mother about how my next bus could be to the town nearest her but I've got to press on. She says sure, she won't bother putting the kettle on then, she understands I don't love her any more, ha ha. A Peruvian panpipe busker outside Phones4U battles with 'Unchained Melody' by the Righteous Brothers, and since one of his high pipes is a bit off things get painful. At the back of House of Fraser some delivery drivers flirt with an attractive young office worker on her cigarette break. They obviously know her, and though she's half their age and the banter gets quite suggestive somehow there's nothing at all seedy about it. The Brits do this very well. Seaside postcard time again.

The stops from which I can choose my next destination are on Corporation Street. After weighing up the options I plump for Lichfield – it's slightly north-east of here, and looks well placed to give me a further shove up the middle of Britain. I have to double-check that this is indeed the correct place to wait, as there's a notice warning of imminent changes to the 'Stop Information Totems'. (Wouldn't it be great if they meant that literally? Bus stops would be so much better made of wood with Native American faces carved into them.) Assurance comes that yes, a 112 will be along shortly, so I settle back for the wait, leaning against the wall of the building outside which the stops are arranged.

It's a large chain pub, popular with – let us be kind here – 'dedicated' drinkers. The bus queues intermingle slightly with patrons who've come outside for a fag. Two of them are working on a newspaper crossword.

'I reckon it's "buck",' says one, a Brummie Phil Mitchell, though he's plump rather than stocky. 'A male rabbit is a buck . . . the "u" fits there . . . see?'

'Now, let's not be getting ahead of ourselves here,' replies the other, an Irish Telly Savalas (bald head, tinted glasses). 'It might be . . .' He goes silent.

Phil runs through his thinking again, calmly and politely.

'I've said, now . . . ' snaps Telly, before recovering his poise. 'Let's just be thinking about this.'

He fights for a few more minutes, but when another answer supplies the initial 'b' he's forced to admit defeat. I wouldn't want to be between these two when they've had another few pints.

To my left, on the roundabout where Corporation Street meets another big road, is a large statue of Tony Hancock. It's a flat (the third dimension no more than a few inches), six-foot-tall version of the famous photo of him in his Homburg hat, hunched miserably over a cup of tea. This wasn't here when

I was a kid, and it's only now that I learn Hancock was born in Birmingham. His family soon moved to Bournemouth, but even so, the hangdog persona seems a natural fit. There's true Brummieness in the note he left when he committed suicide at 44: 'Things just seemed to go wrong too many times.'[18] It had to be Birmingham that marked the millennium by lighting a beacon called the Flame of Hope, then was forced to turn it off because of funding problems.

For my entire adult life this has been my image of the city. I couldn't help agreeing with Mrs Elton in Jane Austen's *Emma*: 'One has no great hopes of Birmingham.' Today, though, it feels different. These people, all shuffles and sniffles and shopping trolleys, don't depress me like they used to. Instead of things going wrong too many times, the Hancock quote that fits my mood is one *about* him, unattributed, on the bottom of the statue: 'I do not think I ever met a man so modest and humble.' Why should Brummies shout in joy if they don't want to? Perhaps they're quietly proud of their city – they've plenty of reason to be so. As if custard powder wasn't great enough, they also invented celluloid, took the first ever X-ray and gave us the copper British penny. The coin, which lasted until decimalisation in 1971, was first minted by Matthew Boulton, a genius whose work on steam power and other ideas fuelled much of the Industrial Revolution.[19] W. H. Auden was

18. His ashes were brought back from Australia by Willie Rushton, who said: 'My session with the Customs was a *Hancock Half Hour* in itself.'

19. He operated from Birmingham's Soho district. As in New York (and unlike in London, where 'soho' was a hunting cry), the name is an abbreviation. Manhattan's is South of Houston Street, Birmingham's South House.

from Birmingham. Washington Irving wrote *Rip Van Winkle* here. Okay, not a great example if you're trying to dispel the sleepy image. But you take the point. Or at least I take it, on this drizzly Friday afternoon: I've been too hard on the place.

Perhaps it's just because it was where I ran from. You can't, in the end, though, can you? You can't run from yourself. I feel like that bus yesterday, the one that carried me into Worcester, racing its own shadow along the hedges.

4

In which we learn how Marmite was invented, visit Britain's
biggest war memorial and muse on why it might be that
Charlie Watts draws every hotel room he ever sleeps in

Gravelly Hill Interchange, they call it. 'They' being
officials from the Department of Transport. The rest
of us call it Spaghetti Junction.

When I was about eight, there was a report on the news
about this engineering marvel/1960s eyesore (delete as
appropriate) not being totally safe. Something to do with cost-
cutting measures during its construction, concrete starting to
decay, that type of thing. For several years, whenever we drove
through it I was terrified, expecting one of the 559 pillars[1] to
collapse at precisely that moment, bringing the M6 or the A38
or the A5127 or one of the several other roads that make up
the junction crashing down on us, subjecting my family to
what would surely be simultaneously the most terrifying and
most laughable deaths you could imagine. Killed by spaghetti.
Today my bus takes me through the junction, just after it
leaves Birmingham City Centre and passes the stadium of
Aston Villa FC, the club whose first-ever match, in 1874, was
for some reason played as a rugby game in the first half and a
football match in the second. Even now, as the massive grey
columns pass by on either side, the roadway weaving between

---

1. That is not a made-up figure.

them like a rollercoaster, I find myself getting tense. You can never tell which way you're going to come out of this place. Even the driver doesn't seem too sure – I think he just puts his foot down and hopes for the best.

Soon we're in Erdington. This suburb's shops include Mobilicious and Phone Junkies, so it's no surprise to see a Community Police Support Officer flicking distractedly through the messages on her iPhone. The more affluent Wylde Green is home to Fiji Colon Hydrotherapy. They also do eyelash extensions. Then a smart wooden sign on a well-tended roundabout announces 'The Royal Town of Sutton Coldfield'. If you grew up where I did, this is one of those mythical places just far enough away that you never went there, but near enough that you were aware of the local jokes about how posh it was compared to the rest of Birmingham. The jokes seem to be well founded: the Baptist Church Centre looks to be an important presence, and though the town has gone a bit zeitgeist (one pub is called the Hairy Lemon) the locals can't be too happy when our driver, ahead of the timetable by a minute or two, gets out, leaves his engine idling, and enjoys a few crafty puffs on a fag. He hops from foot to foot, looking like Private Walker, the spiv in *Dad's Army*.

And then comes the point on the trip I've been waiting for, the point that reveals Overcrowded Britain. There's only one problem: it reveals it to be a myth. Ever since the West Country I've been waiting for the countryside to end, for all the towns and cities to merge into one, creating a choking claustrophobia. The map has told me that this is where it's going to happen, where the Midlands becomes all 'middle' and no 'land', where industry has crushed nature. But the map has lied. At least this one, at this scale, has; the road atlas in which one A3 page covers everything from Stratford up to Nottingham. It *makes* everything look squashed together. Out here, though, on the ground, you realise how much space there is in Britain. Here, just half an hour from the centre of the country's second-biggest conurbation (half a *bus* hour at that), I find myself entirely surrounded by Nothing. On either side of the village of Shenstone I spend long stretches staring at a horizon that is dozens of miles away, and yet there is nothing between me and it but fields. At one point our road passes over the M6 Toll motorway, but that's about as big-time as it gets.[2]

You can understand why some people make the mistake of thinking we're a crowded island. If they've come here from somewhere else, for instance, like J. G. Ballard, arriving by ship from China and wondering why lots of coal scuttles were moving around on the Portsmouth docks, only to realise as he got nearer that they were tiny British cars. Used to the enormous Cadillacs of Shanghai, Ballard came to see Britain's vehicles as exemplifying how cramped the country was. Surely we native Brits, though, must realise the truth? Apparently not. So much of the issue gets clouded (if not crowded) by the debate on immigration. No room at the inn, send 'em all back, etc. I'm sorry to inflict a second unprovoked mention of Noel Edmonds on you, but his phrase does seem appropriate for this trip: 'I'm very straightforward on immigration – the bus is full.' It really isn't, you know. Easy to make the mistake, though. Travelling about as we all do, seeing a stretch of

---

2. This is the motorway, incidentally, that contains 2.5 million pulped Mills & Boon novels. Perhaps romance is dead after all.

greenery here, a yawning landscape there, it's tempting to think: 'Yeah, *this* bit of Britain is empty, but the rest of it's crowded – it must be, they said so on the news.' Perhaps it's a hangover from the nineteenth century, at the beginning of which 80 per cent of us lived in the countryside, and at the end of which 80 per cent of us lived in towns and cities. Maybe modern Brits just have a very urban mindset. Either way, it's only now, travelling across the country in one concerted effort, that it hits me how much room we've got. If we all just *spread out* a bit . . .

Lichfield's welcome sign reminds us that it was the birthplace of Dr Johnson. A car totally ignores a red light, and only by some skilful steering and braking does our driver avoid ploughing into it. As the collected sighs of his passengers die away, he emits a single, perfectly dignified *sotto voce* 'twat'. We arrive at the bus station at 1.34 p.m. Don't know why, but I'd always imagined this to be a rather nice place so I'm disappointed to find it mundane and even a little scruffy. Few, if any, of the inhabitants are quaffing port and firing off the *bons mots*; old Samuel would be very disappointed. The only extended monologue I hear between the station and the main shopping area is from another British archetype: the Person Who Has Been Asked Directions and Proceeds to Repeat Them an Unnecessary Number of Times. This man, fiftyish and mac-clad, tells a couple they need to carry on to the end of this street, turn right, go past the card shop, then look for a little turning on the left.

'Thank you,' they reply, backing away.

'That's to the end . . .' he repeats.

They half pause, politeness getting the better of them.

'Then right, past . . .'

'Past the card shop,' completes the woman, nodding, taking another step backwards.

'Aye. Then it's on the left.'

'Thank you,' call the couple over their shoulders.

'Don't go as far as the Guildhall,' calls the man, 'or you'll have gone too far.' But there's no reply.

Henry James referred to Lichfield's 'smallness' as well as its 'dulness' (*sic*), saying they explained Dr Johnson moving to the city he was most famously associated with, one that which also begins with 'L'.[3] Okay, the people don't seem too inspiring – but there are some lovely buildings, one of which, a solid three-storey job on Market Street where Samuel was born, now acts as the Johnson Birthplace Museum. It reveals that he was great friends with Lichfield's other favourite son, the actor David Garrick, despite the fact that Garrick (a) did a cruel impression of him, and (b) kept a pet puma. Only a couple of hours after my chat with Caroline about dictionaries and the French, it's amusing to learn that Johnson's famous work wasn't as all-inclusive as his reputation might have us believe. Essentially, he didn't want too many French words in it, believing that England was 'deviating towards a Gallick structure and phraseology' that would 'reduce us to babble a dialect of France'. He therefore refused to allow 'blonde', 'bourgeois' or 'champagne' into his masterpiece. 'Ruse', on the other hand, did get the nod, on the grounds that it was 'a French word neither elegant nor necessary'.

Drizzle accompanies me back to the station, where I find

---

3. Actually Johnson's first trip to the capital was at the age of two – suffering from scrofula, he was taken to London to be touched by the Queen.

that the furthest one can strike northwards from here is Burton. This is good, as I'm beginning to get an idea of where I'd like to spend tonight, and Burton is on the way there. This journey (a number 7, on a green-and-yellow Arriva single-decker) will be covered by the day pass I bought on the last bus, which now sits snugly (smugly?) in my pocket, along with all the trip's other tickets. In order. A few months ago, if you'd told me I would end up as the proud owner of a sequential collection of bus tickets I'd have chinned you. Now they're cherished possessions, documents of discovery, the record of my odyssey across the country. I relish the maths of it all; for instance, the fact that the 'day pass' phenomenon means although this is my eighteenth bus, it's still only my thirteenth piece of paper. I may even put them in a scrapbook when I get home. And I don't care who knows that.

There's still a while before the bus leaves, but in view of the weather the driver lets us get on and wait. 'Us' comprises myself and three American ladies, and for the life of me I can't work out what they're doing on a bus in Staffordshire. They're all in their sixties, quite graceful (leisure wear, but stylish leisure wear), with lovely mid-West accents. It's the Golden Girls minus the power hair. All three have collected several bags of shopping, so take a double seat each along the right of the bus (I'm on the left) and examine their purchases. Poundstretcher and the charity shops have taken a big hit.

'D'ya get that for Steve?' asks Woman at Front as Woman at Back flicks through a 2003 copy of *Record Collector*.

'Uh-huh. I bet ya he'll love it.' She finds an article on Tina Turner. 'D'ya see her lately? She can dance right across the stage even now. Warmed me up just watching her.'

Meanwhile Woman in Middle is examining her purse.

'D'either of ya have a twenty pence? I'm trying to get one coin of every denomination.' Woman in Front obliges.

We set off a touch before 3 p.m., and the vehicle's gently lumbering motion soon has the three of them closing their eyes and dipping their heads. A tractor on the A38 becomes the project's second overtaking victim, then we're in the village of Fradley, which contains a brand-new housing estate – several dozen dead-ends and cul-de-sacs of mini-executive homes. Eventually the driver has to execute a three-point turn. As it becomes a 17-point turn his muttered complaints and the crunching gears wake up Woman at Back. 'Aah,' she says, 'look how cute the houses are.'

St Stephen's displays a multicoloured sign: 'This Sunday – Messy Church'. One shudders to think. (In half an hour's time Barton-under-Needwood Christadelphians will ask: 'This Sunday – What's in the Box?') Woman in Front asks another passenger if this is Alrewas. 'No, that's the next village.' I've never known how to pronounce Alrewas, and now, because it's an American who's said it, I still don't. (Later checking reveals that it's 'Oll-ree-wass' – as near to logical as you can expect in this country.) When the time comes the three collect their bags and depart, taking with them the mystery of their presence here. Americans just don't *do* holidays like this.

Out in the countryside again, off a side road triangled between the A38 and A513, we stop at something called the National Memorial Arboretum. It's a huge site, acre after acre of trees and plants, its coach park full of vehicles from all over the country. Near the bus stop is a huge plastic poppy. I've never heard of this place, but it turns out to be Britain's 'year-round centre of remembrance' – a green successor, in other words, to the Cenotaph in London.[4] This is, in effect, the nation's biggest war memorial. As our engine idles away, the driver waiting for anyone who might emerge from the main building, I remember the very first night of this trip: the memorial in Wadebridge, my feelings of guilt. It's the extremes that bother me, I think. Mass slaughter and mass grief. We've never held back from a scrap, that's for sure. A thousand years ago a boy could swear allegiance to the king when he was 12 years old. 'The more blood they shed,' wrote a Frenchman who saw our troops carving their way through his country in the fifteenth century, 'the crueller and more ruthless they become.' Shrapnel is named after an Englishman,[5] and there wasn't a single year of Queen Victoria's reign in which her troops weren't fighting somewhere in the world. Of the 196 countries in the world today, the British have at some point in their history invaded all but 22. Even now the battlefield calls. Reading 'England Your England' I laughed at George Orwell's comment that English soldiers were being trained for World War II with the bayonet, 'a weapon entirely useless except for opening tins'. But later on in the trip I'll read a newspaper story about British soldiers decorated during the current Afghanistan campaign. One of them got the Military Cross for charging a member of the Taliban with his bayonet.

---

4. A suitably Middle Britain site for it, too – we're just a couple of miles to the west of Coton in the Elms, that 'furthest point from the sea' village.

5. Henry Shrapnel, 1761–1842, inventor of a cannonball that shattered in mid-air, spraying lead shot in all directions. The government awarded him £1,200 a year for life – about sixty grand in today's money.

And yet there's always been another strain in there, the awkward squad. Sometimes they're exhibiting a quaint streak of British fair play, as when Sir Howard Kingsley Wood, Secretary of State for Air in the early days of World War II, was instructed to bomb German munitions stores in the Black Forest. 'Are you aware,' he asked, 'that it's private property?' But often they cut deeper, right to the bleakness of it all. 'Do we intend to kill all our young men?' asked one government minister during World War I. As part of his trip to Birmingham in *English Journey*, J. B. Priestley visits the city's Hall of Memory, 'built to commemorate the 14,000 Birmingham men who were killed in the Great War, some of them possibly with bits of Birmingham metal'. And sometimes the contradiction gets coated in good, old-fashioned hypocrisy. Rudyard Kipling, whose only son died in that 'Great' war, was later asked to write the epitaph for the nation's dead. He did, and included the line: 'Had our fathers not lied to us, so many of us would not be here [i.e. in their graves].' The authorities cut it out.

Here, on a number 7 bus, with very ordinary British rain being whipped against our windows by very ordinary British wind, feels the best place to think about all this. I wasn't expecting to come here; it isn't a special trip. This makes death itself seem ordinary, which of course it is: we're all born to die. But being British we never talk about it. That's why we never know what to say at funerals. Every November, to honour our war dead, what do we have? A two-minute silence. Just not a fit subject for conversation, the Big Sleep. Perhaps that's why we love murder mysteries so much – our subconscious has to deal with the issue somehow.

We should be more like Gertrude. Today I've been

reading the bit of her book where she heads northwards from Birmingham. As she's coming from London and I've come from the south-west it's the first place our paths have crossed. Like me she visits Lichfield and Burton. To tell the truth, I've been getting a bit miffed at how inane Gertrude can be. She's always 'chatting' to people, and they're always very 'friendly' or 'nice'. A banal love of contact for its own sake, it's been getting on my nerves. Peering out of the window now, though, at a reminder of what happens when the talking stops, I feel revoltingly cynical. On one bus the woman sitting next to Gertrude begins to point things out as they pass them. 'She smiled and frowned and gesticulated, and I realised that she was dumb, but wanted to show me the sights.' At first Gertrude feels awkward, but then tells the woman about her aim of getting to John O'Groats. 'Her eyes lit up with obvious pleasure, and turning round to the seat behind her she conveyed to her friends something about me in deaf and dumb signs . . . They laughed and made signs, and shook me by the hand.'

In the end no one does leave or join our bus here. We pull slowly out of the car park, the trees dwindling in our rear-view mirror. At least they're a sober commemoration of war, not a glorification of it. Unlike the trees at Blenheim Palace. The 1st Duke of Marlborough was given the residence for winning the Battle of Blenheim, and instructed Capability Brown to base the planting of the trees in its grounds on his victorious troop formations. A combination of war and gardening: surely that's as British as you can get.

In Barton-under-Needwood – home to those Christadelphians, as well as a shop called Liquor 'n' Allsorts – we're invaded by schoolchildren. As the first wave sweeps forward I feel a bit like Michael Caine in *Zulu*, but thankfully a special school bus soon appears, taking some of the heat off. Every one of the seats is taken, though, and soon every window is covered in condensation. Someone writes 'NY' in it (travel's a universal dream), while another girl opts for 'Julie'. Her friend reaches across and adds 'What about me?' The first girl scrubs it out. All good-natured (I think). At the back a group sing Stevie Wonder's 'Happy Birthday', followed by 'I'm Just a Teenage Dirtbag, Baby'. The young Indian girl next to me doesn't talk to anyone, but seems content in her separateness. The accent round here is noticeably different from the West Midlands twang of earlier. A group over the aisle talk about 'arse school' – only after a moment do I realise they mean 'high school'. All in all it's another reminder, as in Cornwall, that today's kids are just as noisy, boisterous and vulgar as those of yesteryear, and the only time we should worry will be when they're not.

Creating my own window in the condensation I note that the countryside has uglified. There's a derelict factory, concrete farm buildings. Lots of the houses have grey rooftiles that bring the mood down. Even the crops are unattractive – a field of corn looks messy, the stems of the plants broken, their leaves dishevelled. A man getting off the bus is asked by the driver if he wants the newspaper he left by the ticket machine when boarding. 'No, thanks,' comes the reply. 'Actually it wasn't mine.' But in a moment of awkwardness he takes it anyway.

We pass through Branston (effectively a suburb of Burton), where the legendary pickle was first made in what had originally been the National Machine Gun Factory; nice twist on the 'swords into ploughshares' theory – guns into ploughman's. Even more legendary, though, is the foodstuff that was invented (and is still made) in Burton itself. It's a foodstuff so British that Jonathan Agnew packs a jar of it whenever he goes abroad for *Test Match Special*, just as various Great Train Robbers once pined for it on their Acapulco sunbeds and Rio beaches. Fifty million jars of it are produced each year, with only 15 per cent of those going overseas. It is the spread, nay the British institution, known as Marmite. Devastating to learn, therefore, that in yet *another* example of Gallic influence the name comes from a French earthenware cooking pot (look on your jar and you'll see a picture of one on the label). On the city's ring road we pass an old petrol station that has been turned into a 'drive-thru dry cleaner's' – how much cleaning can one medium-sized Staffordshire town generate? The driver waves to his equivalent from a rival firm heading in the opposite direction; nice to know this tradition crosses commercial boundaries.

Burton-upon-Trent, said he, kindly passing over its place in 1960s rhyming slang,[6] is most famous for its beer (hence all that lovely Marmite-yielding yeast). Indeed it was the first place to call said liquid 'bitter'; before that there had only been the darker stuff known as 'porter'. Bearing this in mind I've been looking forward to a cosy town centre brimming with hostelries serving foaming pints of best, all consumed by trusty old souls who sneer at the carbonated urine (all right, if you must – 'lager') beloved of Australians and other ex-colonials. Quite possibly a warming log fire or two as well. I'm not terribly over the moon, therefore, to discover a town

---

6. 'Rent', as in 'boy'.

centre brimming with dated shopping arcades serving mid-range trainers and novelty key-rings. There are some pubs, of course, but none of them looks very inviting in this 4.30 p.m. window between lunchtime-lingering and Friday-night-outery.

So instead I find myself dodging the raindrops, dashing from arcade to arcade – being careful in one of them to avoid the gaze of the 'win this car' raffle-ticket seller. It's not difficult – he's staring at his shoes, perhaps in the hope that by looking at his own reflection for long enough he can somehow mimic that bit at the end of *2001: A Space Odyssey* and transport himself forward in time. I need to send an email but my iPad won't co-operate. 'It's the signal – you'll never get one in here,' says the woman in the mobile phone shop. This, I feel, says everything about Burton.

As the town is another one without a bus station, I find the stop I need round the corner on the high street. My destination on this, the day's last journey, is the city whose eponymous earl won the toss of a coin in 1779 and so had a horse-race named after him. If he'd lost it then Britain's gamblers would, every June, place bets on the Bunbury instead of the Derby. The bus is the V3, the letter standing for 'Villager', after the nature of its route. 'Welcome to the Villager,' goes its branding, 'the really good link between Derby and Burton.' Not 'outstanding', you'll notice. Not 'stunning' or 'brilliant'. Just 'really good'. You can accuse Middle England of many things, but hyperbole isn't one of them.

Unsurprisingly, considering the weather, the bus shelter is nigh-on full, but with some shuffling and nudging and squeezing and 'sorry'-ing I just manage to squeeze myself in. As I carefully pack away my pocket-sized umbrella a 60-ish woman at the far end says to her friend: 'Int it incredible 'ow umbrellas fold down now?'

'Arr,' comes the reply. 'You can even get ones wi' two bits now, so they don't blow inside out. "Double-skin", they're called.'

'Bet they're expensive.'

'Arr.' The friend thinks for a moment. 'Still, it'd make a lovely present for someone.'

In the confines of the shelter their voices are hypnotic, lulling me into an alternative universe where things are *almost* the same as in this one but not quite. A Muslim woman walks past wearing a burkha. 'Who was it who wore one of those kaftan things?' asks the first woman. 'Denis, er . . .'

'Denis Beckham?'

'Nar, not him. He wore a skirt. Nar, Denis . . . Denis Roussoff, that's it.'

'Oh, arr. The Singing Greek.'

'That's him. He were good, wunt he?'

'Arr. And that Nana Maskuria.'

Their talk ranges from swearing ('y'ere it all the time, dun't ya – they say that "peeved" off, except they don't say "peeved", if you know what I mean'), through the internet (neither of them approve), to *Bullseye*: 'That bloke, I dun't think he could add up – I think he'd got that dyslexia.' Part of me wants to stay for more, because I'm sure the conversation would reveal deep and fundamental truths, but no, the V3 is here, and I'm getting on it and the women aren't. With a heavy heart I take my leave, forking out £3.20 to do so because the Arriva pass isn't valid on this service. Worth it, though – the villages we pass through are beautiful, the roads that link them dipping and weaving through some great countryside. Raindrops fall from the huge cedar trees lining the route; this weather suits nature better than it did poor old Burton. A young woman joining us in Repton has very good legs, which the middle-aged woman in the shelter behind her surveys half in envy, half in disapproval. Okay, the younger woman is wearing a short skirt, but she's pretty not tarty, and I can't help disliking the older woman for her reaction.

We hit Derby at rush-hour, traffic slowing us so much that the couple behind me experience real alarm as to whether they'll be home in time for *The One Show*. Part of the city's ring road, it transpires, is called Lara Croft Way: the computer designer who fathered her was based in Derby. In fact they do a tidy line in road names round here – the stretch of the A52 from Derby to Nottingham is known as Brian Clough Way, after the man who managed football teams in both cities. As I step off the bus and look upwards, I think of Conrad Hilton. It's hard to imagine that when he opened his first hotel in 1919 in Cisco, Texas, he ever thought that nigh on a century later his name would appear on a building above a bus station in the English Midlands. But it does: the location of Derby's Hampton-by-Hilton means I can find myself a berth for the night suffering only the merest hint of dampness en route as I dash the few yards round the station before taking a lift up to reception.

My room, several floors higher still, offers a panoramic view of the city. Mostly shopping centres, it has to be said, but also a church or two, and parkland surrounding the River Derwent. They know their stuff on that score here – the designers of New York's Central Park were inspired by Derby Arboretum. That was around the time the city's MP was Samuel Plimsoll, he of the line down the side of a ship telling you which point you can safely load to, and, by extension, the item of footwear: the join between the rubber sole and canvas upper was said to resemble a Plimsoll line, and if water came above that line your foot would get wet. Timely trivia.

I call home, catching Jo just before she puts Barney to bed for the night. My son and I have a chat, then Jo tucks him up and goes downstairs. Filling her in on the day's progress I mention Coton in the Elms, which leads to a conversation about the sea.

'You've got it all wrong,' she says. Jo already knows my feelings on the subject.

'No, I haven't. The sea's boring.'

'How can you say that? It's beautiful.'

'But it's all the same. It's all just . . . water.'

'Really? Thanks, David Attenborough.'

I'm not to know it now, but before the trip is over it'll have converted me to Jo's way of thinking. This evening, though, as we finish our conversation and I turn on *Channel 4 News*, I start to feel lonely. Since Bristol that feeling of the project as a job has been there, so during the working week it has seemed the right thing to be doing. But now it's Friday night. The thought of staying away from Jo and Barney for the weekend, and beyond, gives my wanderlust pause for thought.

Distraction, that's what I need. When I venture back out I find that the rain has stopped, and that for all that I label it part of the Midlands, Derby clearly thinks itself part of the North: no one's wearing a jacket against the evening chill. Groups of shirt-clad young men pass by, each one leaving a faint mist of Lynx in his wake. My first task is to indulge in tonight's British Culinary Staple: a Chinese. The restaurant is hidden away in a factory-lined street a little way out of the city centre (I have to ask three separate times for directions). It does me some very nice deep-fried won-ton followed by chicken with cashew nuts. The female owner skilfully switches between taking orders, bantering with regulars and coaching the slightly-behind-the-game local girl who is clearly on her first-ever waitressing shift.

Back into the city centre for some post-dinner beer. It isn't just the lack of coats that tells you you've left the South behind – it's the way there are people from every age mixing happily. People up here never really change their idea of what makes for a good night out as they grow older, so in a party of eight you'll have representatives from two or even three generations – a sort of Club 18–60. The karaoke machine in the first pub is up and running, though purely as a jukebox rather than for its intended purpose. This is another great British invention, for which we must thank Roy Brooke of Stockport in 1975. He called it 'Roy's Singalong Machine'; it was only when a Japanese company bought it off him and gave it the name which literally means 'empty orchestra' that world domination was achieved. At this relatively early point in the evening's proceedings the small dance floor only has one occupant, a man in an expensive shirt, jeans and shoes, displaying moves as slick as his hair. They're so well rehearsed that it's a few bars before you notice they bear absolutely no relation whatsoever to the music.

The Derby accent is fascinating me. It's so uncool that it could simply never be threatening; the police dotted around the city centre in groups of four or five look bored, and they're clearly in for a very quiet night. A voiceover artist I know once received an email asking if she could do a Derbyshire accent: 'Baslow area – definitely *don't* want Bakewell. Can provide grid reference if necessary.' I continue my studies in the Slug and Lettuce, where a young Spanish member of staff collecting empties politely pushes her way through a crowd. Funny to hear the phrase 'beep beep' in that accent.

After this I pinball from pub to bar to pub in a line leading roughly in the right direction for my hotel. At one point I pass a group that includes a transvestite almost as unconvincing as the one in Worcester – strapless dress, enormous hair, sturdy legs – then feel guilty when I realise it isn't a transvestite after all. I also get a reminder of the sort of wisdom you can overhear on a Friday night out in a provincial English city: American Deep Heat, it seems, is greatly superior to the English variety. It will, my source reveals to his colleague, make your balls sting for an hour.

The next morning, getting ready to leave, I do the usual paranoid routine of checking every drawer twice even though I know I haven't used any of them. Then, at the door, the other custom: pausing to look at the room one last time, knowing I'll never see it again. Hotel rooms always get me like this, no matter how luxurious or how grotty, no matter how long I've stayed there or why. I always think of Charlie Watts, who when the Rolling Stones are on tour sketches every hotel room he stays in. He has done for years, though he never looks at the results. 'It's more a record,' he says, 'to know I've got it. I'll look at them all one day.' It's mortality, I reckon. Not many of life's 'lasts' ever announce themselves to you, but the final sight of a hotel room always makes me think of the big journey.

Downstairs it's a brief walk round to the bus station

with bright sunlight hitting yesterday's few remaining puddles. There's even a hint of warmth in the air as I survey the timetables and decide on the 9.40 a.m. departure to Chesterfield, due north of here. The bus, though small, is positively luxurious, more of a coach really; it's even got leather seats. But the driver assures me that it's definitely a local bus, so it fits the project's parameters. Further confirmation comes from the pensioners' passes he accepts, including that of a man who sits on the front row. When another man asks if he minds him sitting next to him, the pensioner replies: 'Okay. If you behave yourself.'

As the hour-long journey progresses, the hills become more noticeable: England's duvet is starting to ruffle. One particularly impressive field contains a dozen white sheep and two black ones, like a giant chess game that someone's about to lose. The sky is defiantly blue now, just a few fluffy *Simpsons* clouds floating along beside us. A big swap-over of shoppers at Alfreton's huge Tesco brings a chorus of greetings, many of them 'all rart, me duck'. Derbyshire leaves you in no doubt that it's a very modest county – Ashbourne, for instance, holds the World Toe Wrestling Championship every June. And in 1665 the village of Eyam took 'self-effacing' to new levels when it voluntarily isolated itself to prevent the plague spreading; all but 83 of its 350 residents died. Derbyshire has a very different character from the county I'm going to reach at lunchtime, on the bus after this one . . .

On the outskirts of Chesterfield I get my first view of the church's crooked spire, and for once a famous landmark isn't a letdown: the spire looks more incredible in reality than it ever has in my imagination – it's as though it's been drawn by a child. A bus driver coming the other way does a royal wave instead of the customary brief acknowledgement, holding the back of his hand outwards and rotating his wrist. We pass a hairdresser's offering 'Vibro-station Power Plate' (your guess is as good as mine), then we're into the town centre itself. Chesterfield is bigger than I'd imagined, plenty of big-name stores lining the streets off the market square, thousands of shoppers doing what Saturday morning was made for. The fruit-sellers on the market itself shout their patter: 'Two for a parnd, ladies, come on, two for a *parnd*.' One man is selling mops with detachable heads you can put in a washing machine: 'If yer not too posh, you can give it a wash.' A woman asks for a demonstration on the specially cut section of laminated flooring the man has brought along, then shows no interest at all as he carries it out. She is quite obviously his wife.

The bendy church (St Mary and All Saints, to give it its proper name) is a couple of minutes' walk east of the shops. I head past surely the only women's clothes shop in the world to advertise 'Flossy plimsoll shoes, now in stock' while simultaneously displaying a T-shirt saying, in big black letters, 'I HATE YOU'. Then there's the Chesterfield branch of Burton's; it was in this town (though not on this site) that Montague Burton opened his first-ever store in 1903. After World War II, demobbed soldiers got their civvy suits there (hence 'going for a Burton'), while the chain's offer of a complete set of clothes including shirt and underwear gave us the phrase 'the full Monty'.[7] Up close the church's spire looks even more bizarre than before, like a huge lead rendition of

7. The town's other contribution to the English language is the sofa that bears its name, a design first commissioned by the 4th Earl of Chesterfield in the 1700s.

a Mr Whippy ice-cream. Apparently the unskilled craftsmen who put it up in the 1360s (your proper workers having succumbed to the Black Death) used unseasoned timber, which then warped; others prefer the story that when a virgin married here the spire was so surprised it twisted round to look at her. Inside, the building is lovely, offering the peace and shade that always tempt even atheist souls like me to take a look. The Devil may have the best tunes, but God's got the best buildings. As ever, the little slips of paper pinned to the prayer board make compelling reading. Someone asks for a soldier to complete a safe tour of Afghanistan. A child's handwriting tells an uncle: 'I wish you'd come and see me again.' Someone mentions Richard III, whose bones have just been found in a car park in Leicester, asking God to bless 'the LAST ENGLISH king'.

There are notices about forthcoming events, too. All in all the Church of England is performing its usual role of social-club-cum-architectural-landmark without letting that awkward thing called 'religion' get too much in the way.[8] I like this, a nation in which the so-called 'established' church hasn't retained much of an influence on anything beyond our language. Point-to-points, for instance, got their name because horses originally raced between neighbouring villages, and in those days only the church steeples were tall enough to see. As for the King James Bible, it gave us dozens of terms, everything from 'the skin of my teeth' and 'nothing new under the sun' to 'a fly in the ointment' and 'pour out

---

8. My local church in Suffolk once asked pensioners to sign up for a lunch; in the column headed 'Special dietary requirements' someone had written: 'New potatoes'.

one's heart'. The 1717 edition is known as the Vinegar Bible because a misprint in Luke 20 changed the Parable of the Vineyard to the Parable of the Vinegar. Not as bad as the 1631 edition, mind you, which missed the third word out of 'thou shalt not commit adultery', landing the printers with a £300 fine. I don't think the Church of England has ever really believed in itself – how can it, when it knows it was only invented because Henry VIII couldn't get a divorce? There's been the odd bit of silly jingoism, as when John Milton said of the Reformation that God had revealed himself 'to his servants, and as is his manner, first to his Englishmen'. These days it's mostly paperwork: John Sentamu, Archbishop of York, has said that 'when the last trumpet shall sound, a commission will be set up on the significance of the trumpet, the financial implications of that trumpet, and for a report to come back in ten years' time'.

Returning to the station I find the white, blue and orange double-decker that Stagecoach call the X17 and I call the route out of Derbyshire. The driver is silent bordering on surly, refusing to acknowledge people's passes as they board; only when forward momentum carries them onwards do they lower them. (Neither, once the journey starts, will he acknowledge the 'thank you's of departing passengers.) But the sunshine stops him dragging anyone's mood down. There are smiles on the ring road when we pass a man walking his young daughter home from ballet class; she's still wearing her pink tutu and dancing shoes. A poster outside Chesterfield FC's stadium advertises the forthcoming appearance there of hypnotist Christopher Caress; I'm sure he's very good, but is that the wisest choice of name for someone in his line of work?

This is a relatively short trip, just a 12-miler, but by now we know that even that's enough for Britain's omnipresent countryside to put in an appearance. To our left, as the A61 carries us northwards, the Peak District lives up to its name. In fact even when we enter the city that is this bus's destination, the greenery never really ends. This is the place that claims the highest ratio of trees to people of any city in Europe, one of those silly things you read in tourist literature, but which in this case turns out to be noticeably true. Just like another of the city's boasts: like Rome, it is built on seven hills. Its southern suburbs are all tree-shrouded slopes and hollows, houses added seemingly as an afterthought. As the road dips through areas with names like Woodseats you're constantly aware of how closely nature's pressing in on you. Yes, the main road is lined with businesses – including plenty of discount stores (Lidl and B&M Bargains are both *vast*, set back from the road and with their own car parks, like DIY stores), and there is Passion By Desire Licensed Adult Store, offering 'DVDs, Adult Toys, Erotic Clothing'; its other sign, apparently without irony, promises 'Parking to the Rear' – but the streets off to the side offer only a few terraced houses before breaking out into acre after acre of oaks, pines, elms and God knows what else. Sebastian Coe loved growing up in this city because he could run from its centre and within minutes he'd be up on the moors. Yes, moors. This city is Sheffield.

Which means that this county is Yorkshire.

5

In which we witness wedding guests threatening violence, venture into the Rhubarb Triangle and learn how the beer mat was born

Perhaps I can best communicate my feelings about Yorkshire by relating the scenario that would form my worst nightmare. Michael Parkinson has returned to hosting chat shows, and is launching his new series with a 90-minute special – the recording of which I have been forced to attend – featuring just himself and two guests: Geoff Boycott and Dickie Bird. The three of them put the world to rights, covering topics as diverse as the merits of yesteryear and the merits of yesteryear, but never avoiding for very long the period in the 1950s when all three of them played as batsmen for the same cricket team in Barnsley. Which is a coincidence, because my instinctive reaction to this scenario also involves a cricket bat.

For a certain sort of Yorkshireman it is not enough simply to hold an opinion: you have to brandish it. Topping the list of those opinions is the one about Yorkshire being the only place on earth with any merit to it whatsoever. The 'Y' word isn't just a county, it's a state of mind. As Nick Jowett in the BBC Olympic comedy *Twenty Twelve* repeatedly puts it: 'I don't care what you say – I'm from Yorkshire.' You would simply never hear the sentence: 'I don't care what you say – I'm from Derbyshire.' Much of my reading for this part of the trip has backed up the impression. Not content with labelling their patch 'God's own county', some natives even try to beat the Almighty by pointing out that Yorkshire has more acres than there are letters in the Bible.[1] It is, as noted earlier, England's largest county, and also has the highest number of cities: seven (Bradford, Hull, Leeds, Ripon, Sheffield, Wakefield and York). Yorkshire people apparently have more sex than anyone else in the country, at 128 times a year (though it's Midlanders who indulge in the most bondage, keen as ever for something to complain about). The only Roman Emperor who died in Britain – Septimius Severus – did so while he was in York.

That *Twenty Twelve* character, of course, echoes the most famous fictional Yorkshiremen of all, the Monty Python 'you think *you* had it hard?' brigade. There's also the joke about the one who finds a pub offering a pie, a pint and a woman for £1. 'That can't be right,' he says suspiciously. 'Whose pies are they?' Such humour only works because it chimes with reality in some way. Yorkshire folk proudly call themselves 'tykes', an old Viking word meaning a vicious dog. To this day Osset in the west of the county hosts the world coal-carrying championship, in which men and women have to carry 120 pounds of the stuff uphill for nearly a mile. And as for meanness: in the nineteenth century there was Old John Mealy Face of Topcliffe, who ensured no one stole his flour by pressing his face into it when going out, so he could check the impression matched when he returned home. These days

---

1. 3,923,359 to 3,566,840. That's on the 'pre-1974 boundary changes' definition. Which is the only definition that would interest Messrs Parkinson, Boycott and Bird.

there is the 'Pigeon Bermuda Triangle' between Thirsk, Wetherby and Consett, where more of the racing birds go missing than anywhere else in the world.

Mainly, though, it's the 'I speak as I find, even if you haven't asked me' attitude that always gets on my nerves. As the historian A. J. P. Taylor put it: 'Northern people in every country like to think of themselves as more honest and straightforward than those further south.' There are many, many reasons to worship Humphrey Lyttelton, but few more compelling than the story of him doing a gig with his jazz band in Yorkshire and being approached afterwards by a member of the audience. 'Mr Lyttelton,' he started, 'I'm a plain-talking man . . .' 'So am I,' Humph interrupted. 'Piss off.' And yet today, trundling into the county on a double-decker bus on which the accents have gradually mutated from Derbyshire into Yorkshire, my hackles have descended almost as quickly as they sprang up. Perhaps it's the nature of the people you get on buses – gentle souls, in the main, nary a saloon-bar pontificator among them. But I've got a nagging fear there's another explanation. Not for the first time the trip is stitching the country together for me, every bus ride another square in the quilt. So this morning Yorkshire belongs very much to Britain. In fact, the uncomfortable thought occurs that Yorkshire could just be an exaggerated version *of* Britain. The way its residents seem to the rest of the country is probably how the British as a whole seem to the rest of the world – certainly the bits we marched into and painted pink. Is my antipathy to the Tykes a case of what psychotherapists call 'projection'? Am I subconsciously recoiling from the aggressiveness in my own character? Those thoughts about hate on my night-time walk in Bristol come back, as does my lack of ease around war memorials.

We're approaching the city centre now, or, as Sheffield's street signs put it, the 'Heart of the City'. That kind of corporate rebranding normally induces nausea, but somehow I find myself liking this phrase. An old London Routemaster passes us, beautifully repainted in cream and red, a ribbon on its bonnet and 'Wed' on the destination board. I once went to a wedding in London where we were ferried from ceremony to reception in a Routemaster. We had been given champagne after the service, and there was more on the bus. When a hold-up occurred at the venue, the bus was told to keep circling. The consequence was inevitable. Eventually our bladders could take the strain no longer, and virtually to a man and woman we charged off the vehicle. There is an alleyway near the Mansion House that I haven't revisited to this day, for fear of the memories it might evoke. At 12.06 p.m. we reach Sheffield's bus station, down at the bottom of one of those seven hills. Perhaps this is a kidney of the city; in any case, to reach its heart I have to follow the other disembarkers up a series of sloping streets.

We pass a pub where football fans have spilled out on to the sun-drenched pavement. Bolton Wanderers are being hosted by Sheffield Wednesday, the team named after the day on which they originally played their matches. (Still not my favourite name, though – that belongs to Crewe Alexandra, who adopted the title in 1877 as a tribute to the princess of that name, wife of the future Edward VII.) As ever where more than eight footie supporters gather together with drinks in their hands there's a faint static buzz of menace, of the angry British. The scared British, too, or at least the scared English, as Bill Buford's account of hooligans during the 1990 World Cup shows: 'Having fled in panic, some of the supporters would then remember that they were English and this was important, and they would remind the others that they too were English, and this was important, and with renewed sense of national identity, they would come abruptly to a halt, turn round, and charge the Italian police.' We even manage to include the game in our real wars: the start of the Battle of the Somme was signalled by a Captain Nevill kicking a football towards the German lines. As with many British traditions, though, what we love about football the most is the opportunity it gives us to complain. 'Nearly everything possible has been done to spoil this game,' someone once wrote. 'The heavy financial interests; the absurd transfer and player-selling system; the lack of any birth or residential qualifications for the players; the betting . . . the absurd publicity given to every feature of it by the press . . .' That was J. B. Priestley, in 1933.

An initial lap of the city centre reveals it to be, like Birmingham, incoherent. It isn't really centred on a particular square or street. You turn every corner expecting it to make sense of your journey, but all it does is lead you on to the next corner. Unlike Birmingham, however, Sheffield does have attitude; the sense of a place where important things have happened and could still happen in the future. The Lloyds No. 1 Bar occupies a forthright Victorian building whose sandstone blocks are engraved with the date 1867 and the words 'Sheffield Water Works Company'. Jessica Ennis has been honoured, like all British winners in the recent Olympics, with a golden post box in her home city – a couple insist that their unimpressed young son stands for a photo in front of

168

it. And all the time you're aware that this was the capital, when David Blunkett led the city council in the 1980s, of the People's Republic of South Yorkshire. This campaigning tradition continues at a series of trestle tables on Fargate, one of the main pedestrianised shopping streets. The *Socialist Worker* team have positioned themselves outside HSBC, though police rather than bankers are their target today, posters displaying the word 'Hillsborough' and a man with a megaphone calling for 'justice for the ninety-six'. Further along two young Muslim lads promote the 'Truth About Islam Project'. The table in between is occupied by someone trying to sign people up for a local paintballing experience. They all compete for attention with several buskers. At one point someone goes past on a unicycle; he turns out not to be a street-performer, just a bloke doing his shopping. He has bought a curtain pole. It looks like a de-nuded companion for his mode of transport.

Round the corner, in the square outside the Town Hall (another grandiose gift from the Victorian era), a group of students march against university funding cuts. Unfortunately the group numbers precisely 14, so to give the word 'march' any meaning they have to proceed in single file. The guy at the front with the loudhailer calls out: 'Education for the masses . . .' His followers repeat this. '. . . not just for the ruling classes.' They duly echo him again. These are the only two lines the group has, but even with so little to concentrate on the leader still manages to go round a large wooden flower tub in too tight a turn, so joining up with the tail of his own march. Having rectified this, he leads the students to the far side of the hall, where he proceeds to give a speech. This is a generous term for his performance, not so much because he's only got an audience of 13, but more because he mumbles, reading his words from several closely written pages of A4 held right in front of his face. His hands are shaking so much he has to use both of them to keep the paper still. Loudhailer-holding duties, therefore, have passed to his second-in-command, which in turn reduces the audience by one. Second-in-Command makes up for this by nodding approvingly at every possible chance.

Despite his inadequacies, or rather because of them, I can't help liking the leader. He's quite clearly one of the more privileged students on the march, but has done his best to counter his M&S trousers and sensible shoes by wearing a green mod jacket (though even this is new, and quite possibly from M&S). He has also attempted a beard; to spare his blushes, the most I'll say about this is that you can still see his blushes. He's noticeably shorter than Second-in-Command, and infinitely less cool, but no one, least of all Second-in-Command, seems to want to point this out. They all listen respectfully to the words of wisdom, delivered without intonation and with an anger that is genuine but self-defeating. 'This government has sought the agreement of the public for these c— This government has *not* sought the agreement of the public for these cuts.'

A few yards away, some guests are gathering for a wedding that is to take place in the Town Hall itself. To say that a recording of *The Jeremy Kyle Show* is short of a few participants today would perhaps be unfair, but there are very few natural fibres on show in their brightly coloured outfits. Of the 15 or so people awaiting the bride's arrival, every last one is smoking. The men all have short, gelled hair, while the women's tattoos don't exactly match Samantha Cameron's for subtlety. Indeed some of them stretch all the way across the backs exposed by their satin-effect dresses (and that is a long way to stretch). The party are not happy that their big day is being impinged on by a budding Che Guevara. There are stony looks. Finally one of the men, slightly older and smaller than some of the others, goes over to have a word.

He can't be heard, but Leader's reply comes through the loudhailer: 'I'll be two minutes. Two minutes.'

The wedding party aren't completely happy with this, but they settle for it. When three minutes pass and Leader is still going, the looks get stonier. After four minutes, one of the burlier men goes over. Before he even has a chance to say anything, Leader cuts him off with: 'Two minutes. Honestly, two minutes.' The wedding guest, influenced by an agitated look from his wife, restrains his urge towards violence (just), and returns to the Town Hall steps.

By this stage Leader's audience and Second-in-Command are obviously willing him to wrap things up, and *now*. But though he's skipping the odd paragraph, anger and pride won't let him abandon the speech altogether. Burly's wife goes across and tries to reason with Second-in-Command, who, having greater people skills than Leader, manages to keep her talking while continuing to hold the loudhailer. Some sort of deal is brokered, but even as Mrs Burly returns to explain it to the wedding party, Leader breaks off from his speech to berate Second-in-Command for fraternising with the enemy. After a brief argument he insists on continuing, but nervous sideways glances show him that Burly is clenching and unclenching his fists. 'The Liberal so-called Democrats have broken promise after prom— . . . two minutes, all right? . . . promise. This coalition cannot be allowed to ruin the educational opport—

. . . two minutes, two minutes . . . educational opportunities of a whole generation. All the while the bankers who brought this country to its knees . . . two minutes . . . get billions of pounds of public . . . two minutes . . . money which they . . .'

At this point Burly takes a step towards him. It is only a single step, but it's enough for the protestors, who all break into applause. Leader eyes them for a minute before realising the game is up. He acknowledges the praise and puts away the still-unread sheets of paper, his eyes revealing frustration at the System and his comrades in equal measure.

Thus does British socialism make another small advance.

Heading back down the hill to the bus station, I receive an email from the person I'm trying to meet up with tonight. We arrange the rendezvous for early evening in a city due north of here, which my newfound busser's instinct tells me should be perfectly reachable. Routes allowing, of course. And even if they're not, the person says, we can always change the venue accordingly; he's pretty mobile. The first stepping stone is none other than Barnsley. Birthplace not just of Parkinson, Boycott and Bird, not just of Arthur Scargill and football manager Mick McCarthy, all of whom you might expect, but also of Jenni Murray, whom you certainly wouldn't. (Don't you just long for an edition of *Woman's Hour* in the Yorkshire accent?) The 265 that will take me there is operated, like today's first two buses, by Stagecoach. The driver on the first one said my cheapest way of getting to Sheffield was an £11.10 day pass. I show it to the driver of this one and ask if it's valid. He peers at it for a moment, seeing that it was issued in Derby. 'Never seen one o' them before,' he says with a shrug. 'But go on, just sit yer'sen down, mate.'

We depart at 1.50 p.m. With her croaky high-pitched voice the woman behind me sounds exactly like John Shuttleworth's manager Ken Worthington. She tells a friend about her new TV arrangements, repeatedly referring to her set-top box as her 'boxset'. An elderly Pakistani man in scruffy clothes and a peaked cap gets on, standing at the front and talking loudly and aggressively in his native language on his mobile phone. We stop in traffic for a moment, next to a car going in the other direction but also currently stationary. Its male driver and female passenger both stare furiously ahead, the woman pressing herself against the door to maximise the distance between them.

Soon we're village-hopping. It's an uneventful journey, and my mood takes its cue from the field full of ponies staring vacantly over their fence at the M1 below us. There are a few reminders of how much better we treat our animals than our fellow humans in this country: Mucky Pups Grooming Salon and Boutique, Pets Are Pals and the like. If you do want to treat yourself, though, the village of Birdwell has a tanning salon called Skin and Tonic. At one point a teenage girl gets on, deliberately looking at the floor as she takes a seat near the front. ''Allo, Laura,' comes a male voice from the back. She grudgingly half turns her head and says, 'Ay up, Dave.' This concludes the conversation. History there.

At 2.55 p.m. we roll into Barnsley bus station. Correction: Barnsley *Interchange*. This is no ordinary bus station, it is a light, airy, renewable-timber-struts-supporting-a-metal-and-glass-roof bus station. One of its pastel-coloured walls bears a plaque saying it was opened in 2007 by the then Transport Secretary Douglas Alexander. Unfortunately it seems to be the only decent building constructed in Barnsley during the last . . . er, well, ever. The hill up to the town centre isn't of Sheffield proportions, but it's steep enough for Geoff Boycott to remember climbing it every day from the bus station to his first job at the Ministry of Pensions and National Insurance (1958–63). The only structure that's genuinely beautiful is an underground Gents whose white porcelain urinals bear the logo 'J. Duckett & Son'. Even the huge 1930s Town Hall is oppressive rather than impressive. It looks down on the town in every sense, and I can see why George Orwell criticised it in *The Road to Wigan Pier*, saying the council should have spent the money helping miners instead.

Most of the shopping is being done in a *very* unpretty indoor market. It offers knitting wool, tacky fancy-dress costumes and cheap carpets. You could call the market and its contents old-fashioned, but that would be an insult to fashion: Barnsley and everything and everyone in it seem always to have existed outside fashion. The town's only distinction, as far as I can discover, is that in 1977 it installed Britain's first bottle bank.

Barnsley is so demoralising that it sets up a rare exception to the trip's 'continualist' theme: a journey that takes me from chalk to cheese. My destination, the day's last but one, is Wakefield. Joining me on the 59, a single-decker, are a host of shoppers, including an old couple who have bickered for so long while queuing that he's now got nothing left to say apart from indecipherable muttering. 'Oh, just sit there and eat your chocolates,' says his wife. Another man carries his only purchase of the day, a second-hand ironing board. No one is smiling. Except, as if to hint at better times to come, a group of teenaged girls comparing notes about who has been invited to which party. It's all very sweet – no bitchiness, just interest. 'He were a very good friend, weren't he, before the whole Joe thing?' The 'whole' is pronounced 'herl', and there are several cries of 'You're *jerk*ing!' It reminds me of a girl I knew at university who was from Hull. We got her to practise the sentence: 'Oh, hello, I don't know you won't go.' This sounds like bear-baiting – I promise you it wasn't. Christine was, if anything, keener on the scheme than we were. Try as she might, however, she never quite managed it. 'Oh, hello,' she would say, carefully clipping each syllable, 'I don't . . . know . . . you won't . . . ger – *ER, NER*!'

Barnsley recedes behind us and we're out on to the moors. There are rough-looking horses in rough-looking paddocks, huge industrial works with ugly pipes and chimneys, angled conveyor belts linking storehouses and factories that seem derelict but are apparently still in use. Whenever we reach the top of a hill you can see Doncaster to the east, Pontefract and Wakefield itself to the north. Most of the houses we pass, no matter their age or size, are constructed of dark stone, which does nothing for the spirits. But then we reach Newmillerdam, a gorgeous village dominated by a large lake that was dammed in the thirteenth century to power a grain mill. Eight centuries after the water gave the place its name it still defines it, stopping at what's now the main road in a pleasingly bizarre fashion. Then we're into Wakefield itself, where there's more rejuvenating H_2O – warehouse conversions overlook the River Calder and a canal basin. The brand new Hepworth Art Gallery honours local girl Barbara. I know now what Daniel Defoe meant when he toured these parts. The place I've just come from was known as 'Black Barnsley', famed for its iron and steel production, though the nickname actually came from 'the black hue or colour of the moors'. Wakefield, by contrast, he finds 'a large, handsome, rich clothing town, full of people, and full of trade'.

Indeed within seconds of getting off the bus it's clear that the difference between my twenty-second and twenty-third destinations is just as great as it was in Defoe's time. I've never really believed in places having characters, not actual personalities that last down the centuries, but this city makes me reconsider. As far back as the Middle Ages it was known as 'Merrie Wakefield', 'wake' itself meaning 'holiday'.[2] And, yes, today there does seem to be an air of optimism here, a cheery disposition. The people complement the bright sunshine, whereas in Barnsley they challenged it. Even when the weather isn't like this Wakefield finds a way to thrive: it's the centre of the Rhubarb Triangle. The fruit, a native of Siberia, loves the cold, wet winters in this part of Yorkshire, and farmers have become adept at 'forcing' it. Wakefield also has the big-name stores and coffee chains that were missing in Barnsley. It has an indoor market too, but unlike Barnsley's this one is new, interestingly angled in black metal.

The main difference, though, isn't physical, it's one of attitude. The kids riding their bikes outside the cathedral have spirit. A busker playing heavy rock guitar to a backing track has attracted a small audience. It's challenging stuff – he finger-taps the fretboard like Eddie van Halen – but technically very accomplished. Even though it's not my sort of thing I stop to admire the skill, moved not by the lad's music but by the effort he has made, both in learning the instrument

2. As in the tradition of 'Wakes Week', when northern towns would close all their factories at the same time to allow workers to holiday together.

and in coming out here today. Others around me, I sense, feel the same way.

I want to linger, but by now it's half-past five and the day's final bus is waiting. It's a double-decker, and buoyed by my time in Wakefield I find myself springing up the stairs for only the second time on the trip. The first part of the journey is due west, meaning that the slowly setting sun fills the large front window, bathing the few of us up here in a warm Jaffa glow. The shadows over St Michael's Cricket Club are three times as long as the players; it's 175 for 6, and you can tell by the crouch of the fielders that there's still all to play for. As a woman departs the front seat just in front of me I notice it bears the first bit of graffiti I've seen on any of the buses. Let the magic-markered record state that as of 2012, Pecka loved Kealy (though given the nature of these things this may well no longer be true). A flicker of nostalgia stirs in my breast, a yearning for the days when buses were covered in graffiti, before on-board CCTV came along and put a stop to it. It showed that Britain was a place with *spirit*, with some edge to it, not the sterile, bland, passively plastic country it has bec— Then I tell myself to shut up. How absurd, longing for a bygone age that far from being golden was just piss-coloured, quite often literally. Who do I think I am, Michael Parkinson? Oh well, at least in eulogising the past I'm being properly British. The Americans write songs like 'Tomorrow'. This country's most successful-ever song is called 'Yesterday'.

A mother gets on with her two sons, the elder of whom (perhaps six) is a fidgeter. It's not serious, but it is constant. 'Mum, when can we buy some more Fruit Strings?'

'When you start behaving. I've told you, no more sweets till then.'

'But they're *not* sweets. They're made with fruit.'

He quietens down. She gets out her pink-covered Kindle and begins to read. Over her shoulder I see that it's *Fifty Shades of Grey*.

Through Ossett, which has a sign announcing that Woodbine Street leads to Rustic Cottages and Sharon Cottages. It also has a Darby and Joan Welfare Hall; fitting, as the original Darby and Joan were a blissfully married couple from Healaugh, north-east of the city I'm heading for. A tiny front garden is entirely filled by a triangular washing line covered in clothes – all you can see are the hands of the small woman in the middle, reaching up to remove the first peg. Next is Dewsbury, which has a John Ormsby V.C. Way and a Horace Waller V.C. Way. Like statues, street names always have me reaching for the history books. Ormsby and Waller were both local boys, and both received their Victoria Cross for bravery in World War I. But there was one big difference: Ormsby lived to collect his, only dying in 1952. He's buried in the town's cemetery. Waller lies in France, where he died aged 20. They and only 1,351 others have received the VC since it was introduced in 1856, every medal made from the same Russian cannon captured during the Crimean War. It resides, somewhat prosaically, in Telford.

For once the countryside doesn't really assert itself on this journey: the towns have all effectively joined up. That's not to say you're not constantly aware of nature – there are fields with a few horses here, a few cows there. In Batley a man takes his pony for a walk in the park; the kids in the playground pay no attention, so it's obviously a regular event. A semi-detached house nearby is covered in Christmas lights; today is 22 September. We pull into the huge White Rose Shopping

Centre, a brand new out-of-towner (if that makes sense in terrain like this); it has eight bus stands, against only six in the town of Ossett. I realise this is how I now judge a place.

And then we're at a big roundabout with a floral display in its centre, the plants spelling out a simple message: 'Welcome to Leeds'.

There is always something exciting about a large British city at 6.45 p.m. on a Saturday evening. Smart clobber has been donned ('Sunday best' has shifted forwards a day), aftershave has been dabbed, make-up applied. Bathrooms and kitchens in a 10-mile radius have echoed to radio stations offering two-hour 'Disco Frenzy' shows, and now minicabs are being booked and meeting places texted. Meanwhile in the city centre itself the advance guard is getting proceedings underway. Everyone is quietly excited, wondering what the evening will bring, and indeed whom. The whole thing floats on a sea of anticipation. That's anticipation spelled a-l-c-o-h-o-l.

Exploring Britain and its history without exploring our love of booze would be like writing a biography of Stan Laurel without mentioning Oliver Hardy. In the twelfth century John of Salisbury wrote that 'the English are noted among foreigners for their persistent drinking'. Elizabeth I loved beer so strong that according to the Earl of Leicester 'there was no man able to drink it'. Children at London's St Bartholomew's Hospital in the 1600s would drink three pints of beer a day (though it was much weaker then – lightweights), and at the Battle of Waterloo our injured officers cried out for Guinness. William Gladstone drank bitter every day, and while giving the longest Budget speech ever (1853, 4 hours,

45 minutes) he quaffed sherry and beaten egg. The Library is positively sloshing around in references to drink: Beryl Bainbridge, for example, complains on her very first night away, in Southampton, about having to eat dinner while she consumes her alcohol: 'it takes ages on a full stomach to get any benefit from drink'.

And of course when we talk Britain and drink, we're really talking the pub, that ubiquitous fixture which the nineteenth-century social researcher Charles Booth called 'the primordial cell of British life'. It's gone under other names over the centuries – Dr Johnson said that 'There is nothing which has yet been contrived by man, by which so much happiness is produced as by a good tavern' – but every aspect of social life has revolved around it. Sport, for instance. It's no coincidence that most sporting trophies are cups. As Hilaire Belloc put it: 'When you have lost your inns, drown your empty selves, for you will have lost the last of England!' So it's only proper that this evening's rendezvous – to examine Britain through the bottom of a metaphorical pint glass, as well as a couple of real ones – should take place inside a pub. The recommendation (the Scarbrough, a beautiful Victorian place not far from the railway station) has come from the man I'm meeting. He's really the only man you can meet to talk about the British and their pubs: Pete Brown.

If you were told that someone was the country's leading beer writer, having started by advertising the stuff and then going on to write books like *Man Walks into a Pub* that win awards from the British Guild of Beer Writers, that he writes the annual Cask Ale Report (the definitive guide to the real ale market), that he's worked as a consultant to brewers including Marston's, Fuller's, Magners and Greene King, and indeed that he was called Pete, you'd probably form a certain image of him. It would not be that he was from Cobham in Surrey, practised transcendental meditation, followed a strict vegan diet and, being a teetotaller, only ever tasted rather than swallowed the beer that was an inherent part of his job, spitting it out afterwards just as wine connoisseurs sometimes do. Which is just as well, because Pete is from Barnsley in Yorkshire and likes a pint or three as much as the next man, as long as the next man *really* likes a pint or three. While his figure is trimmer than might be expected of someone who has spent many of his 43 years sampling bitters and lagers and ciders and stouts (as indeed his beard is trimmer than that of the stereotypical real ale fan), it certainly isn't the figure of a transcendentally meditating vegan.

Pete, who now lives in London, is back in his native county seeing old friends. Given my itinerary today, it's natural that he greets me with an enquiry about how I'm finding Yorkshire. Erm . . . Starting with the positives, I eulogise Wakefield. But it doesn't take long for Barnsley to come up. I can tell that Pete can tell that I wasn't exactly impressed. I can also tell, though, that there are no fists about to be raised, no cries of 'How dare you say that about my hometown?!' So I risk a couple more comments, including that sense of Barnsley being outside fashion.

Pete shrugs sadly. 'Harsh but fair, as they say. It's simply a defeated place. I think a lot of that came from the miners' strike, which totally ripped the heart out of the community. But having said that, Barnsley has always been curiously insular, in a way other places nearby haven't. When mass immigration happened in other parts of the North – for mills and so on – no one came to Barnsley to go down the pit.

Whenever you mention you're from Barnsley, no one ever says they've been there. They've all been past it.'

Like me Pete moved away from his childhood home. 'That's something hardly anyone ever does with Barnsley,' he says. 'Places like Leeds and Sheffield, and Liverpool and Newcastle and Manchester for that matter, have stories of people forming bands to escape. Bands get formed in Barnsley, but they stay there. That seems to be the limit of their ambition.' There's sorrow rather than disdain in his voice, but Pete does agree about the 'fashion' point. 'Show a Barnsley person a designer label and they'll sniff and say, "You can get coats cheaper than that on Barnsley Market." '

Having armed us with pints of Tetley's (Pete's recommendation), I sit down, take a sip, and emit that satisfied 'ahh' sound middle-aged blokes always do when they find themselves in front of a glass of beer in an establishment like this. 'What *is* it about the British pub?' I ask.

Pete laughs. 'How long have you got? There's never a simple answer to these things, is there? When we were doing history at school the teacher said, "There were seven causes of the French Revolution." No, there weren't, there were hundreds! It's the same with pubs. But I think you can pull out some aspects we've got that other nations haven't. The pub is more informal than bars abroad, for a start. Or bars here, in fact. It's more anarchic, more personal. For me, and lots of people I've interviewed about the subject, the pub is somewhere the landlord's personality makes unique. It's *his* place. The pub is a social contract between him and his regulars, and that's what gives it atmosphere. Whenever there's a survey about what makes a perfect pub, people always put atmosphere above range of beers or food or prices or whatever.'

One thing that definitely marks us out is the habit of buying rounds. Frederick Hackwood, in his 1910 book *Inns, Ales and Drinking Customs of Old England*, called the practice 'characteristically stupid, in that it leads to unnecessary drinking'. Pete tells me that it used to be known as 'treating'. 'They actually included it in the World War I licensing laws, the famous ones introduced to stop munitions workers getting hammered all the time. Lloyd George said, "We are fighting Germany, Austria and drink, and as far as I can see the greatest of these deadly foes is drink." The anti-treating law was part of all that. A guy in Bristol was even convicted for buying his wife a drink.' Pete, however, thinks round-buying is a force for good rather than the opposite. 'It encourages socialising. Drinking in a group is good, drinking on your own is bad. And we don't do it like the Irish do it – over there if there are seven of you and someone buys a round you'll be having seven pints, and if someone gets an eighth it'll be fourteen. We're more casual than that. If you don't get someone a drink back they'll say, "It's all right, get me one next time." You know it averages out in the long term. It's a very unifying thing.'

We compare tales of that dreaded British archetype, the Person Who Never Gets Their Round In. Pete grew up with one who gradually made himself a pariah. In my experience it's usually the richest person in any given group. The worst offenders I ever encountered were two people in a group of eight, both of whom (I happened to know) earned more than the rest of us put together. This didn't stop the rest of us having to buy the first six rounds. After we'd sat there with empty glasses for about ten minutes (the phenomenon had been noted), one of the two turned to his colleague and said: 'What do you reckon — shall we share a round between us?'[3]

The Scarbrough isn't one of those plush Victorian pubs with ornate glasswork and padded red banquettes, but its dark wood and friendly service make it a very comforting place to be. Almost womb-like, I say to Pete. He agrees. 'Beer is a very female thing, for all its associations with men. Centuries ago, when people used to brew their own beer at home, it was always the job of the women. They became known as "ale-wives". And that's more than just Dark Ages sexism. In virtually every ancient society the mythologies said that beer was a gift from a goddess, never a male god.'

For most Brits, it strikes me, the ultimate goddess is their country itself. Britain is always 'she' — hence Britannia. John of Gaunt's speech about England in *Richard II*, the one that calls it 'this blessed plot, this earth, this realm', goes on to call it 'this nurse, this teeming womb of royal kings'. Our men have always gone abroad and made war, but they come back to Mummy in the end.

'How come,' I say to Pete, 'when we're sitting in a place like this, which is obviously doing good business, and when most of the pubs I ever find myself in are obviously doing good business, the only thing about pubs you read in the papers these days is how loads of them are shutting down?'

He nods. 'The decline of the pub has been moaned about almost as long as the pub has been around. Do you know when their number actually started dropping? In 1877. When

---

3. They needn't have worried — Kate Fox's studies for *Watching the English* show that those who buy the first round end up no worse off, and very often better off, than stragglers.

Austen Chamberlain gave his 1905 Budget speech he said they couldn't expect beer revenues to keep going up because of all the other leisure options people had, like sport. When radio came in there was less need to go to the pub, because it made staying at home so much cheerier.' Between 1918 and 1938 the number of pubs fell by over 4,000. 'That's how the beer mat was invented – Watney printed them to advertise themselves, to try and keep up business. Beer in cans, too. That was invented by a Welsh brewery, so that even if people weren't drinking in pubs they could drink at home. Unfortunately their can's design was crap – it had a screw top and looked like a Brasso can, so no one bought it.'

Brewers have always been as determined in their efforts to sell beer as customers have to drink it. 'The world's first-ever registered trademark,' Pete continues, 'was Bass's red triangle. The 1875 Trademarks Registration Act came into effect on the first of January 1876, so the bloke from Bass spent New Year's Eve sleeping on the steps of the new office to make sure he was in there first. Even the word "brand" comes from the old practice of burning a firm's symbol into its wooden barrels.'

We continue touring the byways of British history with alcohol as our guide. Pete tells me that part of the reason King Harold lost to William the Bastard in 1066 was that a few days previously he'd resisted an attempted Viking invasion up north, and had allowed his troops to 'over-celebrate'. One historian of the time said the troops had a habit of 'drinking till they were sick'. I hear about sport in pubs; of how Courage's cockerel logo dates from the days of cock-fighting, and how Henry VIII was a dab hand at shove ha'penny. As for pub names, it's not just the Royal Oak denoting Charles II's hiding place which has an interesting back story. There's the Goat and Compasses, for instance, derived from 'God encompass us'. 'Lots of our religious history comes through in pub names,' says Pete. 'Before Henry VIII split from Rome and dissolved the monasteries there were lots of places called the Pope's Head. Surprise, surprise, they all decided that wasn't such a good name any more, so they changed to the King's Head. Or to the Rose, after Henry's flower. If they really wanted to suck up to the King they called themselves the Rose and Crown.' Others, though, wanted to show they were still loyal to the Catholic Church. 'So they found a coded way of doing it – they called themselves the Angel, or the Bells.'

Then there are the unusual pub names. Mauchline in Ayrshire has the Poosy Nancies, named after a lady companion of Robert the Bruce. Bolton has the Lion of Vienna, honouring footballer Stanley Matthews. There's the Jolly Taxpayer in Plymouth, the Bucket of Blood in Cornwall, the Donkey on Fire in Ramsgate and the Round of Carrots in Hertfordshire. Stalybridge near Manchester has Britain's longest pub name: the Old Thirteenth Century Cheshire Astley Volunteer Rifleman Corps Inn. Not content with that, it also has the shortest: Q.

It's thirsty work, this talking about pubs, so Pete gets another round in. He's not convinced by the Tetley's – 'Nothing wrong with it at all, it's just not the Tetley's I grew up with' – so to honour my home county we switch to Adnams. When Pete gets back he's been reminded of something else that's very British, or rather English, about pubs: the way they're arranged. 'I think they're set up as they are because the English are an emotionally repressed race. We need excuses to interact socially. That's why we're made to buy drinks at the bar rather than be served at our table. As you're waiting you get into conversation with people, something we find it very hard to do in the street, at bus stops or wherever.'

As he continues we each open a packet of the crisps he's bought: you need something to line your stomach. 'Even when you're out with mates the pub encourages you to open up. Arguing with them – about football or music or whatever it is – allows us to be demonstrative, to get closer to each other. But in a way that still allows us to pretend we're doing neither of those things. We are English, old chap, after all.'

As Ford Madox Ford put it in his 1907 book *The Spirit of the People: An Analysis of the English Mind*, we will discuss any subject except those 'from which one can digress into anything moving'. The irony of this is that the English are acknowledged – by the rest of the world as well as by ourselves – as masters of language. Nowhere does that show more clearly than in the language of drink, and specifically the language of having had too much to drink. 'I've got a database of different words for "drunk",' says Pete. 'Thirteen hundred of them. There are the obvious ones – "pissed", "wankered" and so on. The Navy has given us loads. "Three sheets to the wind" is the obvious one, but there are also some real gems like "half seas over".' Others in Pete's collection include 'mizzled', 'scoobied' and 'shedded'. 'I've got a friend who says you can take any word, add "-ed" to it, and people will assume you mean "drunk". "God, I was curtained last night." "You should have seen us, we were absolutely tabled."'

Some of the examples Pete mentions are beautiful. 'Pot valiant', for instance. That's poetry. Even something like 'rat-arsed' – you hear it so often you take the inventiveness for granted. And yet, as Pete says, we never use that verbal skill to talk with those closest to us, at least not about things that really matter. Pink Floyd's drummer Nick Mason has described how the band reacted to Syd Barrett's final descent into madness, the increasingly erratic and provocative behaviour that would eventually lead to his departure. The atmosphere in those weeks, according to Mason, was poisonous, vicious, horrible. 'It was so bad,' he added, 'that we almost said something.' And that's just a band; as for the average British family . . . Haven't we all got niggles and secrets, bubbling pots of resentment between ourselves and those we share our genes with? Even the most articulate of families – as much as I love Radio 4, I've got a horrible feeling that its purpose in lots of houses is to provide the conversations that wouldn't happen any other way. As I sit here with Pete I sense he's very similar to me: a British bloke in his early forties who feels very much part of his country, but also can't help stepping away from it – away from himself, perhaps – to examine things from the outside. The other night in Worcester comes back to me, that idea of Britain as a middle-aged friend, looking back on its youth, its days of vigour, of wanting to conquer the world. Come to think of it that was after I'd had a pint, too.

We move on to the subject of temperance. I mention to Pete the passage from *English Journey* where J. B. Priestley, on a bus between Coventry and Birmingham, notices the efforts some pubs have made to attract more custom: bowling greens, food, music. They'd do even more, he says, but for teetotallers, 'those people who say they object to public-houses because you can do nothing in them but drink, but at the same time strenuously oppose the publicans who offer to give their customers anything but drink'.

'I know,' says Pete. 'And it's not even as though the Temperance Movement wanted to ban drink, not originally. It just wanted people to cut *down* on their drinking. That's what the word means — "temper" your intake. When Joseph Livesey started the movement in the 1830s they only wanted people to refrain from drinking spirits.' But the movement gradually grew more militant, as shown from the titles of its publications: the *Preston Temperance Advocate* (1834), the *Teetotal Progressionist* (1852), and finally, in 1867, the *Staunch Teetotaller*.[4]

Pete takes a sip of his Adnams. 'I give up booze every January, and I never miss it. I feel fantastic. I still sometimes go to the pub in January — I'll just drink lime and soda. Someone told me once that you should give up alcohol a day a week, a week a month and a month a year. That sounds very sensible.' Another sip. 'I'm not sure I could do it, though.'

Worrying about other people's drinking, like a lot of the moral crusades in Britain, seems to me to be a very middle-class hobby. While the upper and lower classes happily get stuck into the port and the WKD respectively, Middle England sits at home fretting. It's that 'inward-looking phase of our history' thing again. Nothing left for Angst Ridden of Tunbridge Wells to do but gaze into his navel, stressing about what he finds there. It's also the 'define who you are by who you're not' thing again. During the 2010 general election David Cameron copied Barack Obama and declared that Britain wanted 'hope not fear'. As someone said at the time:

---

4. Thomas Cook owed his travel agency business to the movement. His first trip, in 1841, took a group of temperance campaigners from Leicester to a rally in Loughborough.

'No, we don't. We *like* fear in this country. Why do you think the *Daily Mail* sells so many copies?'[5]

Over the rest of our chat Pete gives me more insights from the Drinker's Guide to British History. Beer remains the defining word, of course, proving once and for all that we're essentially an Anglo-Saxon race; when the Germanic tribes invaded in the fifth century AD they brought their drink with them, seeing off the wine-loving Romans once and for all. 'It's there all the way through,' says Pete. 'The Prince Regent, before he became George IV, said, "Beer and beef have made us what we are." Everyone knows about Hogarth's *Gin Lane*, but you never hear about the companion picture called *Beer Street*. Everyone in that is healthy and happy. Basically the message is "gin is bad for you but beer is good for you".' There's also a sense of British fair play associated with beer. 'In the Chester Miracle Plays, from the fourteenth century, there's only one character who Christ won't redeem – a landlord who was selling short measures.'

The French, on the other hand, have used beer in a divisive way. 'When they lost the Franco-Prussian War in 1871,' says Pete, appealing very much to the part of me still smarting from the discovery that Marmite has a French name, 'Louis Pasteur vowed to avenge the defeat with beer. He decided to topple the German beers, which were seen as the best, from their perch. He knew a lot about fermentation, and so he set about creating a new way of using it in brewing. He proposed that beers made this way should be called "*Bières de*

---

5. Like me, Pete will chuckle a couple of months after our chat when the manager of Britain's last surviving temperance bar – Fitzpatrick's in Rawtenstall, Lancashire – pleads guilty to drink driving.

la Revanche Nationale" – "Beers of the National Revenge".'

Eventually Pete and I have to part, he to continue his round of socialising, I to find a hotel for the night. I leave him with something from *In Search of England*. H. V. Morton has visited the Warren Tor pub on Dartmoor, intrigued by the boast that its fire has been burning for a hundred years. The flames are indeed roaring. 'Suppose,' Morton says to the innkeeper, 'someone let it out?' A 'sharp look of anger' appears on the innkeeper's face. 'Not while I'm here!' he cries, and brings his hand crashing down on the counter. That, thinks Morton, is why England will never be a republic.

After securing a hotel room (big chain place, overpriced, fake mahogany desk – yet again a city has filled up, so I have to take it), I go on the prowl for grub. Tonight's British Culinary Staple is, for the first time since the trip's opening dinner, British. It is a dish that was invented in around 1860 by, depending on who you believe, a Mr Malin of London or a Mr Lees of Mossley near Manchester. So important to national morale did it become that a trade body of its suppliers claimed after World War I that 'we stood . . . more than any other trade in the country, between the very poorest of our population and famine and revolt', while during World War II it was one of the few foods not subject to rationing. In the video for her song 'We Found Love' Rihanna is seen dancing on the table of an establishment that sells it, while prior to swimming the Thames David Walliams ate it to boost his energy levels. But if you really want to know what this dish means us, listen to the Paras: they used it as their codeword to identify friend from foe in darkness at the D-Day landings. One soldier would say 'fish', the other would reply 'chips'.

Yet for something that's part of our landscape, part of our history, part of *us*, a decent chippy, whenever I try to find one in an unfamiliar place, always proves elusive. There are always plenty of places offering *fries* – Maccy D's, kebab shops and so on. But proper chips of sufficient dimensions – a tougher call. And so it proves tonight. Even a group of policemen I consult are unsure; what has it come to when a British bobby can't point you in the direction of a British chippy? Eventually, though, the search bears fruit (well, you know what I mean) in a quiet, unglamorous thoroughfare with the incongruous name of New York Street.[6] The Golden Fisheries is everything you want from a chippy – gorgeous smell, bottle of vinegar and pot of salt on the counter, Formica and metal fittings, including that little bit that keeps the sausages and Pukka pies hot. To stand here is literally to stand inside a British tradition, a real one that continues to live, not a fake tradition like morris dancing or international football. It's now a quarter past nine, and in the lull between dinnertime and the post-pub surge I'm the only customer. When I ask for cod and chips, the man behind the counter asks if I want him to cook the fish from fresh. 'It will be much nicer.'

'How long will that take?'

'Four minutes,' he says, with professional pride at the exactness of his answer.

'Sure, why not?' I reply. It's relaxing to watch his carefully practised moves – dipping the fish in the batter, placing

6. Actually we should remember that the American city gets its name from Yorkshire's county city. When we nicked New Amsterdam off the Dutch Charles II renamed it in honour of his brother the Duke of York and Albany. The second bit of the title was used for the place that is now New York's state capital.

it carefully in the bubbling oil, monitoring the chips that are already in there. I've noticed that his accent is very un-Yorkshire. 'Where are you from, if you don't mind my asking?'

'Kurdistan.'

'How long have you been over here?'

'Eight years.'

'And how do you like it?'

A wrinkle of the nose. 'Is all right.'

We both laugh. His presence here, he's implying, says more about Kurdistan than it does about Britain. But still, I feel that we've bonded over fish and chips – my love of eating them, his mastery of making them. If you 'get' fish and chips you're British; if you don't you're not, even if you were born here. Hence everyone's delight in the story about Peter Mandelson visiting a chippy during an election campaign, and on seeing the jar of mushy peas asking for 'some of that guacamole'.[7] A few weeks after my trip there will be another story in the news, one that I would like to nominate for the award of Most British Thing That Anyone Has Done Ever:[8] a

---

7. In reality the comment was made by an American helping out on the campaign. But the fact people *want* to believe it tells you everything about how Mandelson is perceived.

8. If I'm allowed another nomination for the same award, can I choose Bertrand Russell? In 1948 the great philosopher was flying to Trondheim to deliver a lecture, when his plane crashed into the sea just off the coast of Norway. Nineteen people died, but Russell swam to safety. What's so British about this is not that he was 76 at the time, not that he clung on to the briefcase containing his notes for the lecture, but that he attributed his survival to being a smoker. It was only the people in the non-smoking seats, he noted, who had died.

man in Cambridgeshire successfully fought off four attackers outside a pub – one of whom stabbed him in the chest with a screwdriver – *without dropping his fish and chips*. It was the most-read story on the BBC News website. On the day that the Pope resigned.

As I wait those four tantalising minutes I examine a poster on the wall showing different types of sea fish. It has been issued by the National Federation of Fish Friers, whose headquarters – and it's at moments like this that you realise the universe is running to a perfectly choreographed plan, of which you are merely a passive and contented part – is in Leeds. Then I wander the streets, savouring the chips (perfect mix of grease and crispy bits), observing a Saturday night coming happily to the boil. When Daniel Defoe visited Leeds he noted the strange 'profound silence' of the cloth market, customers being served in whispers so that one trader 'should not know what another does'. The volume levels tonight are somewhat different. Lads roar and girls screech, and sometimes girls roar and lads screech, and as I'm a few pints behind them all it's fun to watch. Leeds is a great city, with wide streets and wide arms. There are lots of solid nineteenth-century buildings that are reinventing themselves, notably in the Victoria Quarter (there's a Harvey Nicks, donchaknow). Further south at 25 Briggate is the building where, in 1865 (its original first-floor signage announces), the clockmaker John Dyson was to be found; now it's a very smart Indian restaurant. I observe this from the Hourglass pub over the road, where I wash down the fish supper with a Guinness. The stand where the DJ rests his deck (well, his iPod) is sponsored by Red Bull. To ring the changes I also have a more refined bottle of Peroni in a more refined bar called 1871, which has vintage film posters and exposed air conditioning.

Back out on to the streets. It's 11 now, and the town is being painted a very comprehensive red.[9] Certain pedestrians are not taking the quickest line down the middle of the pavement, and the odd high heel is wobbling. There's at least one example of that British archetype, the Girl Who Has Put On a Skirt Which Is an Inch Shorter Than She Now Feels Comfortable With So Spends the Whole Night Reaching Round to Pull It Down. There's bellowing, and there's football chanting. But there's no trouble. When you stop and think about it, there very rarely is (give or take the odd screwdriver in Cambridgeshire). We may like invading the rest of the world, but at home we keep it calm. Even people who do go out looking for trouble tend to find it with each other, rather than targeting innocent merry-makers. Someone who knows Newmarket well told me that the fights there are actually arranged. 'We're starting at ten-thirty,' you'll be told as you arrive in a pub. You drink happily with each other until that time, then beat the hell out of each other, then go back to drinking again. On most nights in most towns and cities, if you want to be safe then you will be. But as always Britain likes its fears, its prickly comfort blankets.

I stop opposite Yates's Wine Lodge, on the corner of two streets and with large windows on both frontages. The DJ plays 'Shake Your Tailfeather' from *The Blues Brothers*, and the whole place erupts. Everyone bends at the waist and

---

9. The metaphor actually comes from Melton Mowbray, where one night in 1837 the 3rd Marquess of Waterford got drunk with some friends, found several tins of red paint and redecorated the high street.

waggles their backsides. They jump to one side, re-bend and re-waggle with even more fervour. It's a crescendo of shaking bottoms. Then they straighten again and shimmy like majestic loons.

Some of the smokers on the pavement outside have been copying the moves, while those inside and nearest the window turn so that their backsides would touch were it not for the glass. Then the two groups face each other, 'touching' palms like prisoners separated from visitors by a screen.

Even as he lights another fag, one of the smokers can't stop dancing.

6

In which we finish Sunday lunch too quickly, visit the home of the pencil and discover why James Bond refused to drink tea

When Ossie Ardiles and Ricky Villa signed for Tottenham Hotspur in 1978, there were many aspects of British life they found different from their native Argentina. Of the two players, Ardiles found it easier to adjust, working hard at understanding the culture and traditions of the strange new country. He went to the cinema, he read British newspapers, he ate our 'overcooked' roast beef. The thing he found weirdest of all, however, the thing that nobody had warned him about, was that the shops didn't open on Sunday. 'We would play on Saturday,' he says, 'go out in the evening – and then on Sunday there was nothing to do.'

Much has changed these last thirty-odd years, Ossie. The shops do open now, though because a certain strain of Middle England wants to pretend we're still in the 1950s the bigger ones, the ones most people actually use, aren't allowed to trade for more than a certain number of hours. One thing that hasn't got better on a Sunday, however, is the frequency of the buses. Or, on many routes, the presence of the buses full stop. An increasingly frustrating session on the iPad over breakfast this morning reveals timetable after timetable saying 'No Sunday service'. And where routes do run, they lead to dead-ends. There is a combination of buses, for instance, that could get me to Hawes today, a fair distance to the north. It's tempting to see what this place is like – if only because of William Hague's story about mis-dialling a phone number in his Yorkshire constituency and saying: 'I'm sorry, I was trying to reach a Hawes number' – but there are no onward buses from there. Even when normal service resumes tomorrow I'd be stranded.

It turns out the best I can do is Ilkley, about 15 miles north-west of here. Tomorrow I'll be able to get from there to Skipton, and from Skipton up into the Lake District. Newcastle calls like the brash, heart-warming siren that she is, but that's not what this trip is about: I want to see the places I *haven't* been to. The only view of the Lakes I've ever had has been from a train on the way back from Glasgow. Even at the speed of rail it seemed to take hours to get through that incredible landscape, every last brook and valley bathed by a gorgeous sunset. But train lines stick to their straight, uninterrupted routes, buses don't. It'll be nice to go through the towns and villages, to see the humans who call the Lake District home. All of this planning, incidentally, is done by 8.30 a.m. I'm now at the end of my first week away, but the sleep patterns instilled in you by a three-year-old child take longer than that to fade. There's an Ilkley bus leaving at 9.40 – I might as well get that, then spend my enforced leisure hours walking in the Dales: the fresh air and exercise will do me good.

There is no silence quite like that of a British city centre at 8.45 a.m. on a Sunday morning. The only signs of last night's revelry are the discarded drinks bottles and kebab wrappers, and even they're about to be dealt with by a rubbish collector.

His first act is to take off his belt. He lays it on the pavement, then positions a pile of bin liners at *exactly* the right point for them to hang properly, then puts the belt back on. Actually, there are two other remnants from last night – the Asian girls who sit dejected on the steps of an office building, false fingernails tapping listlessly at smartphones, their skimpy black dresses offering scant protection from the morning chill. The only vehicles on the road are buses. Whenever one passes, its engine echoes round the empty streets like the roar of a prehistoric beast. Then silence resumes. I pass Dr Herman's Hed Shop, offering 'scales, seeds, blunts, skins, bongs, grinders and more'. In the middle of the list 'legal highs' has been scrubbed out – obviously the authorities have changed a classification. The staff of a furniture store have assembled for an early team talk from the manageress; lined up on a sofa they look like naughty children.

There is, unsurprisingly, precious little activity around the bus station, the only display of energy coming from a small guy in his forties who seems to be surgically attached to a BMX. You see men like this occasionally; like lots of kids in the early eighties they had the bike, but for some reason never grew out of it. Now they circle car parks, unable to stop in case, like a shark, they die. The X84 bus is at its stand, and soon it's carrying me out of Leeds. At several stops in the city's suburbs we're joined by walkers of a certain age, with brightly coloured rucksacks and those walking poles everyone seems to have nowadays. The first decent-sized valley (sorry, dale) that appears to our right is filled with fog, though out of twenty cows in a field only three are lying down, backing up the weather forecast which says the torrential rain heading for the rest of England won't quite reach us up here. Let's hope they're right: it's severe warning stuff, an 'only travel if you have to' situation.

The stones are getting darker again now, like the ones north of Barnsley, giving buildings an ominous appearance. This doesn't bode well for Ilkley, the place whose very name defies *joie de vivre*. Of course the famous song is running round my head, together with the extra words a friend from Hull has told me are traditionally added by locals: 'On Ilkley Moor bah't 'at . . . where the ducks play football.' What does that *mean*? My friend didn't know, so what chance have I got? *League of Gentlemen* strangeness lurks, I fear. If I see a single whippet I'm off.

What I actually find is that someone has picked up Cheltenham and carried it 150 miles north. There are yummy mummies steering Bugaboo buggies, and Tommy Hilfiger-clad men steering VW Touaregs. The coffee chain requests run to at least four words, one of which is often 'soya'. Le Bistro Pierre at the Crescent Inn have roasted their mini-chorizos in honey; if anyone has too many they can always work them off at the Ilkley Lawn Tennis and Squash Club. The roads crossing at right angles to form the town's centre are both very wide, and with the number of 4×4s cruising them there's an American feel to Ilkley. A town in the Hamptons perhaps, or rather (given the surrounding hills) somewhere in the Midwest. No one's hurrying; everyone's confident and assured. The only rough edges are to be found down on the football pitches by the riverside, though even there the cries of 'fuckin' 'ell, ref' are watched by a manager sipping his tea from an Emma Bridgewater mug. My own tea has been provided by Costa; I can't remember which of their 378 blends I opted for. But before we get all 'how ponceyfied and complex our national beverage has become', remember that as far back as 1946 George Orwell was *very* finickety about how to make the perfect cuppa. 'Indian or Ceylonese leaves' (rather than Chinese), and definitely no sugar. James Bond, meanwhile, refuses to drink the stuff at all: he sticks to coffee, blaming tea for the downfall of the British Empire.

There's a freshness to the breeze, so just in case John Kettley's got it wrong I buy a disposable poncho from Mountain Warehouse, a rather swish camping shop, and set off towards them there hills. A footpath along the wide and white-foaming River Wharfe soon leads to some splendid isolation, broken only by occasional encounters with other walkers. Two of them form a British archetype, the Couple Who Look Exactly the Same As Each Other (in this case: short, with cropped dark hair and round wire-framed glasses on round faces, making them look like Venn diagrams). The Sloanification evident in Ilkley continues out here with signs asking you to pick up your dog's poo, even though the fields are full of sheep poo. Oh, well, I suppose it is a footpath rather than just a field. And it's not as ridiculous as the woman who wrote to my local newspaper in Suffolk demanding that horse owners should be made to pick up their animals' dung in bin liners.

An hour or so of this has my appetite perking up, so I circle back towards Ilkley, planning on lunch then another bout of pedestrianism this afternoon. With due respect to the mini-chorizos, there is only one dish it can possibly be on this day and in this county: roast beef and Yorkshire pudding. The meal was introduced to Britain as a Sunday lunch by Edward VII, which means that if your roast potatoes are King Edwards you're paying him a double tribute (the spud was named for his Coronation in 1902). He did a lot to shape Britain, old Eddie. There was Crewe naming their football team after his missus, of course, plus quite a few sartorial touches – such as leaving the bottom button of your waistcoat undone, in his case because of a 48-inch waist. Trouser turn-ups, too: according to one wag these were to catch any crumbs he dropped.

Choosing a pub that looks as though it'll keep things traditional without going all the way back to the Ossie Ardiles era, I order the full-trimmings option. Only as I pocket my change do I realise that I now say 'Could I get . . .' instead of 'Could I have . . .' Another bit of verbal pollen that has flown across the Atlantic and germinated, like losing the 'and' from 'vodka and tonic'. The meal is delicious, the Yorkshire pudding making a particular effort on home turf, and within not many minutes at all there's a plate in front of me that very possibly won't need washing. Sitting there sated, I look over and notice that the posh group at a nearby table, who were served before me, have still not finished eating. This makes me feel piggish and unrefined. Posh people never seem that interested in food, certainly not in troughing it as quickly as possible. They talk to each other instead, occasionally glancing down as if to say: 'Oh, look – there's some food there. I might even eat some of it in a bit.' Is it in the genes, a deep-rooted certainty that the next meal is never in doubt?

Up on my feet again. As I'm tootling round the town trying to decide which hill to tackle (and also keeping an eye out for likely-looking B&Bs), I notice a bus stop. The word 'Sunday' leaps out from a timetable and just to confirm that it's followed by the words 'no service', I stop for a look. But no – there are some times underneath. It must be an old copy

. . . er, no: it's the summer 2012 timetable, valid for another month. According to this there will, at 16.15 hours, be either an 884 or an 871 leaving for Skipton. That's only a little further along, but it's where I was aiming to get to tomorrow morning – now I can get there tonight instead. I kill the time with a truncated walk, then return at the designated hour to find that, yes, the Dales Bus company is indeed prepared to take £3 of my money and convey me to Skipton. So Google, who this morning provided a seemingly exhaustive account of every bus service in this part of the country, missed one out. I find this simultaneously worrying and refreshing.

The countryside has become very rugged now. The rolling dales are full of rocky outcrops, as though a green-and-red rug has been daubed with patches of tar. There are some impressive inclines, and our driver hurtles the short single-decker down them at top speed, always knowing just when to brake. (Incidentally, my favourite British hill remains one I've never seen, outside the village of Aston Clinton in Buckinghamshire, where Lionel Martin used to test his early cars; Mrs M suggested combining 'Aston' and their surname as the company's title because it would put them at the start of alphabetical lists.) The sheep look very hardy indeed. There are now dry-stone walls around too, though the dryness doesn't seem all it's cracked up to be – most of the walls have got at least a few stones missing, and some have fallen down completely. They just make everywhere look a mess to me. A journalist friend of mine confessed in a national newspaper that despite living in dry-stone wall territory in Derbyshire, he's never liked the things. From the reaction he got you'd think he'd called for the National Trust to change its logo to the swastika.

Touchdown is a shade before 5 p.m. Skipton is very similar to Ilkley in its market-town appearance, if very different in the number of people wearing designer rimless specs. Though I won't find this out until later, there not being anyone around at the moment: the rainclouds have put on a sudden northward surge, and a fine but persistent drizzle is falling. I choose a B&B and on being shown to my room by the wise-cracking owner find I have chosen well: handing me a breakfast slip, he says, 'I 'ope you don't like croissants.' Guests are to place their slips on the hall table, having first deleted from a long list of fried ingredients the ones they don't want. This, you'll notice, rather than ticking the ones they do. The room itself is entertainingly twee; the light switch has a picture frame built round it.

Rainy Sunday evenings are meant for reflection. They are also meant for Timothy Taylor's Dark Mild, so I head round to the Woolly Sheep Inn just off the high street and avail myself of both. Including the day spent getting from Suffolk to Land's End, I have now been away for a week. I have taken 26 buses, spent £89.10 on fares, and covered 539.8 miles. The journeys feel like 26 squares across a quilt. They've now brought me, I read as I drink, to the town where, in 1852, Thomas Spencer was born. In 1894 he met Michael Marks, and British shopping was never the same again. I also discover that Yorkshire gave us the 'doh-re-mi' musical notation system: its inventor was born here (I think Julie Andrews should have done it in the local accent). It invented the seaside resort too, Scarborough being the first town developed as such, and the first in the world to boast a Grand Hotel. What's more, Scarborough features in the sentence designed to remind us just how illogical the English language is, which contains eight pronunciations of the syllable '-ough': 'A dough-faced, thoughtful ploughman strode through the streets of Scarborough; after falling into a slough, he coughed and hiccoughed.'

Hanging in the pub is a copy of a *Times* article from 1997 listing some of the reasons for 'taking a pride in being English'. It's here because Timothy Taylor beer gets a nod, but among the others are 'The Lark Ascending', Double Gloucester, the Bash Street Kids, fig rolls, 'Penny Lane', the V-sign, 617 Squadron and Basil Brush. We could all compile our own versions of this list; for what it's worth mine would include *Wisden*, purple Quality Streets and Joe Brown's song 'Free Inside' from the film of *Porridge*. But whatever your choices, soaking in the warm psychological bath they provide is just another way of savouring your country's history and the way it has formed the identity you possess. This is a collective thing, of course, binding you not only to the people you know today but also to those who are long dead. This is something I'm more aware of the older I get, and especially since I became a parent. When we're younger some of us run away from the closeness of family life; the British actress Rachel Ward emigrated to Australia because 'divulging information on who one danced with often provoked such killjoy spoilers as: "I knew his father. He had a famously small cock."' Then you have a child, which you think is all about looking to the future, but which actually makes you look to the past. You realise just how few generations link you to the Industrial Revolution, the Civil War, Magna Carta.[1] The last person alive in Britain with a

---

1. Some parents with a real awareness of history were those of the actor Windsor Davies. His brothers are called Tudor and Stuart.

parent born in the eighteenth century was Alice Grigg of Kent, who died in 1970. Her father William had been born in 1799.

At a table in the corner of the pub are two lads and a girl, all in their early twenties. Their voices provide a soothing background to my reading. They call a cup of tea a 'brew'. They agree that 'it were great when Damon got his arse handed to him on Friday'. One of them reminisces about a vending machine at college in which he used to get rid of his small change, pressing the 'cancel' button so it returned large denomination coins. There's no Yorkshire opinionating here, no bragging, no front. In fact, now I think back, there hasn't been any in Yorkshire full stop. What's happened? I've come to Yorkshire, that's what, rather than Yorkshire coming to me. Caroline spoke of this county's fierce sense of identity, comparing it to that of Liverpool. When I visited that city a few years ago, prickling from a lifetime's irritation at the touchiness of Scousers, I was disarmed by how untouchy they were. You don't often get comparisons between Scousers and wine, but it struck me that perhaps, like certain vintages, the people of Liverpool don't travel well. On home ground they're relaxed, among their own kind with nothing to prove. But when they're away the insecurities creep in, and defensiveness brings up its shield of aggression. Are Yorkshire folk the same?

Who am I kidding? We're *all* the same. Certainly if we're English we are. That's why we compile lists of reasons for taking pride in being English, why we pack jars of Marmite when we go abroad, why we invaded every country in the world but 22, renamed all the cities Victoria and made them as much like England as possible. We all feel insecure when we travel, it's just a question of how you cope with it. Marmite, fine – mass invasions, not so much.

That's what life's all about, really. You've got to learn how to travel well.

The whole reason people come to the Lake District is to see water, so I can't really complain about how much of it I see today. You think I mean rain, don't you? No. For whole chunks of this epically wet Monday I don't even see the rain. The condensation inside the buses covers the windows so completely that they might as well be frosted. It gets to the stage that at each destination I stock up on paper napkins with which to wipe viewing holes; there's only so much punishment a coat sleeve can take.

Today proves to be the first really consistent one of the trip, where all the destinations are essentially the same as each other, sitting nicely together like a collection of novels by the same author on a shelf. None of that bleak Barnsley/ merry Wakefield malarkey. The Lake District makes *sense*. I reach it through Settle, which is at the other end of the 580 bus route from Skipton. Waiting for it I hide from the rain that's already lashing down at 9.30 in the morning by sheltering in a passageway near the stop. I see another bus that probably isn't mine but might be going the same way, so decide to flag it down anyway.

'You don't go to Skipton, do you?' My tone is meant to convey that I'm almost certain he doesn't but I just want to make sure. This while trying to deploy a very small umbrella against a very large amount of rain.

The driver – bushy ginger beard, no stranger to a pork pie – laughs in small-town incomprehension that there are people not from his small town. I might as well have asked if he goes to Jupiter. 'No,' he says condescendingly, and for the first time on the trip I feel angry with a driver.

'Fine,' I say. 'Thank you for the clarification.'

He drives off without another word.

When it finally does appear the 580 is easily the oldest bus of the trip so far, an orange 1980s specimen with a ticket machine like a pre-ZX Spectrum computer, and those big clunky switches all over the dashboard that look like you'll need both hands to press them. Some of them bear bits of yellow sticky tape with writing on them. Once I'm on board we motor through terrain similar to yesterday's, only even more bleak because of the weather. The Highland cattle look *really* pissed off.

Settle, like Ilkley, lets the hills crowd right round it, nature not so much on its doorstep as squatting in its front hall. I invest in a £6 golf umbrella, wondering how strong it can be for that sort of money. Also a £1 pair of shoes from a charity shop; my trainers are already hinting soggily that they don't much fancy the fight. The shoes are black, seemingly watertight, and entirely without style. I don't mind this – it'll make it easier to get rid of them after the trip. The need to travel light has really brought home how anti-possessions I'm getting. In my twenties I worked with a woman in her forties who said her ambition was to get rid of everything she owned, giving away her last possession on the day she died. I never got it then – I do now. Money should give you memories, not things. Twenty-seven bus fares have been a good investment.

Although tempted by the Settle Down Café, I nonetheless plump for Ye Olde Naked Man Café, eager to understand its name. The waitress brings me a tea but no explanation, there not being one, other than the (quite modest) depiction of a chap in the buff on the building's first-floor frontage. It bears the date 1663; this has been a café ever since, and indeed claims to be the country's oldest. This morning there's as much steam coming off the damp customers as off the hot drinks, but I wave it aside and read the diaries of Alan Bennett, who has a home not far from here. On 25 July 1985 he popped into Settle for fish and chips, and was alarmed by someone asking if the kestrel under the counter was for sale, until he realised it was the name of a lager. On 3 March 1982, getting a script photocopied here, the shop-owner said: 'Glancing at this I see you dabble in playwriting.' Bennett thinks that although 'this just about sums it up', the comment is like a nurse saying: 'I see, watching you undress, that your legs are nothing to write home about.' Of course he's being overly modest. If we take him at his word for a moment, though, Bennett is admitting to being crap but getting a laugh out of it: the very definition of post-World War II Britishness. It's there in everything from *Lucky Jim* to *Miranda*.

But the most fascinating entry is from 15 June 1982. Margaret Thatcher has announced Britain's victory in the Falklands. 'Not English, I feel now,' writes Bennett. 'This is just where I happen to have been put down. No country, no party, no church, no voice. And now they're singing *Britannia Rules the Waves* outside Downing Street. It's the Last Night of the Proms erected into a policy.' Keen history boy that he is, Bennett will know he meant to write 'Britannia *Rule* the Waves', Britons singing it in the 1740s because they wanted the Navy to get their act together. But anyway, we take his point. The trouble, Alan, is that's what belonging is all about, and why it's so problematic. If you define yourself by your membership of a group numbering tens of millions, there are bound to be times when some of the others do something you don't agree with. Lots of people felt *more* English because of the Falklands, and indeed because of Margaret Thatcher. It's like when Chris Donald of *Viz* was criticised for being rude about the Royal Family. 'You can't say that!' people would tell him. 'She's our Queen!' 'But she's my Queen too,' Donald would reply.

Back outside again. The rain is still at cats-and-dogs level. The next step of today's north-westerly journey is the 581 to Kirkby Lonsdale. It's operated, the timetable reveals, by the Little Red Bus company, so the bus that appears at 11.30 a.m. is, of course, white. It is little, at least; a minibus bearing absolutely no insignia or markings of any kind. The only clue to its identity is a laminated sheet of A4 paper propped on the dashboard with '581' on it in very large type. It's the trip's first undercover bus. Boarding it I feel like an American cop. Well, slightly.

Two minutes down the road is Giggleswick. Its graveyard is home to Russell Harty, who was not only Alan Bennett's friend but also Richard Whiteley's teacher at the school here, much as Socrates was Plato's teacher. That's the way we do things in this country: the Ancient Greeks invented philosophy, we mastered light entertainment television.[2] The remoteness of this part of the country is really noticeable now, not just out of the window but on the map: whole stretches of white, with just the occasional road laid across them like string

---

2. There's another reminder of this world up near Kirkby Lonsdale, where there are two places called High Biggins and Low Biggins. Poor love, him and his mood swings.

on a tablecloth. Not far away is the tiny village of Kettlewell, where the parson once asked a woman why he never saw her any more. 'Oh, I used to like going into Kettlewell about once a week,' she replied, 'but now I can't stand t'racket.' When I see the sign on the A65 saying it's 13 miles to Kirkby Lonsdale I get the first stomach-knot of panic since the West Country. *Thirteen miles!* And that's the quick way, staying on the main road, not constantly heading off it to village-mop as we'll be doing. I have to concentrate on my breathing for a moment, slow it down, to reattain a state of Bus.

For the final 20 minutes of this journey we're joined by a young woman who starts every sentence on her mobile – *every* sentence – with the phrase 'Tell you what . . .' And for the final five minutes by an old man who holds out both hands to balance himself against the bus's movements as he finds a seat. He looks like Tommy Cooper impersonating Frankenstein. In Kirkby Lonsdale a few of us keep dry in the market square's beautiful hexagonal stone shelter, peering out at the stop a few yards away to make sure the 567 to Kendal doesn't arrive and leave without us. Two of my companions, both women in their sixties, see me cross-referencing timetables with my road atlas, and we get talking. It turns out they once did the same run as me (Skipton up to Windermere) on their free passes, to surprise someone they'd met on a holiday. They've even been as far as Blackpool. I plant the seed of a possible Lejog trip. They laugh about it – who knows if it will ever happen? But there are glints in their eyes. I like the cut of their jibs, and indeed their headscarves.

I still haven't seen any actual lakes yet, apart from the one by the luggage rack of the 567 where shopping trolleys and umbrellas quite literally pool their resources, but the ride to Kendal is lush, with trees and bushes and shrubs and hedges all drip-drip-dripping, as though a million taps had all been *nearly* turned off. In the village of Barrows Green one householder has failed to trim his trees and hedges: irritating for neighbours anywhere, but especially round here where rainfall is a way of life. I can't help thinking of Leighton Hall near Welshpool in Wales, the nineteenth-century home of banker Christopher Leyland. It was there that two different strains of cypress plant were first cross-pollinated to produce the beast that would one day lead to court cases, and which still bears the banker's name: the Leylandii.

Kendal itself is the day's first 'takes more than five minutes to walk around' destination, and as it's now 1.08 p.m. I decide to make it the venue for lunch. First, though, in the indoor market very close to the station, I purchase a £10 golf umbrella. (There's your answer to how strong a £6 one can be.) I also invest in some waterproof trousers, and put them on straightaway. The town centre is largely pedestrianised, making the search for a café relatively free from splashes by passing traffic, though it's still a case of door-hopping, pausing, catching my breath, then diving out again. Coming out of one mini-shopping centre I hold the door for a man who doesn't say thank you. Somehow the weather makes it seem even ruder than usual. I once saved a man from drowning and he didn't say thanks. He just sat on the deserted Suffolk riverbank next to me, both of us drying out, him moaning about how was he going to get his paddle back, it had drifted off when his canoe overturned, and was his phone still working in the waterproof pouch he'd been trying in his pocket, plus a dozen other grumbles. I wanted to reply: Never mind about waterproof pouches.

Don't you think a lifejacket might be an idea, seeing as we've established that you can't swim and it was bloody lucky I happened to be walking my dog here? Of course I didn't. Nor did I point out the lack of thanks. I just got up, said bye, and carried on with a now very squelchy dog walk. Not saying thank you is an increasingly British habit. Being embarrassed about confronting people who don't say thank you is an even more British one.

Examining the list of possible lunches outside one café, I hear the following exchange:

Customer: 'Do you do your coffees to take away?'

Woman behind till: 'Yes, we do – what would you like?'

Customer: 'Could I have a latté?'

Woman: 'We only do filter.'

I move on, and find somewhere else. The cheese sandwich has to be followed by a slice of the famous Kendal mint cake, though I can only manage a couple of mouthfuls. This is not just because they remind me how much I dislike mint, but also because any more of the energy-giving stuff and I'll be bouncing off the walls of the next bus – it got Edmund Hillary up Everest, for God's sake. Even the sugar from the two morsels I've had needs walking off. On Branthwaite Brow (a cobbled street of some steepness) I'm surprised to see a rainbow sign. Wow, even somewhere as conservative as Kendal has now got a gay bar. Except they haven't: it's an office supplies shop called Rainbow.

Round the corner in a charity shop an older sales assistant coaches a young recruit. 'You have to develop a feel for the prices,' she tells him. 'If you get a designer jacket, for example, and it's got a two-ninety-nine tag on it, you know there's been a mistake.' She takes a sip of her tea. 'That's the art of retail.'

The second 555 of the project, from Kendal to Keswick, is where the Lakes really become the lakes. Our double-decker passes a sign that says: 'Welcome to Windermere – A Fair Trade Town'. Trade is the only thing about the town that is fair. There's more than just the odd dark stone and bit of flint around now – everything in sight is built from the stuff: the railway station, the huge Windermere Hotel opposite, the churches, the houses, the walls that line the road as it winds down into the town. Even the sheep we'll see later in the journey are black. We all know what Wordsworth thought of the Lakes, but Defoe was unimpressed, referring to the district's 'unpassable hills, whose tops, covered with snow, seemed to tell us all the pleasant part of England was at an end'. It's too wet and warm for the snow today, of course. Pity – it would lighten the colour scheme a touch.

We call at a huge school, taking 15 minutes to inch our way round the mini-island in its forecourt and back out again, while other designated buses, coaches and cars collect chattering pupils. We take on so many of them that the condensation starts forming its own micro-climate, and the driver has to put the air-con on full blast. Together with the noise from the engine and the kids it's deafening. Eventually we escape, and reach Lake Windermere itself. This was the inspiration for the lake in Arthur Ransome's *Swallows and Amazons*, though things are slightly less grazed-knees-and-lemonade these days: more Ayurvedic-yoga-and-Chablis, from the appearance of the boats and yachts moored here. Further along the shore, at the lake's northern end, we reach Waterhead Boutique Hotel and Dining.

Ambleside is equally *à la mode*, especially when a French

mother and her teenage daughter get on, heading for Grasmere. They depart at the stop nearest Dove Cottage and the Wordsworth Museum, over the road from which a new hotel has just opened, called the Daffodil. I'm surprised by how small the cottage itself is, a humble whitewashed (how was that allowed round here?) structure with a grey slate roof. Then I remember that just because a world-famous poet lived in a cottage it doesn't stop being a cottage. Certainly the geese in the nearby meadow don't seem very impressed. They honk grumpily.

The hills are getting serious now. Not just taller and steeper but rockier, with streams flowing down them so fast they foam white, even forming mini-waterfalls. The bracken, ferns and moss give a red tone to the landscape, complementing the rich green of tall pine and spruce trees. The next big body of water is Thirlmere, whose eastern edge the road skirts for what seems an age. This long, thin reservoir was created in the 1890s from two natural lakes, specifically to supply fast-growing Manchester with water. There's an aqueduct linking it to the city through the hills; at 96 miles it claims to be the longest tunnel in the world. Whether or not that's true it's a miracle of engineering, built to slope slightly downwards the whole way so that not a single pump is required; gravity does everything. At 4 m.p.h. the water takes slightly over a day to reach Manchester, a travelling pace that makes me feel like we could bond. Just the other side of the reservoir is Seathwaite, which holds the title of Britain's wettest inhabited place. They get 140 inches of rain a year there, nearly six times as much as London. On a day like this it feels like they're trying for all 140 in one go, but before I get all 'we Brits beat the world at crap weather', I should note that the world champion is

Cherrapunji in India, with an average yearly rainfall of 463 inches. You could stand a double-decker bus in that, put another one on its roof and still be ten feet from the surface.

On the way into Keswick we pass a group of dedicated walkers, kitted out in all the gear, including hoods pulled tightly around their faces with drawstrings; they look like shrink-wrapped action toys. The town itself, which we reach at 4.20 p.m., is like Kendal: a proper working place, rather than a decorative one like Windermere. A slackening of the rain's strength from 'lashing' to 'irritating' allows for a stroll around. A chippy offers free gravy to pupils of a certain school (nice change from the usual 'no more than two schoolchildren at one time' grouchiness), while the pupils' predecessors, a plaque reveals, formed the PUPS (Pushing Young People Society) in 1928. They published an annual with useful tips – to prevent toffee papers crackling in church, for instance, an overnight soaking in olive oil and treacle was recommended (can we pass that on to modern cinema-goers?). Old silk stockings, meanwhile, were 'grand for polishing the car . . . but be careful to keep them in your pocket. Some people may not believe you.'

A pub displays a notice saying they want to use local produce wherever possible and are willing to barter, offering beer tokens in return; this week they're looking for courgettes, runner beans and fresh flowers. Outside the Moot Hall – an old churchy-looking building in the market place which used to be the Town Hall but is now the tourist information centre – a weather forecast for tomorrow has been printed off the internet and displayed (summary: 'crap but not quite as crap as today'). An old couple are struggling with the small print, so I read it out for them. Reaching the end, I continue with:

'And to the woman who called today saying she'd heard there was going to be a hurricane, don't worry, there certainly isn't.' The couple nod in all seriousness, say 'thank you' and walk off.

I walk back to the bus station, which is essentially a corner of a supermarket's car park (a chain, but a local one – Tesco haven't won yet). A man sitting in a light blue Jaguar, obviously waiting for his wife to finish her shopping, uses nail-scissors to trim his moustache in the rear-view mirror. I fill the time until the X4 to Penrith arrives with some more reading about Keswick. For centuries, I learn, it was the world capital of pencil production, the implement having been invented here in 1546 when a seam of graphite was discovered in nearby Borrowdale and found to be perfect for marking sheep. It was 1770 before the pencil *eraser* was invented, but have no fear – that was an English achievement too. For 200 years people had been using breadcrumbs to rub out their mistakes, until one day an engineer called Edward Nairne accidentally picked up a cube of rubber instead of bread, and realised its properties. I also take in a few pages of Gertrude, including her stop in Keswick: 'I watched a fisherman bring out a little "fella" – quite five inches long. The man looked thoroughly satisfied.' God bless her.

Keswick is the end of the northward drag – the trip turns right now and heads east. A 5.20 p.m. departure means several passengers are on their way home from work. One woman spends the first bit of the journey surreptitiously eating a sausage roll, then openly drinks a Diet Coke. By this stage in the day the puddles are huge, and several times our driver pulls out into the middle of the road – which round here means on to the opposite side of the road – to avoid drenching pedestrians. This journey is only a 40-minute jog, but it marks the end of the Lakes, which are the part of Cumbria that don't call themselves Cumbria. The 'Cumbrian Foodhall' store on the outskirts of Penrith is the first use of the 'C' word I've seen all day. As we pull into Penrith bus station there's only me and a couple of other passengers left, two slightly rough-looking middle-aged guys (makes three of us then, I suppose). One turns to the other and says: 'Have you been to that new tapas bar? It's spot on.'

Ten minutes later I'm standing in the town's main square, alone. It's been one of those days when you develop rain-tinnitus, so it's only as I notice the absence of ever-changing dots on the puddles that I realise the heavens have actually closed at last. Taking down my umbrella, I admire the red sandstone buildings – thank God for some colour at last. Barclays is a particular beauty, and J & J Graham too, the family grocer's dating from 1793. They show that indies can survive if you move with the times: local smuggler's cake nuzzles pancetta in the window. Just about every trading need seems to be taken care of here, from Betfred to Bambinos (baby clothes, since you ask).

My phone goes with a text. It's a friend I haven't seen for a while, asking if I'm around for a drink. I reply, telling him where I am and why. He comes straight back with: '*Please* tell me you're going to the Penrith Tea Rooms.' Of course he does. It's what I would have said, it's what any British film fan of our generation would have said. The sad truth, however, is that the iconic scene in *Withnail and I* wasn't shot here. The part of Penrith was taken by Stony Stratford in Buckinghamshire, and that of the tea rooms by a building that now houses a chemist's. But the reference has put me in the mood for some genteel respectability of the sort verging on crustiness. On the other side of the square is the George Hotel, genteel respectability made sandstone. That's it – tonight's Culinary Staple will be the 'meal at the slightly posh place you wouldn't normally treat yourself to'.

Entering through the pillared porch and turning right in the oak-lined reception area, I find myself in the restaurant. The white linen is crisp, the place settings immaculate. The coal-fire is a fake gas one, just as the Edwardian tiles around it are reproduction, but both are done so well that at first you don't notice. The hushed tones of Westlife are perhaps a trifle out of place, though not so much that they jar. *Quelle surprise*, at 6.15 on a rainy Monday evening they can just squeeze me in. I'm led by the East European maître d' to a table on the far side of the room. He very kindly pretends not to hear the swish of my waterproof trousers, which I've forgotten to take off. Only one of the other tables is occupied; a sixty-something couple are seated in the corner. He is wearing a jacket and tie, and is that British archetype, the Slightly Deaf Man Who's So Used to Saying 'What?' That He Says It After Everything Even When He's Heard You. The maître d' sends across one of his crack team, a local girl who hands me the leather-bound menu and wine list. I decide on a large glass of Shiraz. She goes to fetch it.

'How did it go with Charles today?' says Mrs Genteel to her husband.

'What?'

'How . . .'

'Fine, fine. He says they'll have the paperwork done by Thursday.'

I take out my iPad and research hotels in Carlisle. That

feels like a suitable base from which to launch tomorrow's leg of the trip (if things go to plan it will be a momentous leg indeed). The waitress brings my wine, together with a basket of identical bread rolls which I examine carefully before choosing one, that being the Expected Behaviour in this situation. I also order the braised lamb shank.

'I saw Veronica at the dentist's,' says Mrs Genteel.

'What?'

'I s—'

'Really? How is she?'

When the waitress brings my meal I have a mouthful of wine. Before I can swallow it and say thank you, she says, 'You're welcome.' I eat, and the Genteels silently await their desserts, to the incongruous strains of Craig David running through his week's love-making schedule.

This, I feel confident, was not the early pattern of their own courtship.

'Celtic FC', someone has argued passionately, if briefly. The response is equally to-the-point: 'Fenian Bastards'.

It's not just the graffiti in the Gents – most of the discourse in the Last Orders Inn seems to revolve around sport. Two guys at the table next to me discuss the Ryder Cup preview being shown on the large screen. A group of young lads play pool in the corner. Someone at the bar announces that all modern footballers are 'poofters'. Meanwhile one of the wi-fi networks my phone's picking up is named 'Police Surveylance Vehicle'. Quite what the joke is I'm not sure, but it wouldn't be harmed by some correct spelling. I've decamped here from the George for a post-prandial and pre-cinema pint. With a room at the Carlisle Travelodge safely booked, I want to sample some Cumbrian nightlife. This could be done in Carlisle itself, but the project hasn't yet included a late-night bus, so a longer stopover in Penrith it is.

As that first day in the West Country proved, small local cinemas haven't reached extinction quite yet. The Lonsdale Alhambra inhabits a building with a frontage no bigger than the estate agents and building societies it's filed among on Middlegate. A rugby team could fill its foyer. But the young man who talked me through the options here earlier on had an obvious and genuine love of film that made him a pleasure to deal with, and must give the Lonsdale every chance of adding at least a few more years to the 102 of its lifespan so far. An American comedy showing upstairs on Screen 2, I recall, was described by a Radio 4 reviewer as 'one of the most depressing cinematic experiences of my life', while someone in a respected newspaper was even less diplomatic than that. Slatings always tempt me – just how bad can a movie be? My adviser behind the counter hasn't seen it and so can't comment, but he's lukewarm about the other possibles, so I stump up my £5.80, plus £4 for a bag of Revels and a latté from one of those little machines they always have in places like this.

It's not the greatest surprise in the world when the audience for a movie with reviews like this, on a Monday night like this, in a town like this, numbers just one. But I'm glad. Never before have I had an entire cinema to myself. It's tempting to move around and sit in every one of the 90 seats for a minute at a time, but it might freak the projectionist out, so I stick to the middle of the back row. And you know what? The film isn't that bad. It's not that good either, but after the GBH inflicted by the critics it feels like *The Big Lebowski*. A Ready

Brek glow envelops me, the wonderful sensation of being a long, long way from the national media and their cultural Stasi. I even find myself laughing at Ben Stiller, and if that's not proof that travel broadens the mind then such proof does not exist.

It's a glow that continues as I head to the bus station, where Stagecoach's final 104 of the day is due at half-past ten. The rain's back on duty, and as the drips from the long shelter produce metallic ringing noises, I read a notice from another operator: 'We would like to thank all our passengers for supporting our fledgling service, and hope to see you all again when our exciting new timetable starts at Easter.' A week ago this would have made me laugh. But as I take out the road atlas, and see just how far up Britain's spine these trusty things called local buses have carried me, a timetable seems the most beautiful thing there could be. The driver of the 104 accepts the £10 day-pass I've had since Kendal, bringing today's average fare down to £2.50. It's a mixed crowd who board the vehicle – seemingly restaurant workers heading home, including two young Thai women who spend the entire 19 miles to Carlisle glued to their iPhones, tweeting and texting and occasionally showing each other replies but never actually saying a word. A cool lad sits at the back, wrapped in a pair of large, expensive headphones.

A puddle-cum-lake on the A6 slows us to walking pace, and the pitch-blackness hides the countryside from view. As we pass through villages the sodium sparks of streetlights force their way through the steamed-up side-windows, each one distorted into an exploding sun. But of course the windscreen is kept clear by its wipers, and when we crest a hill after Low Hesket and the lights of Carlisle appear in the distance, it's a bit like that moment at the beginning of *E.T.* when the alien first sees Los Angeles spread out beneath him. On the outskirts of the city a man gets off and bids farewell to the woman he's been talking to since Penrith. He's mentioned that he had to abandon work today because of the rain, and I assumed the case he was carrying was a toolbox. Only now, as I notice it more clearly, do I see it's a tuba.

When we reach the bus station it's 11.14 p.m., and I'm the last passenger left. Unlike everywhere else today Carlisle is a city rather than a town, and slipping into it unnoticed like this, under cover of the late-night drizzle, makes me feel like a character in a John le Carré novel. Asking a cabbie for directions to the hotel, I have to resist an urge to say 'the pigeons fly low over Koblenz'. His reply comes in a Geordie accent, giving the first clue (it'll be confirmed in the morning) that another linguistic boundary has been crossed; no more of the Yorkshire-ish tones that have filled today. But surely Carlisle is north-west rather than north-east? Well, yes it is – it's just that Britain has narrowed so much at this point that it's only 52 miles from here to Newcastle, so west and east don't really mean that much any more.[3]

After five minutes' walk through the deserted streets I'm at the Travelodge, which is an old Royal Mail building of plain bricks and large square windows dating from 1955, a fact gleaned from the 'EIIR' insignia by the front door. That's the only architectural nicety in the entire place, but never mind; the young lad on reception provides a warm welcome. A

---

3. George Stephenson, the inventor of the Rocket, had a Geordie accent so strong that when he went to London he had to take an interpreter.

little too warm, actually, in that he insists on going through the full spiel about emergency exits and breakfast times and procedures if I change my mind about wi-fi vouchers. This could be irritating, but actually he's so nervous I just feel sorry for him, and stand there giving encouraging nods.

Tonight's final bit of reading, undertaken to induce sleep's warm embrace, is from Celia Fiennes's *Through England on a Side Saddle in the Time of William and Mary*. This 1695 trip made Fiennes the first recorded woman to visit every county in England (there were at that point 39 of them). It's a brilliant book, Fiennes encouraging her readers to travel their homeland in order to 'cure the evil Itch of overvalueing fforeign parts', and avoid the dangers of 'ignorance and being strangers to themselves'. Her accommodation in Carlisle is vividly described, though it's only when you reach the bit about the 'young giddy Landlady' who is happy to 'Dress fine and Entertain the soldiers' that you realise Celia is in fact spending the night in a brothel.

Two in the morning. I wake with a jolt. Something troubling is there in the subconscious, pushing to get through. Gradually, as the map of Britain fills my mind, the worry makes itself clear. I'm heading away from home, with a hell of a long way still to go. There comes a point in every trip, every undertaking, where the end seems impossibly far off, and it feels like the middle is going to keep you prisoner for ever. I've reached that point now. Nothing has changed from earlier this evening, only my perception of things. A couple of hours' sleep have made me drop my guard, and now the truth breaks through: I'm feeling low. I'm missing Jo and Barney, and I don't even know exactly when I'll see them again.

It's strange how your psyche can mess you around like this. One of the Lejoggers I've read about had the same problem. Cycling the journey, he stopped for the night at his home in County Durham. Setting off again the next morning, he found it hard: 'Heading away from home had a massive psychological effect on me . . . My determination to succeed was sorely tested.' The next night he was even unsure whether he would continue. 'Only the encouragement and support from Lynda during our daily phone call kept me from throwing in the towel.'

I can't call Jo at this time in the morning. There's nothing I can do except wait for sleep to return. Thankfully it does, eventually. But before I drop off the image filling my mind is of a never-ending bus timetable, one that scrolls away into infinity. The name John O'Groats doesn't appear on it anywhere.

7

In which we learn how Homer Simpson got his 'doh' from Scotland, find solace in a graveyard and eat a deep-fried Mars bar

Day eight starts with my thirty-third bus. It is not a very special bus: a standard-issue single-decker, white with blue-and-orange fittings, operated by Stagecoach. The journey itself will not be special, either – a modest 12.5 miles. There isn't even anything special about the route number: 79. What's special is what this bus is going to *do*. Something that none of the other buses have done. Nor, given the nature of the deed, something that any of the remaining buses will be able to do.

This uniqueness helps counter, if only a little, the depression that's descended upon me. It's tough to get going this morning. I've had a look round Carlisle, the city that was home to mainland Britain's first pillar box, invented by novelist and Post Office employee Anthony Trollope in 1853 (Jersey had the first one a year earlier). A replica now stands near the Old Town Hall. Carlisle is also home to the trucking company and national institution Eddie Stobart Ltd. The 79 will pass the retail park where they're based, though I won't actually see any of the famous trucks, which are all named after women.[1]

---

1. The first four were Twiggy, Tammy (Wynette), Dolly (Parton) and Suzi (Quatro).

On the whole, however, Carlisle doesn't do much to get rid of my gloom. The place has a harsh edge to it; you can sense its past as a military stronghold, not least in the citadel buildings on Botchergate, dark stone replicas of Tudor fortifications which even now seem to act as a city wall through which traffic and pedestrians have to pass. My bus stop is only a few yards away from them.

It's hard to believe, staring at a timetable like any other, that the 79 is going to take me where it's going to take me – and in just 35 minutes to boot. The place where juries have 15 members rather than 12. Where the first printed example of the F-word happened (William Dunbar, 1503). The place that gave us the hypodermic syringe (1853, Alexander Wood, inspired by the way a bee stings), colour photography (1861, James Clerk Maxwell, picture of a tartan ribbon), and, depending on which account you believe, the telephone (1876, Alexander Bell – that's how he was born, the Graham only coming at the age of 11 when he asked his father if he could have a middle name like his two brothers). It's the place that invented golf and from whose people the entire crew of the *Enola Gay* were descended. It's even, in a sense, the place that gave us Homer Simpson's 'doh' – the catchphrase is based on the sound uttered in the Laurel and Hardy films by actor James Finlayson, who was born there. Yes, this bus is going to take me to Scotland.

I've only ever been north of the border by plane or train, so have never really bothered to examine just where that border runs. You might assume that it's due east–west, if only so Hadrian could keep his wall-building to a minimum. But of course borders move over the years, hence Berwick-upon-Tweed being shunted between England and Scotland 14 times in three centuries; they say the town has been besieged more times than anywhere in the world except Jerusalem. It's now English by a couple of miles, though its football team play in the Scottish league. In 2012 a woman in Wooler, just south of the border, gave birth to her first twin at home, then was driven to hospital in Melrose to deliver the other baby, so now little Dylan is English while his sister Hannah is Scottish. That's all over on the east side of Britain, though. Here on the west the border is well south of that, having run in a diagonal from top-right to bottom-left. Carlisle has had its own time as a Scottish rather than an English place, and remained under threat for centuries, hence the city walls and military atmosphere. The border now is just 10 miles north of here. There are clues in the street names – the main north–south one changes from English Street to Scotch Street. Rather touchingly it does this at British Home Stores.

So as I board the single-decker it feels like I should be offering a passport rather than just a £10 note (the price of the 'Explorer' ticket that will be valid beyond Gretna, where this bus will take me).[2] As if to remind us where we're going we pass a health club owned by Duncan Bannatyne, the Scottish dragon (sorry, Dragon), and then later a roadside burger van offering haggis. The country itself is much flatter now, with small messy paddocks containing bored cows and scruffy sheep. The only town we pass through is Longtown, which has a card and gift shop called Thinking of You. At 10.50 a.m. it is still shut. This really doesn't help my mood.

---

2. Fitting that this should be the bus's destination – a woman behind me says to her friend: 'She was pregnant when they got married. I've been to four weddings like that.'

Because of its slope the national border runs due south here, meaning that Longtown is actually north of Gretna, and the A6071, the final bit of highway carrying me out of England, slopes slightly towards the bottom of the page. We cross the River Esk, and then, on a grassy bank just before Gretna Gateway retail park, there it is: the small rectangular sign saying 'Scotland Welcomes You'. It is brown, though there's a small blue circle containing Scotland's emblem of the thistle. First used in the fifteenth century as a symbol of defence, the one word the thistle puts in your head these days is 'prickly'. Though that quality isn't unique to the Scots, of course. Take Alf Ramsey. Flying into Glasgow for a match against the old enemy, the England football manager was greeted by a journalist with the words: 'Welcome to Scotland.' He replied: 'You must be fucking joking.'

Crossing the border like this has reminded me of a sketch from the 1980s Channel 4 programme *Absolutely*. The fanatical Scottish patriot played by Jack Docherty cycles a few yards past the 'Welcome to England' sign in a quiet country lane, steels himself, shouts 'Poofs!' to the empty fields at the top of his voice, then quickly remounts his bike and returns to safety. Less comically there was Hugh MacDiarmid, the twentieth-century poet who said that the English were 'finished as a world power and must be forced back upon their own right little, tight little island, or rather that part of it which is their own'. There's also been plenty of flak flying in the other direction, of course, not all of it from Alf Ramsey. To insert the obligatory Samuel Johnson quote: 'Much may be made of a Scotchman, if he be caught young.' Then there's Somerset Maugham: 'Scotchmen seem to think it's a credit to them to be Scotch.' And P. G. Wodehouse: 'It is never difficult to distinguish between a Scotsman with a grievance and a ray of sunshine.' The Royal Family might love Balmoral, but the hood mascot for any car the Queen ever travels in is St George, not St Andrew.[3] Even geology seems to be determined to stir up trouble: until 400 million years ago Scotland and England weren't even joined – the former was part of the American continent.

Yet this morning the line between these two great rivals isn't even a line, it's just that rectangle of metal. My conclusion is the same as that of everyone in the Library: the border seems totally meaningless. Gertrude, also on a bus between Carlisle and Gretna, comments that there were 'no policemen – no barriers of any kind. We just left England behind as if it were of little consequence'. H. V. Morton permits himself a quick northward turn of the Morris's steering wheel to see Gretna Green, swapping England for 'a country which looked exactly like it, but was not'. And John Hillaby, whose *Journey Through Britain* recounts a Lejog walk of the late 1960s, crosses east of here, from Northumberland towards Jedburgh, and is disappointed to find no 'instant taste of whatever it is that makes Scotland different from anywhere else'. Because of course a border like this is entirely arbitrary. The fields don't know we've drawn a line through them. Indeed, although wars used to rage round here, the worst treatment was often meted out by people on the same side. One Scottish witch, burned at the stake by her own countrymen, was refused a glass of water first because 'the drier ye are ye'll burn the better'.

---

3. Then again St Andrew himself never even visited Scotland. His diagonal cross commemorates the one he was crucified on, saying he wasn't worthy of the same shape as Jesus.

But there was one practical consequence of Gretna being the first place over the border: because Scottish law didn't require parental consent, you could get married here. Gretna Green, the place where runaway couples used to tie the knot, is a little way outside the town itself. So I disembark by the retail park and walk the half-mile or so to the legendary place. In 1782 Lord Westmorland brought Sarah Anne Child here, against the wishes of her father Robert, who chased them. They only made it by Westmorland shooting Mr Child's leading horse as its straining head drew level with the window of his coach. Not much drama of that calibre this morning, as a chilly wind blows across the paved courtyard that's surrounded by half a dozen modern buildings. A handful of tourists mooch dutifully about. Gretna hosts one in six of all the weddings in Scotland, and surely that says 'conveyor belt' rather than 'romance'. (A shop in the town centre is called Gretna One Stop Weddings.)

The only actual couple I encounter are from China, and even their knot is being tied back home rather than here. This, as far as I can tell from their halting English, is just a pre-wedding holiday, a kind of reverse honeymoon. He's in his best suit, she's wearing her white satin wedding dress, but as it leaves her shoulders exposed she's going round clutching a purple Puffa jacket to herself. They ask if I'll take their photo under the wooden sculpture that dominates the courtyard, two 20-foot-high forearms touching hands to form an arch. They proceed to bicker with each other about exactly where they should stand. Start as you mean to go on.

Back at the retail park, waiting for the next bus (destination Dumfries), I keep the cold out with a cup of tea and a slice of whisky cake. Not that I want to perpetuate any myths about the Scots and their drinking, you understand. Though it is true that their great hero Robert Burns died at 37 from a rheumatic condition made worse by his love of the hard stuff. At the next table a very ginger baby attacks some cake, as do her mother, grandmother and great-grandmother. My ears are still getting attuned to the accent; one woman talks of 'the windy', and it's a while before I realise she means 'window'. And as always in Scotland, it surprises me that people really do say 'the noo' for 'now'. 'Have ye got another puppy the noo?' says a shopper to her friend.

The bus arrives, and takes us first through the centre of the town itself, which amounts to not much more than a kids' playground opposite a grim parade of shops. The countryside between here and Dumfries is if anything even less inspiring than today's earlier scenery. The farm buildings are made of pock-marked concrete and dirty corrugated iron. Yards and fields have big piles of stuff in them, but it's impossible to tell what the stuff is because it's covered with huge tarpaulins weighed down with tyres. Through Rigg and Dornock we go, then Annan, a three-bus-stand town. It still has a 'London 2012' banner strung across the main street. Wonder what Hugh MacDiarmid would have made of that?

Needless to say, none of this helps my spirits. But the journey's very lowest moment is still to come, because of a teenage boy who joins the bus in Racks, an almost non-existent place a couple of miles outside Dumfries. It's not his fault, it really isn't. For whatever reason (given the bag he's carrying it's probably college), the lad has to go into town. I can't blame him for that. It's just that the stop he gets on at is very near a farmyard. One whose owner has just finished spraying the surrounding fields with the oldest and most natural fertiliser known to man. In the mere fifteen seconds the doors are open, a quite astonishing smell enters the single-decker bus and fills every last corner of it. No one is safe. Of course we're all too polite to so much as wrinkle a nostril, but the stench is here to stay. For the remaining 20 minutes of the journey it will be our companion, a very real, almost physical presence. This isn't what I need.

Dumfries, in these circumstances, is a hard sell, despite the fact it's offering my lungs some clean air at last. I give it a few minutes, trying to be impressed by the thought that somewhere in this town's outskirts is St Michael's church, final resting place of Robert Burns. And that its nickname, and the name of its football team, is Queen of the South, four words that always caught the imagination during the Final Scores of my childhood. But it's no good. This *isn't* the south, a newborn pedant inside me yells. The southernmost point of Scotland, at least by tradition, is Maidenkirk. That was the equivalent of John O'Groats to Land's End, before the 1707 Act of Union with England: you went from John O'Groats to Maidenkirk. Today, just to be awkward, it's known as Kirkmaiden, but it's still in the same place, near the bottom of the Mull of Galloway, a straggly little bit hanging off Scotland's west coast. It's way south of here, south even of Carlisle, and almost level with Penrith.

Plough on, that's all there is for it. Glasgow is the next big mark to hit, and there's a bus from Dumfries to Cumnock; surely there'll be one from there to Glasgow? The 246 lurches into action, taking us past a mammoth Tesco Extra on the fringes of Dumfries. Didn't the Extras used to be the small ones? Metros are the new small ones, right? Soon they'll be the size of airfields, no doubt. We go through Holywood, which is just a few council houses and a shop with a red plastic sign over its door: look what happens when you lose an 'l'. There are plenty of road signs warning of cattle. After what took place on the last bus, the black silhouettes in the red triangles are scary indeed. The map reveals that there's somewhere east of here called Ae. Assuming a misprint, I look it up, and find that really is its name. It's the shortest place name in the whole of the UK. This information gets emailed to Caroline, who is delighted by it. As the person who was disappointed about there not being any two-letter place names in England I should be delighted too, but that emotion feels out of reach right now. Another place near here sums up the atmosphere much better: Irongray.

As we approach the crossroads in Thornhill the bus slows down. Actually that should be 'the crossroads that *are* Thornhill', there really only being the main road we've followed here (the single-carriageway A76) and Morton Street at right-angles to it. The rest of this tiny place is just padding. We pause at the bus stop. No one gets on, but everyone gets off. (Everyone being the four other passengers.) The driver catches my eye in the mirror. He doesn't say anything. He doesn't have to – his expression says it all.

'You're finishing here?' I ask.

'Aye.'

'Oh. Right.' As I pick up my rucksack and head past him to the pavement, I add: 'Sorry – thought you were going on to Cumnock.'

A shake of the head. 'Nah. You'll be needing the next one for that.'

'How long will that be?'

Fair play to him, he doesn't do the standard 'Thirty-five feet, same as this one' gag. He can't know how much I appreciate that small mercy. He just says: 'Three o'clock.' It's now 1.35.

I step down on to the pavement, wait for the bus to pull away, then survey Thornhill. There's a mini-column at the crossroads, with a mini-winged horse on top of it. There are a couple of cafés and a few shops. There is nothing else. Because of my haste to jump on a bus in Dumfries I didn't read the timetable properly. Because of that mistake I now have to spend an hour and a half here. Crossing the road, I enter a baker's shop that also serves as one of the cafés. A builder in grubby overalls asks his colleague, who is staring out of the window, how many sugars he wants.

'Loads,' he replies, without smiling or shifting his gaze. Not just me in a bad mood, then.

Over a sandwich I don't really want I read about Thornhill. The winged horse is the emblem of the Queensberry family, owners of nearby Drumlanrig Castle. The Marquess of Queensberry Rules which govern boxing (essentially 'no hitting him in the balls') were drawn up by the 9th Marquess, the same one who ruined Oscar Wilde because he wasn't happy about his son, Lord Alfred Douglas, being the writer's beloved 'Bosie'. James Harkness, head of the Church of Scotland between 1995 and 1996, was born here. Even he only merits a mention as a reminder of why there are more Rangers fans than Celtic fans: it's easier to shout 'fuck the Pope' than 'fuck the Moderator of the General Assembly of the Church of Scotland'. Other than that, Thornhill's history cupboard is pretty bare.

I stare at the stop over the road, willing a bus to appear. Perhaps the driver got it wrong. Perhaps I misread the timetable. I go and check. The timetable is sticking to its story. I keep thinking of Jo and Barney, 300 miles away. It's still 250 miles to John O'Groats. Both those figures are in crow-miles. I imagine turning into one and swooping up, away over Glasgow, then the Highlands, finishing the job by this evening. Or indeed just heading south to Suffolk. But wings appear there none. Ditto buses. I can't just stand here for an hour – I'll go mad. It looks, to quote Robert de Niro in *Midnight Run*, like I'm walking.

I head east, telling myself I'll do 25 minutes, then turn around and come back, making the wait for the bus a mere ten-stretch. At least the rain has stopped for now. Within a couple of minutes I've passed all the houses and a school, and the lane is winding its way off towards the Tweedsmuir Hills in the distance. The last thing I pass is a cemetery, on a bit of a slope – a taste of the peaks to come. These places always get me, as it seems they did Beryl Bainbridge too. 'Perhaps it has something to do with the war,' she muses in *English Journey*, 'and hearing at an impressionable age of the massacre of the Jews.' With me it's just the stories. Every gravestone tells one. I open the gate and go through.

There they all are. A couple of hundred stories, most of them told in your imagination, but then sometimes that's the best way. Two of the women here lost their husbands within a few months of each other in the late 1950s. One joined her beloved within weeks; the other lived nearly until the millennium, dying at 82. What happened to the first one? A broken heart, or something more definite? Sometimes details are given, but they only ever prompt more questions: 'Died result of accident at Carronbridge'. There are different words for the same emotion, but placed near each other they can seem like grades of feeling: does 'in loving memory' beat 'in fond remembrance'? Is 'dearly loved' stronger or weaker than 'much loved'? Then there are the different names we give to family ties: 'Granny', 'Dad', 'Papa', 'Great Papa'. Someone here died on Christmas Day. A man died in his fifties, his wife in her eighties; their son had died 'in infancy'.

I realise after a while that being here is lifting my mood. That's not meant to be morbid. It's not even the sense of contrast; the thought that in the midst of death I am in life. It's just a gently growing awareness of how short a day is, or two days, or however many days it's going to take from here to John O'Groats. If it sounds flippant to say that a graveyard is a calming place, I apologise. It's just that here, surrounded by rows of people gazing eternally at the red-mossed hills, it's impossible to feel gloomy, or self-piteous, or indeed anything at all. There's just a sense of being, not of feeling.

It continues as I return to the bus stop, as three o'clock brings a double-decker and a trip further along the now tree-lined A76. Just as on that very first morning in Cornwall the sun turns the bus into a greenhouse, thawing my feelings, as well as nicely toasting the left-hand side of my face. There were short sunny periods this morning, come to think of it; it was just that my mood didn't want to acknowledge them. A very faint and stunted section of rainbow appears to the east, and it makes me laugh, not just because it's a cliché but because rainbows always remind me how barking mad Isaac Newton was. Count the stripes next time you see one: there are six, not seven. Newton only split purple into indigo and violet so he could have his lucky number.[4] Scotland is getting

---

4. Some artists keep it accurate – the spectrum on the cover of Pink Floyd's *Dark Side of the Moon* has six colours, for instance.

very hilly now, with plenty of the slopes covered in spruces and firs and pines. Sometimes they push down to the road, sometimes they allow you a view. One field has been stripped of its trees, save for a three-acre block of dark green firs hemmed in by a stone wall, the outermost branches pushing over it like a beer belly over a belt. Cloud shadows chase each other sedately, then more quickly, then fade away completely. To the left of us the River Nith gurgles happily over its rocks.

And so by the time we reach Cumnock my soul is half-full rather than half-empty. The small town becomes an interesting study in the human drama to be found at 4.09 p.m. on a weekday afternoon. Among the few humans I see on the street are a mother making a call in a phone box while her young son hides from the cold in the adjacent one; she has her back turned to him. For conversations I can listen to, I have to go to the only place people flock to in a town like this: the pub. There's one not far from the café offering 'Wee Breakfast Big Wan All Day'. I *think* I understand that.

It's a modest place, which the woman behind the bar is doing her best to keep clean. She sprays some polish on the shelf holding the Pineapple and Blueberry Breezers (on offer at £1.50 each), only to be snarled at by a man sitting fully 20 feet away: 'I've got a whisky here.' The telly's showing racing from Beverley, though none of the 11 customers pay any attention. There's a sign saying 'Welcome to the Nut House', while others advertise forthcoming appearances by DJ Leske and Sterio. I'm about to order a pint – you just can't do soft drinks in a place like this – when a bronchial wheeze from a joking group of oldies in the corner gets my attention. Turning round, I see they're younger than me.

That does it. 'Coke, please,' I say.

No one bats an eyelid. As long as they can stick to their lagers and chasers they don't care about anyone else. Two guys next to me talk about . . . well, it's hard to say *what* they're talking about, exactly. Not because their accents are thick – they're not, though the men are slurring their words in that habitual way heavy drinkers eventually adopt whether they're drunk or not. (In fact they never really get drunk, do they? They never sober up, but they never fall about.) The problem is that their sentences never end. A lot of them never begin. There are just half-formed thoughts leading to other half-formed thoughts via incomprehensible word associations. If you put this on at the National people would think it was Pinter.

One of the Wheezers comes to the bar. I'm hoping she'll order a Breezer, but sadly it's a Guinness. Halfway through the pint being poured the barrel runs out.

'Good job, love,' says the older of the Slurrers. 'It's fuckin' shite, Guinness.'

She doesn't respond, but Younger Slurrer does. 'Ya dinnae like Guinness then, ya c——?' There's no aggression in the last word. He's been addressing his friend by this title constantly. It's just a reflex.

'Nay, I dinnae,' replies Older Slurrer. 'I've never tried Guinness in my *life*.'

There has been great variety among the British Culinary Staples so far. They have differed in terms of ingredients, country of origin, style of cooking, level of spiciness and formality of the venue where they've been consumed. You'd think that food-wise every base had been covered. You'd be wrong. Because there's one thing I haven't eaten. Tonight

I'm going to put that right. Tonight I'm going to eat an urban myth.

Until arriving in Glasgow I wasn't sure whether my quest could be fulfilled, whether Scotland really had taken the food substance of student lore and made it a reality. But if my researches are to be believed, there's an establishment here which does indeed serve the delight. It's just a few blocks from the Premier Inn that tonight I call home. Having dumped my rucksack at the hotel and made a call about tomorrow morning (when my final appointment for a chat is to occur), I'm on the way to find out. Dodging the puddles (it's monsoon time again), I think back on the bus journey that brought me here from Cumnock. Even though it was the second-longest of the trip to date (38.75 miles, beaten only by the 46.25 of Wadebridge to Exeter), it didn't seem that far, taking not much more than an hour and a half. This was partly due to my first bit of motorway, the M77 into Glasgow itself. Even that was just a two-laner, though, with cows grazing by the side, no different in effect from the bigger A-roads that previous buses have taken.

Most of the passengers on the X76 were people heading home from work, giving the ride that relaxing, day-at-an-end feel. A nice touch was the sign announcing that if the driver can't give you the right change he'll issue a voucher you can use on future journeys: an elegant solution to an old problem. Some horses nuzzled each other's necks near a sign for Prestwick, the place whose airport was the only bit of British soil Elvis Presley's feet ever touched.[5] Kilmarnock

---

5. 1960, fuelling stop on the way home from Germany with the army. The airport now has a lounge named after him.

was the pivot point, the 'one lot empties out, another lot get on' place. A big Victorian building opposite its railway station bore the inscription 'the earth is the Lord's and the fulness thereof'. The majesty of this message was dimmed slightly by a bloke like the tall, fat one in *The Office* sitting in front of me and snoring heavily. The woman behind me talked about her dishwasher, the second syllable rhyming with 'splash'. Kilmarnock also had a Blair Cottage, the first mention of the B-word I'll get very used to over the next few days (it means 'field'). Its use as a surname is a reminder that our former Prime Minister is Scottish (and, incidentally, born on exactly the same day and in the same city – Edinburgh – as the footballer Graeme Souness).

Finally, under a sky that was half fluffy white clouds and half dark grey slate, as though a painter had changed his mind mid-canvas, we hit Glasgow itself. It's a huge city, right from the moment you enter it by crossing the River Clyde, weaving under flyovers and passing roads at different heights which serve different levels of the sloping terrain. It's a *Metropolis* metropolis. Most of the centre is built on a grid system, giving it an American feel, with superb block-long Victorian buildings that look as though they weigh a million tons each. If Manhattan had been built of sandstone, on a gradient like San Francisco's, and had stopped at six storeys, it would be Glasgow. Oh, and if it had a shop near its bus station called News 'n' Chews.

Another big thing about Glasgow is its reputation. Talk to people who have attended football matches between Tottenham and Arsenal, or between Manchester United and Liverpool, and they'll tell you those occasions feel like a Women's Institute meeting compared to a Rangers–Celtic derby. A cabbie from Glasgow once told me he hated the days leading up to a match, choosing the perhaps-unwise phrase 'you can cut the atmosphere with a knife'. Another person who knows the city said that Rangers' 2012 demotion because of financial irregularities had been the worst thing ever for Celtic fans: without those four festivals of hate each year there was nothing to look forward to. And Glasgow's violence extends beyond the terraces. In the 1980s there were the ice-cream wars (the vans used as fronts to sell drugs). Gangs have always been around, though some of them have chosen distinctly unthreatening names: the Antique Mob, the Parlour Boys, the Norman Conks and the Wee Cumbies. Then there are the lone operators. Brian Cox based his portrayal of Hannibal Lecter in the movie *Manhunter* on Peter Manuel, a Glasgow serial killer from the 1950s.

Thankfully my walk northwards (i.e. uphill) to tonight's food provider takes me past no one scarier than students rushing to get out of the rain and into the new residences that have been built for them in this part of the city, which is dominated by the University of Strathclyde. Perhaps that explains why the food provider is here and thriving: it's a chippy. In particular, it's a chippy renowned for its rendering of one very famous, nay notorious dish. Yep: it's the deep-fried Mars bar.

Quite when this delicacy first came into being is unclear. For years Scottish people told me it was a myth, and that they'd never seen anywhere serving one. Very occasionally one might tell me they'd seen it on a menu, but hadn't themselves partaken. Not since the days of Marianne Faithfull had a Mars bar been shrouded in such mystery. The late, great Linda Smith, meanwhile, used to have a line in her act about going to a chippy during the Edinburgh Festival and getting her change in batter. Whatever the truth of the past, however, I can personally vouch that as of September 2012 the deep-fried Mars bar is a reality in at least one Glasgow chip shop.

But of course I can't just have that for my dinner – I need something healthy as a main course. So I have battered haggis. With chips. Meat and one veg, you might call it. The woman serving me is Turkish, and when she takes great pride in frying the haggis *just* right (it's shaped for chippy purposes into a sausage) it reminds me of Mr Kurdistan in Leeds. As well as the usual items for sale – ketchup, pickled eggs, fizzy drinks – there's a shelf of cigarettes, 10-packs of Mayfair. Next to them, waiting to be deployed into boiling hot fat, are the Mars bars.

The place has no seats, and I can hardly stand there eating my dinner in front of the poor woman, so I head back out into the rain. It's not too heavy at first, meaning I can pause outside a pub and watch the TV news with its auto-generated subtitles. There has been 'flooding in the North-East, especially County Durham and Cleaver Land'. Soon, though, God opens the taps up, and I have to run for cover. Where to? A bus shelter, of course. It's written in the stars. There's no one else here, though, so I can enjoy the haggis in peace. It gets a bad press, Scotland's national dish, and indeed it's banned in the USA because it contains chopped lungs. The chopped heart is okay, apparently. How strange we can be about food. Admittedly when you spell out the ingredients like that it does give you pause for thought. Much better to maintain the mystery, as Brazil's customs men did in 1965 when they intercepted a parcel of haggis, had it analysed and decided it was fertiliser. Tonight, happily hungry and smugly watching the rain from a position of dryness, I love every mouthful of my haggis for what it is: nothing more or less than spicy sausage. There's that pleasing game of timing it so the haggis and chips run out at the same time, then it's back for dessert.

'Deep-fried Mars bar, please,' I say to the woman.

She nods slowly, as though she had suspicions about me and they've just been confirmed.

'Sorry,' I say, not really sure why. 'It's just . . . I've never tried one, and . . .'

She smiles. 'Is mainly for students we do them.' She takes down a Mars bar from the shelf. 'Why they like it I not know.' A shrug. She hasn't opened the wrapper yet. 'I can do you lovely baklava.' She indicates the refrigerated display unit containing the enticing Turkish pastries.

'Oh, don't get me wrong, they look great . . . but . . .' My turn to shrug.

She nods, smiling again. Into its bubbling volcanic bath goes the Mars bar. A few minutes later I'm walking back to the main part of town, giving the snack a while to cool. The first bite takes a bit of courage, but then the confusing mix of batter and chocolate and nougat begins to make sense to the taste buds and the brain, until finally you realise: yeah, this works. I don't think I'll go out of my way to have another one, but in principle, what is this foodstuff other than a student profiterole? It's also a melted metaphor for the melting-pot theory of cities: an American chocolate bar cooked in British batter by a Turkish woman. The names change, but the pot keeps steaming. One Sunday morning in the nineteenth century a Glasgow woman saw some boys playing marbles on the street. She asked why they weren't at Sunday school.

'Ach,' came the reply, 'we're what ye call Jews.'

The rain eases again, allowing a lap of the city centre. It's perhaps strange for somewhere whose name means 'dear green place', but Glasgow has that quality that truly great cities display: it really doesn't give a monkey's about you. The trip has only had three (*can* now only have three) places that compare with this in size – Bristol, Birmingham and Leeds – and those were gentler cities, a little less sure of themselves and a little more interested in you. But Glasgow's a cliff face. I love this in a city, an indifference that could be mistaken for hostility, except to be hostile somewhere has to notice you first. London has it, so do New York and Paris. Perhaps the best is Moscow. It means you can watch without getting drawn in. Tonight what really fascinates me is the different ways people hold their cigarettes. Now that people have to stand outside to smoke it's become an activity in itself, almost like a performance you should be judging them on. There's Dainty and Ladylike (fag held between first two fingers, others spread out, smoke with very edge of mouth, remove as quickly as possible) . . . Secondhand Car Dealer (hangs vertically from bottom lip, eye screwed up to avoid the spiralling smoke, concentrate on what your hands are doing, usually sending a text) . . . Protecting Your Face from the Cold (jammed at base of middle and ring fingers, hand held sideways) . . . Groucho Marx (using all your fingers, the better to tap off the ash) . . . the Cradle (hold the filter, fingers all pointing towards yourself) . . . I almost want to hold up scorecards.

I don't though. It wouldn't be a good idea.

As someone who was born in Wales to Northern Irish parents,

grew up in England and now lives in Scotland, Jo Caulfield sounds like the first line of a joke. Though not, it must be said, the sort of joke that she herself has made a career out of. Her stand-up comedy has taken her to clubs and theatres all over the world, as well as on to TV shows like *Mock the Week* and *Have I Got News For You*, plus Radio 4 (other people's shows as well as her own) and Radio 5 Live, which is where I first met her in the late 1990s. She has written for everyone from Joan Rivers to Graham Norton to Ant and Dec. It's a while since I saw her, but with a few emails over the last couple of days we've managed to coincide my morning in Glasgow with a work trip Jo's made here from her home in Edinburgh. And now we sit, at 10 a.m., in a café in the city's Merchant City area (not many deep-fried Mars bars here, let's put it that way).

Jo hasn't changed a bit: she's lean, sharp and quick-witted, not in the way some comics can be – just looking for the next one-liner, the next ego-boost – but genuinely observant. The older I get the more I think comedy is the greatest revealer of truth we have – whenever we laugh it's because something fundamental has chimed inside us. If your living depends on finding those entry points to the common psyche, you get good at it. My experience of spending time with comics is that even in normal conversation they cut straight to the heart of a subject.

Beyond remembering that Jo's husband Kevin is Scottish, I didn't know why they'd moved to Edinburgh from London, so she starts by explaining their thinking. 'We'd been together for sixteen years and had never even thought about it until a couple of years before we did it. We both loved London – still do – but we just didn't want to live there any more. We'd spent a lot of time in New York and liked how easy it was there to walk home or take a short cab ride. You can't do that in London because it's so sprawling. So we started thinking about where we could live like that in Britain. It came down to a shortlist of Brighton, Bristol or Edinburgh.'

'And the winner was Edinburgh because . . . ?'

'Because it's so beautiful. I'm constantly saying things like: "The light is so beautiful." "Did you see the sunset yesterday?" The locals must find me very tedious, I'm sure.' She gestures out of the window. 'I wouldn't have moved here. Glasgow's a great city, but it's a big city, happening and gritty, and I don't want happening and gritty any more. I want pretty and nice. Not a backwater, though. Edinburgh feels cosmopolitan because of all the students and tourists. And you can get loads done in a day because nowhere is more than a twenty-minute walk away.'

How has it been as an English woman living in Scotland?

'Not an issue at all. But everyone down south is obsessed with the weather in Scotland. It's not that cold! Six million people live here and survive quite well. We have central heating. And coats. I've become very defensive about the weather here.' As if to back her up, this morning's sky is a cloud-free zone. There are coats on view, yes, but also plenty of sunglasses. 'Scotland is a great country if you wear the right clothes. The secret is layering. I have never yet worn a pair of open-toed sandals for an entire day.' She stops herself. 'Now I'm sounding like an English person complaining about the weather. I'm not. All I'm saying is, bring a cardi.'

The same 'keep it realistic' advice extends to Jo's accent (which is neutral southern). 'No one ever mentions it. It's perfectly fine living here speaking like I do. Just don't be an idiot. Don't assume people here wish the England football team well.'

How about language, as opposed to accent? I've read in John Hillaby's *Journey Through Britain* that Scottish people of the 1960s said 'butter and bread' instead of 'bread and butter' – has that survived? 'I've never heard it,' says Jo. 'But "wee" – people say that *all* the time. I find it so funny that grown men say "wee". It seems something only old ladies in tea rooms should say.' She laughs at a memory. 'When I put my car in for an MOT the mechanic said, "I'll get you two new wee tyres on there." In my head I couldn't help saying, "What, really? Wee tyres? Not tyres that are the right size?"'

We pause as someone at the counter orders, just on the off-chance they might say 'butter and bread'. But it's not really a butter-on-your-bread place. The chickpea and coriander soup comes with ciabatta, I think.

'I've also found myself adopting Scottish ways of saying things,' continues Jo. ' "Through the house", for instance.'

'Eh?'

'Instead of saying something is "in the kitchen", I'll say it's "through the house" and point to the kitchen. And you always say "house", even if you live in a flat. Another thing is "stay" – I ask "Where do you stay?" rather than "Where do you live?" That's what Scottish people always say.'

Is there anything Jo misses about England?

'Not really. I still go to London a lot for work, usually a couple of times a month. In some ways I don't feel I've left. I probably still meet up with friends as much as when I lived in London. Coming into King's Cross on the train is always exciting, and I feel slightly smug because I have an Oyster card, which means I'm still a Londoner, not a tourist.' Then there's the role of technology. We talk for a while about how email and Twitter and their digital ilk have made Britain – the world – a smaller place, how we stay in touch with friends without having to meet, how we've now all got friends that we've *never* met.

Something Jo does miss about England is its villages. 'Well, I don't miss them as such, because I see them all the time on tour. Real "chocolate-box" ones, all over – Herefordshire, Dorset, Norfolk, Devon. You don't get those up here. I suppose it's made me appreciate them more.' Not, of course, that she doesn't like Scotland's scenery. 'Kevin's from Aberdeen and we go to see his mother there, so I've got to know that part of the country well. Deeside is *stunning*. You can see why the Royal Family have a "holiday home" there.' Balmoral is where the Queen takes her annual turn at doing the washing-up, after the barbecue held during the Prime Minister's traditional summer visit. Her Maj retires to a special hut for the purpose. Margaret Thatcher once insisted that she should do it instead; apparently there was something dangerously close to a scene before the monarch prevailed.

'There's so much countryside to explore here,' says Jo. 'It's so quick to get out to the coast or some mountains. I tell people I go hill-walking, but I don't.'

Something Jo *doesn't* miss is England's licensing regime. 'I was in a pub in Soho recently and couldn't believe that you get unceremoniously thrown out at 11.20 sharp. There's none of that in Scotland. Mind you, it did mean that when I first came to Edinburgh I was continually drinking till one and two in the morning. I assumed if they were still serving it must be before eleven.'

We move on to Jo's work. Apart from appearing in her

own right she has run comedy clubs on both sides of the border. How does the Scottish sense of humour differ from the English?

'I think the Scots, the Irish and the Welsh share something with English people from tough industrial cities – Geordies, for instance – in that they all think southerners, and by that they mean "posh people", should "get over themselves". They're much more able to see through bullshit; they won't politely let people get away with pretentious or arrogant behaviour. I think that's where the myth of the "Glasgow" audience comes from.'

Ah, the Glasgow audience. Its most famous incarnation was at the Empire Theatre, which last night I was disappointed to find has been replaced by an office block. I was hoping to hear the echoes of the boos and catcalls that used to rain down on some performers, especially if they were English. Not for nothing did it earn the nickname of the 'comedian's graveyard'. Des O'Connor got such a pasting he pretended to faint, just so he could be carried off-stage. When Mike and Bernie Winters played there the act started, as usual, with Mike playing a tune on his clarinet. The crowd weren't overly impressed, but they let him get on with it. Then Bernie stuck his face round the curtain and gave his trademark leer. Someone in the audience shouted: 'Oh, fuck, there's two of 'em!'

All good fun, but even though Jo's office is the stage, on this question she's sitting with the audience. 'Glasgow audiences are just hard-working people who have paid their money, so you'd better be funny. Lots of bands have recorded live albums here because actually the crowds are fantastically appreciative. But if they don't like you, don't waste their time – leave.'

I mention the P. G. Wodehouse Scotsman/ray of sunshine quote. What does Jo think of it? 'Argh! I hate people saying that kind of thing. You *want* to be able to tell the difference between someone with a grievance and someone happy, don't you? Although people in Surrey see no need to portray a difference . . . The Scots don't smile without a reason. Is that not a rather sensible national characteristic?' She takes a sip of her coffee, marshalling her thoughts. 'In fact, you can't even talk in terms of "Scottish versus English". Glaswegians are extremely friendly and gregarious, but the east coast is different. Like Aberdeen. Kevin might be considered "dour", but he's one of the funniest people I've ever met. They just don't walk around smiling and "enthusing" about everything. Often because they're too busy making funny remarks. It's a deadpan kind of humour. I would say Jack Dee is a classic Aberdonian, except he's English.' She pauses. 'You see what a mess you can get into with stereotypes?'

We move on to what Ben Elton might call a little bit of politics. There's a referendum-shaped shadow hanging over everything at the moment. A Scottish friend of mine in Suffolk says he doesn't think his countrymen will vote for independence, though 'if you gave the English a vote on it they'd tell the Scots to piss off'. Or, as Jack Straw put it, with the greater formality we might expect from a former Foreign Secretary: 'People's sense of Englishness will become more articulated, and that's partly because of the mirror that devolution provides us with.' What does Jo think?

'Devolution has put the country in an awkward position. English people have come to resent the fact that there's this anomaly of Scotland having a say in two parliaments. There's an anti-Scots feeling because of things like Scotland voting for free prescriptions and against student tuition fees. But I think that's unfair. English people have got to remember that Scotland has never voted for a Conservative government but has been ruled by one for most of the last century.' And as with comedy, the question is never simple. 'There's resentment *within* England, one part against another. I've got friends in Wigan and the London bias of the media drives them nuts.'

Devolution's one thing – what about full independence? 'There are very mixed feelings,' says Jo. 'Emotionally, people might like to be separate. But there's also a feeling that the likes of Alex Salmond are just out for themselves. They want to be bigger fish in a smaller pond, divide up the spoils among a select few.' She shrugs. 'MPs, SMPs, they're all the same breed to me: incompetent and untrustworthy.'

Her words echo Billy Connolly's, who has spoken of 'a new Scottish racism, which I loathe – this thing that everything horrible is English. It's conducted by the great unread and the conceited wankers at the SNP, those dreary little pricks in Parliament who rely on bigotry for support.' They also echo Lord Byron's: 'I have simplified my politics into an utter detestation of all existing governments.' Perhaps he'd have had more time for Andrew Fletcher, a Scottish politician of the eighteenth century, who had a trace of the Edith Cavell: 'Show me a true patriot, and I will show you a lover not merely of his own country, but of all mankind. Show me a spurious patriot, a bombastic fire-eater, and I will show you a rascal.' I like this. Moved as I was at the recent Olympics by Mo Farah and his Mobot, my favourite athlete during the Games was Guor Marial, who ran in the marathon. His country? He didn't have one. He is originally from Sudan, a country torn apart by civil war, and his new state, South

Sudan, isn't recognised by the IOC. However, he was given special dispensation to compete as an independent. He said he was 'representing the whole world'.

Which leads Jo and me to the question of personal identity. What do we feel: English, British, a mix or neither?

'I've always been a mixture,' says Jo, quoting her 'opening line of a joke' status. 'If it's a question of where you come from, I don't really come from anywhere. I've got no concept of what that means. My dad was in the Air Force, so we moved every two years. I suppose that's why I can be easily uprooted. Sure, I've got memories of the places where I spent my teenage years. I loved Derbyshire, where we used to walk in snow and rain over the dales wearing knee socks and school tunics.' She pauses. 'Hang on, wasn't that child cruelty?'

But in terms of identity, Jo sees things much more in terms of who she is and how she fits in, rather than where she grew up. 'I'm always surprised when northerners say I'm a southerner. I know that's what I sound like but that's just my voice, not where I've lived.' The disappearing Midlands, again. 'We went to Northern Ireland every summer to see my cousins. I was aware that we were "the English cousins", but I never felt different from them. I think that's why Scotland does feel very much like home now – the sense of humour is the same. The dry wit feels very familiar. The directness, too. My relatives in Northern Ireland wouldn't give you a straight compliment to save their lives – that way of always taking you down a notch, not letting anyone get away with "airs and graces". But it's done in fun.' Her 'moveability' has another consequence. 'I will quite happily travel the length of the country to see friends. Don't invite me to something presuming I'll say no just because I live in Scotland.'

It's time to head off now. Jo asks what my next destination is, and I say I don't know. 'Sounds fun,' she says. 'I think we should all travel around Britain more. I've been doing it for years with the stand-up. I think it'd be my subject on *Mastermind*. I know all sorts of odd facts about everywhere. Like the Petrifying Well in Matlock. We went there from school, actually. It's a grotto, and they put everyday objects in – there was a boot, I remember, and a pair of trousers – and then the water flows through the limestone and calcifies the objects so it looks like they've turned to stone. I thought it was magic. Then the teacher went and ruined everything by explaining it.'

Jo shares my love of finding new places. 'I'm always surprised if someone mentions somewhere in Britain that I haven't been. Different towns, different areas – they're all fascinating, whether they're twee or shite.' She recently visited Barnard Castle, a town in County Durham. 'I had a curd tart there. My God, it was the best thing I've ever eaten.'

As we part, I think about that Scottish phrase Jo has picked up: 'Where do you stay?' For a lot of people, where they're born *is* where they stay. Jo's done the leaving thing very well, if only because she didn't have anywhere to leave from. A couple of my forty-something male friends share my experience of being the one who left the family turf. It doesn't always make things totally easy with the members who stayed. I envy Jo her uprootability. You still get a sense of belonging, just one that's based on personality rather than geography.

Only one sort of baggage involved.

8

In which we treat ourselves to a luxury hotel, encounter a
horse watching a football match, and learn why the boxes
carried by government ministers are red

I thought England had a lot of countryside. Now that I
stand in Glasgow bus station (a large glass-and-concourses
affair) looking at the map of Britain in my road atlas, I get
a sense of just how much of the stuff there is in Scotland.
There are huge great stretches of nothingness on the page;
massive patches of white and green with only a single road
traversing them, perhaps the occasional village, and very
often not even that. And there's a consequence of this for
the project: up here, 'local' changes its meaning. The buses
themselves don't; local buses are still pay-as-you-board, with
no need to pre-book, and pensioners travel for free. They still
link places with the nearest places to them. It's just that the
gaps between those places are greater. Local is further away.

The first bus of the day (my thirty-eighth in total) is the
M8 from here to Perth. It will take an hour and a half, which
is less time than several of my buses so far. But it'll get me
62 miles, a far greater distance than any of my buses so far.
The bus itself is actually a coach, like the ones you went to
school on when you were a kid, except a bit bigger and more
comfortable. There's even one of those toilets where you
have to go down three little steps. Birmingham City had one
on their team bus when Karren Brady took over as managing

director. She accompanied the team to a game at Newcastle: 'spending all those hours on a bus with 35 men and one small toilet' was why she never repeated the experience. That and the comment from a player as she returned to her seat from one of her 'doomed' toilet visits: 'I can see your tits from here.' 'Well, when I sell you to Crewe you won't be able to see them from there,' came the reply.[1] Fortunately by this stage of the project my drinking habits have been honed well enough to ensure that the call of the bladder never arrives at the wrong time.

About three dozen of us depart, heading past Al's American Diner and the equally transatlantic Destiny Church, which has a 'Go Team' to bring the gospel to the people; wonder what the Scottish ministers of old would think? Soon we're on the M80, very modest as motorways go, but a great way of seeing the Kilsyth Hills to our left, topping up their mossy tan in the bright sunshine. The 'new town' of Cumbernauld isn't exactly the glitziest place in the world, though surely the Scottish Design Awards have been a bit harsh in awarding it two 'Plook on the Plinth' titles? This honour is given to the country's most dismal town centre; the judges compared Cumbernauld to Kabul. Then between here and Stirling there are more fantastic hills. When does a hill become a mountain? It seems there is no set definition around the world, though the UK government's official one is 600 metres (1,968 feet). What we can say for sure is that any Scottish summit over 3,000 feet is known as a Munro, after Sir Hugh Munro, the first man to list them all in 1891. The first man to climb them all, it's generally acknowledged, was the Reverend A. E.

---

1. She did, too.

Robertson, in 1901. Collecting the set is known as 'Munro bagging'. More recently a list of mountains over 150 metres (492 feet) has been compiled. These are known as Marilyns.

Stirling is the journey's pivot point. Its major building of interest, at least to the group of women clustered near me, is the new supermarket that's under construction. No one seems to know *which* supermarket it is.

'I'd heard it was going to be a Waitrose,' says someone.

'But it says "Muir" there,' comes a reply.

'No,' someone else gently points out, 'that's just the name of the builders.'

Stirling has been called the 'brooch which clasps the Lowlands and the Highlands together', and after it the hills certainly do seem to get bigger. One of them, a few miles to the east, bears a hilltop monument. It looks a beauty, a huge Gothic thing, and a quick bit of research tells me it is the Wallace Monument. The 220-foot tower contains old William's sword no less, and is understandably an important building for those who, 700 years later, see themselves as continuing his fight for Scottish independence. The stakes are a little lower, though. Alex Salmond might end up with a red face if his campaign fails: William Wallace ended up with his own bowels being burned in front of him after a partial hanging, before he was finally beheaded. His limbs were later displayed in Newcastle. And Berwick. And Stirling. And Perth. All at the same time. Nice, eh? Perhaps it's the chat with 'four countries in one woman' Jo, but yet again the horror of what 'fighting for your country' can actually entail makes me feel very un-militaristic. Violently so, you might say.

The nothingness is almost oppressive now. There's so much space you don't know how to look at it. Some of the hillsides are bare, some tree-covered – others have just a few clumps left as though they're recovering from a rash. There's a sign for Scone Palace, the site where Scotland's early kings were crowned on the Stone of Scone. Until 1296, that is, when Edward I of England nicked it and took it to Westminster Abbey. The Coronation Chair there, the one on which British monarchs are still crowned, was specially made to contain the stone. As of 1996 the Scottish have been allowed to keep the stone again; it's stored at Edinburgh Castle, though will still be returned to Westminster and slotted into the chair for future coronations. It's a great source of Scottish pride, then – though I can't help noticing there's nothing more quintessentially English than the word 'scone'. Apart, perhaps, from a disagreement about which pronunciation of it is the posh one. The people round here remove themselves from the 'sconn'/'scohne' debate by calling the palace 'Scoon'.

There's a retail park on the outskirts of Perth called, if one of its signs is to be believed, St Catherines's. I'd love to put an Apostrophe Nazi in front of that and watch him explode. We pull into the bus station at 12.42 p.m. It's not very inspiring: just a single 1970s building labelled BUS STATION. The 'U' is hanging off. It has 10 stands, or, as I've discovered they're known in Scotland, 'stances'. Both here and in Glasgow I've heard people directed to 'stance two', 'stance seven', 'stance nine' – it's like being in the middle of a group golf lesson. The short walk into the town centre takes me past a members-only social club. They're obviously trying to create a classy image, because their menu is displayed in one of those fonts that's so italicised it's almost impossible to read. Only by squinting hard do I make out the words 'chicken nuggets'.

If Settle in Yorkshire was hemmed in by nature, Perth is being mugged by it. No matter which way you walk in the town centre, after a couple of minutes you'll be facing the River Tay again, beyond which is a sloping wall of trees. The effect is 'town – NATURE!' I like the place, not least because its motto is 'Make haste slowly', which is exactly what this project's about. Perth contains the Salutation Hotel, a plaque on which announces it to be Scotland's oldest (its exterior paint-job might make the same claim). Through the window of a more modern hotel I see a lecture room filled with OAPs watching a young woman give a slide-show talk about a polar expedition. Most of them are still awake. A kilt shop offers tiny versions of the garment labelled 'bottle dressers' – possibly the most unappealing gift you could imagine. A sporran shop is called 'Janet Eagleton MBE & Son'; I do hope he catches up in the honours stakes one day.[2] The Perth Concert Hall advertises its forthcoming productions with posters whose 'celebrity' names need bracketed explanations of which shows they've been in; always a bad sign. Both *Emmerdale* and *Dancing on Ice* get mentions.

There are several Polish shops; some of the beauty treatments at the Polish hairdressing salon sound terrifying – 'microdermabrasion', 'cavitation peeling', even an 'algae mask'. One tiny street is called Cutlog Vennel, another Oliphant's Vennel. The word is common in Scotland, and is derived from the Old French word *venelle*, meaning 'alley'. On the pedestrianised street is a sculpture that seems to be a silver ring, about eight feet in diameter, hovering at waist

___

2. A BBC local radio presenter received an MBE and insisted that his work email address be changed to incorporate it. No, really.

height while two bronze men stand at opposite sides of it. You soon realise that they're supporting the ring, but the effect is still incredible. Further along a street performer has crafted a sleeping Labrador from damp sand. More conventionally, a guitar-playing busker with his own mic stand and backing track sings 'Mrs Robinson' by Simon and Garfunkel. A few paces away stands an old man in bottle-bottom glasses, tiny bits of tissue paper covering the shaving cuts on his chin. He claps along enthusiastically and entirely randomly, bending slightly at the knees, giving defiant arm thrusts whenever the music reaches a crescendo, and indeed whenever it doesn't. Occasionally he joins in with a single word of the lyrics, usually when the busker is halfway through the next line. It must drive the busker mad, I think. Then I realise the old man is the only reason I've stopped to watch, and the reason I feel obliged to throw a quid into the guitar case.

I have lunch in a café called Delicious run by a woman who looks Thai but sounds 100 per cent Scottish. Sooner or later, surely, I must hit the Scotland of *Local Hero*, of tiny villages with impenetrable accents. The Cairngorms are waiting due north of here – it can't be long, can it? Talking of which, the extreme rurality provides me with an idea for tonight's accommodation. I've done everything from hostel through pub and B&B to chain hotel via quirky independent – the one thing I haven't done is country-house hotel. It's time for a treat, is it not? There's a likely-looking candidate which I must be able to reach on buses from here. In fact, looking at the map it's hard to see how buses could avoid going there: there are really only two roads north from here, which form an 'o' shape with the hotel at the top. I make a call and enquire whether they have a single room for tonight. They do, says the woman. I reserve it. She asks what time I'll be arriving. Afraid I'm not sure yet, I say. Oh, she says, well, drinks and menus for dinner are at 7.15. I say I'll do my best. I put her somewhat terse phone manner down to the fact that she's probably busy, and look forward to a bit of luxury at the end of another hard afternoon on the buses.

Back at the station a suitable itinerary does indeed present itself. Menus and drinks at 7.15 are a distinct possibility, even though the first bus, the M91, is 20 minutes late because of flooding further south. We're taking the left-hand side of the 'o'; the A9 then the A86 (both single-carriageway most of the way). Just north of Perth there's a tiny hamlet called Waterloo, built for the widows of the soldiers who died there. Then Dunkeld, which has a hotel advertising a Rod Stewart tribute night, as well as a building with a huge panda logo outside it, which turns out to be the Scottish headquarters of the World Wildlife Fund; strange to find such a huge organisation in such a tiny place. The Tay flows alongside us to the left, the largest river in Britain by volume. The slopes are getting a bit rockier now, but they're still largely covered with fir trees, making them hills in my book, not mountains. When will the really big furniture start? A bird to the east of us flies into the wind, its flapping wings doing nothing but keeping it stationary. I always envy this: give me the option of being any creature in the world and this is what I would choose. Only today does it hit me that this is a 'journey' thing. We love travel, but equally we know that each step is a step closer to the end. A bird doing this, however, gets the sensation of travelling without actually getting any closer to journey's end. A feathery taste of immortality.

The sheer amount of space surrounding us gives time

for reading, which is why before we reach Pitlochry I know that in a park overlooking Sydney Harbour there's a cairn built with 1,750 stones, one from each parish in Scotland, commemorating the role of Scots in establishing Australia. And that the word 'spree' (as in shopping) comes from *spreidh*, a cattle-stealing raid undertaken by Highland warriors into the Lowlands. And that the Nae Limits activity centre, which we pass just before Pitlochry, offers 'black out bungee jumping'. It's named not for the effect it has on you, but because you do it at night, in the pitch dark.

Pitlochry itself offers the trip's first man in a kilt, though he doesn't look entirely comfortable; some sort of promotional thing going on? The signs advertising retirement apartments sum up the town's overall feel. Pitlochry is also home to Bell's, a reminder that we're now in whisky country (don't you dare put an 'e' before the 'y' — that's the Irish stuff). The Scots are pretty canny at marketing their national drink. At marketing full stop, in fact: the legendary Greyfriars Bobby, the dog who continued to sit by his owner's grave in an Edinburgh cemetery, now turns out to have been two dogs. When the first one died a local restaurant owner, who'd been benefiting from the resultant tourism, quickly had him replaced.

Onwards again, the A9 climbing now, a valley opening up below us to the left. Near Blair Atholl we can see, on the other side of that valley, some sort of refinery or mine; it's the only thing that's spoiled the view all day. Near Dalwhinnie, where there's another distillery, the cloud starts to come down, hitting the top of a hill so that it looks like the ground is on fire and smoking. Due east of here, between us and Balmoral, is a mountain (that's the official word — they still seem hilly to me) called the Devil's Point. Its Gaelic name actually means the Devil's Penis, but Queen Victoria's gamekeeper John Brown was too embarrassed to say that to her, so he thought it up on the spot.[3] There must be something about naming geographical features in this way: Wales has a mountain called Lord Hereford's Knob, while England stays with the satanic theme but changes the anatomy – there's a cave in Derbyshire called the Devil's Arse, because of the flatulent noises made by the water in it.

There's still lots of heather around. Charles and Di lay in the stuff near Balmoral on their honeymoon. He treated her to readings from books by the conservationist Laurens van der Post. (And we wonder why it all went wrong.) Until this trip I'd never really thought that much about our royals, at least not about how much their history is Britain's history. But when one of the country's most popular pub names is based on a tree that had a fleeting connection with a king, you're reminded how crucial they were. You remember how recently it is that they lost their power to govern us. And even now, when the Queen does nothing more than go to Parliament once a year to read out a speech someone else has written for her, they remain the nation's favourite soap opera. What a storyline it's been. In 955 King Eadwig failed to turn up for his own Coronation feast, and was found in bed with a girl and her mother; he was 14 at the time. Queen Anne became so fat through food and drink (acquiring the nickname 'Brandy Nan') that her coffin was square. We've also got the royals to thank for some of our enjoyments – Henry VIII, for instance, installed the first tennis court in Britain, at Hampton Court

---

3. Strange that he should be embarrassed, given the rumours about their relationship. She was buried holding a picture of him.

(it's still used today) and for the occasional repression of our enjoyments: the same king made sodomy illegal with the Buggery Act of 1533.

The royals have literally added colour to the nation's life: the red boxes in which government ministers carry their papers were introduced by Prince Albert, that being the main colour in his family coat-of-arms. And barristers wear black robes because they're in mourning for Queen Mary II (she only died in 1694 – give it time). Okay, the family which has ruled Britain for three centuries can seem barmy (Edward VII had the jeweller Fabergé make precious-stone-encrusted models of his pigs and chickens), and occasionally uncaring, as when Walter Monckton's retirement after 20 years' unpaid service to Edward VIII was marked with a cigarette case on which his name was misspelled. And okay, sometimes the pomp descends into farce: when extra loos were installed in Westminster Abbey for the Queen's 1953 Coronation, a check was performed to ensure that if they were all flushed at the same time the BBC microphones wouldn't pick up the noise. But by and large I feel sorry for the family. When the 10-year-old Princess Elizabeth told her sister in 1936 that their uncle Edward had abdicated, Margaret replied: 'Does this mean you'll be the next queen?' 'Yes, some day,' came the reply. 'Poor you,' said Margaret.

Just before Newtonmore a middle-aged woman gets on, engaged in a heated mobile-phone discussion with her father. It ends, at least as far as her audience on the bus is concerned, when she leaves us in the village itself, the last line we can hear being: 'Dad, I'm not going to argue with you about this now, I need to collect my son then go home to make a chocolate torte.' One of her replacement passengers is an old lady in a purple bobble hat, a red coat and yellow wellies. Somehow she brings it off; Vivienne Westwood would charge thousands for that look. Between here and Kingussie, on the railway line that's been snaking alongside the A9 for chunks of the journey, I finally see a train, a modest two-carriage blue-and-purple Scotrail affair. It prompts thoughts of what I'll be doing at the end of the trip, whenever it comes – taking a sleeper back down to Ingerland. The 'Welcome to Kingussie' sign displays the same message in Gaelic too, just as prominently as the English version. Jo Caulfield and I chatted about this: she said you never hear Gaelic spoken on the mainland, although there are two state schools in Edinburgh that use it. It is spoken on the islands, however, and is much more of a living language than Cornish.

In Kincraig some lads play football in a field as a horse watches over the hedge, looking for all the world like it might shout, 'On me head, son!' Loch Alvie hugs the road just before Aviemore, its stretch of blue to the right making a change from the purple and yellow of the hillsides. The clouds are getting lower now, rolling down one of the hills like a slow-motion avalanche. Finally they unleash their contents, just in time for me to get soaked as I step off the bus in Aviemore. Having established in Kendal that a £6 golf umbrella lasts a couple of minutes, I establish here that a £10 one lasts a couple of days. Oh, well, at least there are several hiking and camping shops opposite the bus stop (no station here), so sourcing a replacement isn't hard. In fact this one-street town has precious little *besides* hiking and camping shops. It's something of a relief when the Grantown bus comes along within 20 minutes. Like today's other two buses it's really a coach, though an older one – those clunky 1980s switches cover the dashboard again.

Only a 16-mile hop this time. The driver's from London, a would-be comedian, his repartee extending all the way from (of the malfunctioning ticket-machine) 'It thinks it's cleverer than us – it isn't!' to (when a woman gets on with a collie dog that shakes itself) 'I've already had a shower today!' We're off the A9 now, which heads north to Inverness; instead we take a succession of minor roads north-eastwards, in the general direction of Elgin (whose 7th Earl had a taste for marbles), and also somewhere with surely the least glamorous name of anywhere in Britain: Keith. In the nineteenth century someone published a history of the town called *The Chronicles of Keith*.[4] The first village we go through, by contrast, delights in the name Boat of Garten; there used to be a ferry over the River Spey here. Today the river is rising almost noticeably because of the rain. The driver and a female passenger notice someone they know fishing on the bank below us.

'There he is again,' says the driver.

'Aye,' replies the woman. She watches the fisherman for a few seconds. 'He's not right in the head.'

The cloud has come down low now, a blanket hovering just over us. In the winding lanes it feels as if everything has suddenly got very small after the massive countryside of earlier today. But that has its own charms. A golf course. Three tiny deer in a field. The driver lets people off at non-stops, and knows them all personally. It strikes me for the first

---

4. On 2 January 1963 the Beatles flew from Hamburg to play the town's tiny Longmore Hall, the first date of a small Scottish tour. Only on arrival did they find that because of bad weather the gig had been cancelled.

time that Scottish people – this seemed true even in Glasgow, never mind up here – don't grumble like English people do. Are they hardier? More stoic? Whatever the reason, minor complaints about minor niggles just haven't been there, which is refreshing. Though perhaps I shouldn't grumble about grumbles. Stanley Baldwin said that, unlike other nations, the English 'grumble, and we have always grumbled, but we never worry . . . By the absence of worry [the Englishman] keeps his nervous system sound and sane, with the result that in times of emergency the nervous system stands when the nervous system of other peoples' breaks.' I'll remember this next time I hear that time-battered phrase 'mustn't grumble'. No, I'll think to myself – you *must*.

We reach the final stop at six o'clock. The hotel is a little way out of the town, but perfectly walkable, especially to someone who's been sitting on buses all day and has a brand new umbrella. By twenty-past six I'm strolling up the driveway of a substantial Victorian pile and ringing the front doorbell. A woman who looks to be in her fifties answers; clearly the one I spoke to on the phone earlier.

'Hello,' I say, giving my name and explaining that I'm the one who made the booking this morn—

'Yes, yes,' she says, standing back to allow me into the hallway. Her thin smile isn't one of welcome as such, rather amusement that I thought an explanation was necessary. I sense that the hotel is far from chocka.

She goes straight to the small table at the base of the stairs and puts a registration form on it, turning to offer me a pen. As I fill it in I explain why I couldn't be sure of my arrival time. She nods, and makes a vaguely interested sound. This is followed by: 'Really? Well, well!' I look up to see that she's been joined by her husband. He and I chat for a minute or two about the project, how long it's taken and so on. She maintains her smile. The captions hover over their heads: 'Unfortunate Manner' and 'Spends His Life Mopping Up After Her'.

My en-suite room is on the first floor. The striped wallpaper might be a touch chintzy, but overall things are rather luxurious. The whole building has a reassuringly solid feel: the doors are heavy and wide, the curtains thick and expensive, the twin beds firm but comfy (one for me, one for my stuff – the dream arrangement). Mr Mopper shows me how to work a TV remote control. He tells me I'm not allowed to have any of my own food or drink in the room. Then he leaves, with a reminder that it's drinks and menus at 7.15.

Lovely. I put on the news, then set about examining the room's finer points. There is a leather folder containing the usual hotel info, as well as a thinner folder of stationery. This is labelled: 'You are welcome to use the CONTENTS of this folder. However, it would be appreciated if you did not use or remove the FOLDER in order that it may be re-filled for our next guests.' Righto. Further reading reveals that smoking is not permitted anywhere on the premises (this has been underlined), and that it is best to open the windows, 'which are extremely heavy', from the bottom rather than the top. However, 'if you wish to open the windows at the top a pole is provided'. I'm also requested not to 'put wet clothes in the trouser press to dry'. The room doesn't have a trouser press. Next to the folder is a kettle and a tray containing an impressive white china teapot and two cups. There is also a small glass dish. 'Guests,' reads a laminated note, 'please place used teabags into the glass dish on the tray and NOT in the room bins.'

At 7.15 I present myself downstairs for drinks and menus.

There are only two other guests in the plushly tasteful lounge, a married couple from the Home Counties. He's tall, shy and distracted, in an intellectual sort of way; she's jolly verging on formidable. They're regulars here, which at least bodes well for the food. He's gone for a gin and tonic as his pre-dinner drink, which inspires me to do the same. We're seated opposite each other on the sofas at right angles to the fireplace. I ask how he's getting on with the novel he's reading; I haven't read it myself, but do know another by the same author, and that's just about enough to get us through a minute or so's stilted conversation. When this finishes he gives several thoughtful 'mmm's, the gaps between them gradually lengthening until they stop completely. I return to the dinner menu, and then to my iPad. Noticing that its battery is about to go, I pop upstairs to get a book. By the time I return the lounge is empty, and Mr Mopper and the Regulars can be heard in the dining room, so I get my drink, and enter. Mr Mopper, seating the Regulars at the window table (there are only five), looks up, alarmed. 'We're not ready for you yet!' he says, turning the alarm into a laugh only in the last couple of words. 'Won't be a moment.'

'Oh,' I say. 'Right.' I return to the lounge, where I have time to read three sentences of my book before Mopper appears in the doorway.

'Okay.' He smiles. 'All ready now.'

I stand up.

'Shall I get a tray for your drink?' he asks.

The glass holding my gin and tonic is a good-quality one, with a pleasing heft, but nevertheless I think I can manage. 'It's all right,' I say. 'Thanks anyway.'

My assigned table is the one between the Regulars and

the door. I'm sitting sideways on to them, in a direct line, so although he's facing me his view of me is blocked by her. Even when I look to my left all I can see is her back. Good – no danger of awkward eye contact.

They get their starters before I get mine (it'll be like this throughout the meal). 'Lovely soup,' she says.

'Is it? Mmm, mmm. Good, good. Mmm.'

'How's your terrine?'

'Excellent. Mmm. Excellent. Just . . . just right. Mmm. Mmm.' Then some more 'mmm's until he again quietens down.

My salad is also excellent. Just right. As, when it comes, is my lamb. By this time, of course, the Regulars have had their main courses for a while, and mutual satisfaction has been confirmed.

'I must remember to book the car into the garage when we get back,' she says.

'Oh, yes,' he replies. 'Of course. Needs looking at. Mmm. Mmm.' The way he peters out after each comment reminds me of the cooling sounds of a recently boiled kettle.

After they've finished their mains he stands up and announces he's going for 'a short walk'. In this weather? But he goes upstairs, not outside. He's taken his *Telegraph* with him. Oh Christ. On his return Mopper enquires if they want any dessert.

Mrs Regular replies that she simply doesn't have room. 'The *thought* of sponge pudding,' she says. 'Be it ever so light.'

My lamb is long-finished now, and I've had my eye on the walnut parfait ever since kick-off, but of course I have to wait until Mr Regular gets his ice-cream before I'm allowed to see the menu again. The parfait's worth waiting for, however.

Mopper asks if I'd like to round things off with a whisky. Not normally my drink, but as we're near the Spey, a river renowned for its whisky-generating qualities, I go (in every sense) with the flow. The Cragganmore, distilled very nearby, gets a good billing: 'on the nose it is fragrant . . . the finish is long and dry with perhaps a hint of peat smoke'. To quote Mr Regular: mmm. It's OK, I suppose, if you like that sort of thing. Which, despite all flow-going efforts, it seems I still don't.

Oh, well. Whoever said luxury was about enjoying yourself?

The woman in the 4×4 parked near Grantown's bus stop is obviously waiting for someone on the 34X, which I'll be taking for the rest of its journey to Inverness. To fill the time she's reading a paperback, the front cover of which shows a buff, bare male chest and the title: *Cocktales*.

The Stagecoach single-decker, very possibly the same bus as last night, arrives at 8.50 on this bright but chilly Thursday morning. It's £5.50 for the 35 miles to Britain's most northerly city. This procures an hour and a half's worth of scenery. It's thickly wooded stuff at first, as we wind westwards through Dulnain Bridge (whose GARAGE sign has a big spanner wrenching the 'E' away) and Carrbridge, whose golf course has a tin hut for a clubhouse. Then it opens out as we reach the A9 and head north. Were we to head south, a partly worn road sign tells us, we would return to 'Pert'. (Don't we all dream of that?) The hills are alive with the sound of rockfall, or at least they would be if it weren't for the wire netting covering the bits of rockface that loom at the sides of the road. (Still no proper mountains, though. Do I get those after Inverness?

And do I get *Local Hero* there too?) This is the craggy beauty that has people coming to Scotland from all over the globe. The only bit of rock that isn't quite as beautiful is the one on which someone's graffitied INDEPENDENCE NOW in white paint.

Now call me thick (I've had worse), but I've never put the 'Ness' in 'Loch Ness' together with the one in 'Inverness'. Only today, as I monitor the map and see signs for businesses like Loch Ness Leather, does the watery penny drop. The city's name means 'Mouth of the River Ness', the river that connects it to the loch running south-west from here for over 20 miles. This still doesn't make it Scotland's biggest by surface area (that's Loch Lomond), but its incredible depth – it could hide the Blackpool Tower with over 200 feet to spare – does give it the volume record.[5] Plenty of room, then, for Nessie to spread her flippers. The monster is a protected species under the 1912 Protection of Animals Scotland Act.

The first part of Inverness we reach today is an industrial area, including a metal-detector factory. Somehow that feels reassuringly old-fashioned, a connection with the days when Britain actually *made* things. These days you can probably get an app that turns your iPhone into a metal detector.

By this point I've got used to hearing all the things you think are Scottish linguistic myths but aren't: 'sh' instead of 's', for example, as in 'pish'. The only one left gets ticked off by an old lady who leaves the bus with me at Inverness station. To the driver's 'See you again soon' she replies, 'Och aye.' (A friend of mine once saw a factory in Scotland owned by a Japanese firm called Okai. Oriental humour?)

---

5. It could hold all the water from all the lakes in England and Wales combined.

Inverness was the first place other than London ever to host a British Cabinet meeting. It happened in 1921, to discuss an emergency situation in Ireland – David Lloyd George was on holiday in Scotland, and as he was the PM everyone else had to come to him rather than vice versa. The city's motto is 'a hundred thousand welcomes'. This means two from each of its inhabitants. It doesn't feel like a city at all, in fact, more of a town; somewhere like Nuneaton (although Nuneaton has a higher population). There's one small modern shopping centre but overall this place seems to have settled not just for 'town' but for 'town of the mid-1980s'. Not in a bad way, though – there's just a feeling that when you're this far north of everything, what's the point in a city being trendy? The effort would look ridiculous.

The map splits Scotland into three potato-shaped sections, each sloping bottom-left to top-right: everything from the border up to Glasgow and Edinburgh, then everything up to Inverness, and then everything north of here. Inverness belongs to the top potato, not to the middle one. The street signs are in Gaelic as well as English.

I wander for a while, relishing the out-of-date atmosphere that sometimes verges on the surreal. The indoor market has the usual stalls (beauty products, gifts, jokes), but also a cosmetic denture design firm. There's a plaque about the 1889 fire here, in which the only life lost was that of a guard-dog which refused to leave. Greyfriars Bobby, anyone? A poster advertises a boxing event, the fighters including Willie Limond, a man nicknamed 'the Highlander' but also someone called Jasper. Perched on the internal balcony of a café are four full-sized motorbikes. There's a shop offering mugs that bear Scottish definitions ('glaikit' means 'stupid', 'scunnered' is 'extremely fed-up'), and, within easy reach of kids, humorous condoms. 'Blow my pipe,' says one. Another, whose packet depicts Nessie, asks: 'Want to see the monster?' Flicking through the local paper I find an article about the city's male MP wearing high heels (it was for charity), plus one in the nature section headlined: 'Tomatin – home of unique great tits'. I genuinely can't tell if the pun is intended.[6]

Perhaps the most unexpected thing of all is that there's a Jamaican restaurant here. It's called 'Kool Runnings', after the film about the Jamaican bobsleigh team who entered the 1988 Winter Olympics. Its owner is the only black person I'll see in Inverness (or indeed for the rest of the trip). He's proudly sweeping the pavement outside his establishment, and gives me a cheery 'A-rite?' Pity it's too early for lunch – I quite fancy adding Caribbean to the list of British Culinary Staples.

In front of the small railway station is the war memorial. This one doesn't make me feel sad, or guilty, or any of the usual things. It fits in with the rest of Inverness and makes me feel slightly surreal. There's a list of people who were 'killed up the Nile'. The farce of war is shown by the Battle of Khartoum, where three were 'killed and died of wounds' while twenty 'died of diseases'. Perhaps that's the best way to deal with war – just think about the bizarre bits. The myth about carrots giving you good eyesight, for instance: that was concocted during World War II to cover the fact that we'd invented radar. All these German planes, went the story, were being spotted by RAF pilots who'd been munching

---

6. Just as I never can with my local paper, which proclaims itself 'Suffolk and proud'.

on the vegetable. The word 'banger' for sausage also dates from that war – their water content was so high they used to explode. But perhaps my favourite tale from the conflict is of Wing Commander Ken Gatward. It was 1942, and although we couldn't yet prise the Germans out of France, we could do something to raise the morale of captured Paris, which was suffering the indignity of daily Nazi parades. Gatward popped over the Channel, flew down the Champs-Élysées at second-floor height, then dropped a French Tricolor over the Arc de Triomphe. He also strafed the Gestapo HQ for good measure, at which the Germans 'came out and shook their fists at him'. The only casualty was the crow that got sucked into Gatward's engine. On his return to RAF Northolt he removed the bird and 'laid it to rest'.

There really is only one possible route now – the A9 up the east coast. The road atlas offers a whole page of places I've never heard of: nothing to their left but white expanse peppered with little black triangles denoting mountains, nothing to their right but the blue of the North Sea. Actually that's not quite true: I've heard of John O'Groats, of course, and also Wick, the last place of any size before it. That was the only bus I checked before the project; no point getting all that way then not being able to do the last leg. But between here and Wick – a complete mystery. Its first chapter is Inverness to Dornoch. The 25X will do the job, a single-decker (proper bus rather than coach again now). Within minutes it's brought a smile to my face, as we pass the Caledonian Stadium, home to Inverness Caledonian Thistle, commonly known as Caley Thistle. The first word is pronounced 'Cally', which is a good job, because it allowed the best British newspaper headline ever. In 2000 the lowly strugglers beat the mighty Celtic in the Scottish FA Cup, allowing the *Sun* to announce: 'Super Caley Go Ballistic, Celtic Are Atrocious'.

The fiddly coastline means we take bridges over two huge expanses of water, the Moray Firth and then the Cromarty Firth. Fields stretch up to the hills, some of them covered with bright yellow bales of straw catching the midday light. On the other side of the water is the Black Isle (actually a peninsula, joined to the mainland by one of the coastline's fiddles), so called because the snow never settles there during winter. It'll be in the news in a couple of weeks' time, when the last-ever speaker of its native dialect, Bobby Hogg, dies at 92. There will be the usual mourning for 'another precious part of our linguistic heritage, etc., etc.', ignoring the fact that new parts spring up all the time. Perhaps Bobby would have preferred some mourning for him, especially seeing as at the end he had no one to talk to. The dialect had three sets of words for 'second fishing line'.

We travel on through Alness, with its bike shop called Mellow Velo, and Invergordon with its Purple Turtle Bistro. A woman takes out her mobile, dials a number, waits, says, 'I'm on the one o'clock bus,' waits again, then hangs up: that's the way to do it. The scenery is spoiled for a while by rusting oil rigs squatting in the firth (they're round, like wedding cakes that have rotted), then, in Milton, by the trip's only seriously vandalised bus shelter. Its plastic glass is moss-stained and cracked, its metal frame graffitied by (I'm assuming this is a tag) 'Pink'. Presumably 'F.T.P' refers to what Rangers fans say about the Pope. In Tain, which has a carpet shop called Cutting Corners, we pass a schoolboy smoking while his friend eats chips, the latter watched carefully from a nearby rooftop by a seagull so huge that it seems unnatural. Although we're nearly at Dornoch by now, we pause here for another trip 'only': a change of driver. The woman we've had so far seems to live in Tain. Just as she has allowed the odd passenger off at non-stops, so the company doesn't mind her finishing a shift mid-journey.

For much of this journey the A9 has been like a B-road. As it has narrowed, so too has Britain; the hills of Scotland's west coast are visible in the distance. They still don't qualify for 'mountain' though, not to my mind. The ones over here on the east coast are even more modest, and now the truth starts to dawn: there aren't *going* to be any mountains. The figures next to those little black triangles on the map get ever smaller north of here. Gertrude's route took her past Ben Nevis, Britain's tallest peak, and even then she couldn't really tell which one it was; the conductor had to point it out to her. Proper mountains are grey, pointy and covered in snow. They're Everest, they're the Alps. We just don't do that in Britain, even up here. We have things that are green and red and brown, with just the occasional dab of rock if you're lucky. Their tops are round, not pointy, and even though they sometimes get covered with snow in the winter, that still doesn't qualify them for the M-word. They're hills. We do hills here, not mountains. Because we are Britain. Our only M-words are 'modest' and 'medium' and 'middling'.

And if that sounds defeatist, that isn't how it's meant. Today, near the end of this journey across my home country, it feels very comforting. It feels just fine.

There is a breed of chicken called the Dorking. It's called that because the Surrey town of the same name bred a lot of them in the nineteenth century, although the breed was actually first introduced to Britain by Julius Caesar. This information comes from the booklet *Know Your Chickens*, which I find in a Dornoch gift shop.

The town has character, not to mention a hotel in what remains of its castle, but under normal circumstances (i.e. if I were driving) I wouldn't have chosen to spend two hours here. But the trip has hardened my resolve in the face of two-hour waits. They are now a stroll in the park. Or rather, in this case, a stroll round the town that forms part of the Scottish county of Sutherland, which despite its location on the map actually means 'southern land' in Norse (the Vikings once having ruled here). Southern, that is, compared to Caithness, the only county north of here. Everything depends on where you're standing.

Even the drizzle can't get me down. I have a cup of tea in one of the cafés catering to the mainly American tourists who keep Dornoch going – though only a few of them are around today. I survey the church that bills itself as 'Scotland's smallest cathedral', which is rather like Danny de Vito billing himself as 'the world's smallest giant'. A respectful half-dozen of us shuffle around it, taking it in turns to examine the building's various points of interest. A large woman audibly breaks wind. Dornoch also boasts a museum of its history, the sort that's just a single room of stuff with a VHS playing on a loop. People are doing what people always do in British museums – shuffling along, spending ages painstakingly reading every word of the text beside each exhibit, then having a two-second glance at the exhibit itself before shuffling to the next thing. I adopt my usual tactic of starting at the end; this way you don't feel you're on a production line.

The museum's quite good, actually. You learn that

Dornoch's golf course is rated in the world's top 15; Tom Watson said it gave him 'the most fun he'd ever had on a golf course', though what he got up to isn't specified. You learn about nearby Skibo Castle, which in 2000 hosted the wedding of Madonna and Guy Ritchie, presided over by the Reverend Susan Brown, minister at Scotland's smallest cathedral. The castle was built by Andrew Carnegie, the local boy who had moved to America and made his fortune from steel.[7] Impressive as Skibo looks, the best castle round here is surely Carbisdale, known as the 'castle of spite'. It was built on a hilltop in 1907 by the Duchess of Sutherland, who had fallen out with her family. Its tower has clocks on three sides, but not the side facing Sutherland, as she literally didn't want to give the time of day to her relatives.

Eventually, at 3.30, the X99 to Helmsdale looms into Dornoch's main square to collect me and several school-children. We pass through Fourpenny, which despite the lovely name is one of those non-existent places. Fair enough; who'd want to build anything to spoil the scenery round here? The land is flat now, all the way from here on the coast to a few miles inland, where the hills start. A flock of geese swoops in a perfect parabola to our right, as if to see us on our way. For miles and miles of the approach to Golspie you can see a monument on a hill overlooking the town. Known locally as 'the Mannie', it's a 100-foot plinth and statue of the 1st Duke of Sutherland, who in the early nineteenth century booted thousands of local farmers off their inland properties to make way for sheep. The farmers were forced out to the coast,

---

7. He sold his company in 1901 for $480 million. Not in today's prices – 480 million of your 1901 dollars.

despite massive and violent protests. Incredible, then, that the monument should have been built by public subscription – though in recent decades people have been trying to knock it down again. In 1994 someone had a go with dynamite.

On the hills overlooking the next town, Brora, are several dozen electricity pylons, marching away into the distance in spindly single-file; you feel that at any minute they're going to lose their balance. Brora itself has a women's clothes shop called Pandora's Emporium, and an ice-cream shop called Capaldi's, which used to be owned by the family of actor Peter Capaldi; what wouldn't we give to see his most famous creation, foul-mouthed Malcolm Tucker, serving the rum 'n' raisin? Brora is most famous, though, for its wool industry, which is still thriving today. They don't seem to have needed the protectionist measures offered to their English counterparts in the seventeenth century: the Burial in Woollen Acts made it illegal not to be buried in the stuff. You even had to have your coffin lined with it.

Several firsts happen on the run-in to Helmsdale. The first stretch of beach appears on our right. It's fairly grubby, but it is sandy and it does have waves breaking on it. The first fishing trawler appears, quite a distance out to sea. And we see the trip's first house with a Scottish flag flying on a pole in the garden.[8] But none of these things really catch my attention, because I'm too busy dealing with a last rather than a first. Just west of Helmsdale, we reach the edge of page 57 in my road atlas. So I turn over to page 58. Helmsdale's at the bottom-left. Most of the page's right-hand side is, of course,

---

8. For all the talk (and indeed graffiti) about 'independence now', it'll be the trip's *only* one.

sea. And there, in the top right-hand corner, where the white of the land slopes eastwards to push back the blue, are those three little words: John O'Groats. That's it. I have turned my last page. This is a momentous event in itself; to map junkies, seeing your destination on the page means a little part of you has done the journey already. But there's something of more practical significance – I realise just how few towns, and therefore buses, stand between me and journey's end. It hits me what today is going to be: the last full day of the trip. Tonight we dine in Wick; tomorrow morning my Le will acquire its Jog. For a few minutes I feel slightly deflated – how can the top of Britain have appeared so quickly? Suddenly I don't want the trip to finish, not now I've discovered the Tao of Bus. Then I remember that this is the trick long journeys always play on you; only by refusing to look for the end can you survive them, but that allows the end to jump out and surprise you. Everything has to finish sometime. This trip is going to finish tomorrow.

And here in Helmsdale I have, surely, found my *Local Hero*. It's a fishing village – just a collection of houses gathered below hills that have surged back to the coast after their inland digression. The A9 crosses a bridge high over the Helmsdale river as it flows out to sea, then the village is on the left. Disembarking, I smell the salt of the sea for the first time since Cornwall. Two trawlers are chugging back into harbour. All that's needed is for Burt Lancaster to fly in by helicopter and the movie will be complete. I do a circuit of the village, taking in the fishing tackle shop (closed – it's just gone five now), the fish and chip shop (not yet open) and the convenience store. There's also a 'collectables' shop, one of those where unless you're interested in collecting junk there's probably not much for you.

A hearty breakfast this morning meant no lunch for me, which in turn now means an urgent need for dinner. One of the two pubs (modern, converted from a terrace of houses, has a pool table) does me a vegetarian bake, the only disappointing thing about it being that the woman behind the bar who brings it to me is from London. We get talking, and I ask how she ended up here.

'Just fancied a change of pace.'

I tell her about the woman in charge of the museum in Dornoch. She was from London too. She'd 'followed a friend up here'.

'Yeah. You get a lot of that. People come from northern cities too – Manchester, Leeds, all over. People want to get away from the violence.' Uh-oh. Something tells me *Local Hero* is disappearing off the bill here. 'I'd say . . . what? Forty-five per cent of this village is English now.'

And there I'd been hoping they'd all be like the pub's only other occupant, a friendly old boozer at the bar whose Scottish brogue might as well be Ukrainian for all I can understand it. I eat, he speaks, I laugh and nod in what I hope are appropriate places. The woman can obviously understand him, and occasionally replies, more to keep me abreast of the one-sided conversation than anything else. We all get something from the experience, each corner of the triangle enjoying it in its own way. It reminds me of the subtitles American cinemas had to add when they showed *Trainspotting*.

But then over the road at the other pub the dream finally dies. There are a dozen people in there. The woman behind the bar is a Brummie, and almost all the others are builders from Darn Sarf. The TV is showing a quiz show I've never seen before, its gimmick, apparently, that it mixes very difficult questions with very easy ones.

'In fluid dynamics, which Greek letter represents the von Karman constant?'

Silence, both on the screen and in the pub.

'Which minor key signature is identified by two flats, B flat and E flat?'

Silence in the pub. Someone on the screen says E minor. It's G minor.

'Mr Blobby has yellow spots on what colour skin?'

'PINK!' choruses the entire pub.

A guy near the telly turns round. 'We've found the level, haven't we, chaps?'

Oh, well. No mountains, now no *Local Hero* either. But who cares? As Oscar Wilde never said, the only thing better than having your preconceptions proved right is having your preconceptions smashed into a million tiny slivers. All of a sudden Alex Salmond looks even more posturing than Billy Connolly makes him out to be. What can independence mean when the mix of people on the ground is so madly unpredictable as this? We know that the Scots have been invading London for generations, often ending up as presenters on Radio 4, but the flow in the other direction was a secret. At least it was to me. This evening, finishing my pint and taking another stroll round the village, the discovery makes me laugh.

I cross the bridge back over the river, intrigued by a sculpture on the other side that caught my eye as the bus sped past. On a patch of open ground, with nothing else nearby, it's of a man and woman with their young son and baby, clearly looking into the distance. It's called *The Emigrants*, and is a tribute to the people forced off their land by the Duke of Sutherland. The plaque attached to its plinth talks of how 'they and their descendants went forth and explored continents'. And I realise I'm losing a hero here. There's a bit of *In Search of England* where H. V. Morton sings the praises of St Anthony in Roseland, a tiny village in Cornwall. It has no young people left, and its school has closed, but that doesn't seem to bother him. The fact that it's an unchanged English village is all he's interested in. He moans elsewhere in the book that 'the average city family has disappeared into racial anaemia'. Towards the end of his life he too left Britain, going to live in South Africa. Now okay, it would be silly to get all right-on about this. Values don't always travel easily over the decades, and there's still a place in my heart for Morton's essays about London. But in his writings on England I can't help seeing the worst sort of patriot, the one who wants to preserve the version of it that dates from five years before they were born.

It's the same elsewhere in the Library. Beryl Bainbridge complains that Salisbury has knocked down a theatre she remembers, replacing it with a supermarket. 'There should be a rule against change,' she writes, and it's hard to make out any irony. Similarly in *English Ribbon* Jack Hilton observes the post-war German and East European immigrants in his native Rochdale: 'I regard them as basically different from us, and like not their kind of smartness and would prefer more humility . . . [They] are a poor substitute for the number of healthy youths who are being attracted by the prospects in the dominions.' Like a lot of supposed radicals, he's actually very conservative. I can't imagine he'd like the comparison with Lord Falkland, a Royalist in the English

Civil War (and ancestor of the man the islands were named after), but I think it's a fair one. It was Falkland who uttered the words you still hear quoted with approval by some Conservatives: 'Where it is not necessary to change, it is necessary not to change.'

Balls. It's always necessary to change. People *and* countries.

The most dangerous road in Europe – that's what I'm on now, according to the guy at the bus stop in Helmsdale. This has nothing to do with drink-driving, he explained as we waited for this bus to Dunbeath, it's just that it's easy to lose concentration because the drive is so boring. Really? A dramatic coastal road rising and falling and weaving like this? Drama, it would seem, gets tedious when you watch the same one every day. But for my first-timer's money (£4.40), this stretch of coast is a thrill a minute. Either side of Berriedale the terrain gets *seriously* steep. At one point we're as high as the hill-clipping clouds inland to our left. These vicious bends make a paperclip look like a ruler, and there's nothing to protect us from the sheer drop on our right but a tiny fence. As this bus is another coach, my mind is constantly replaying the final scene of *The Italian Job*.

There is stuff to distract me, though – the ugliness of some of the remote buildings, for instance. Apparently many of the architects round here were members of the 'Grim Bungalow' movement. Then there's the hardiness of the sheep, stoically accepting the weather that's now at the heavy end of 'dreich'.[9] The pensioner in front of me has protected herself from the elements with one of those brilliantly old-fashioned see-through plastic headscarfs, the sort an elderly

_____

9. The famous Scots word deriving from the Gaelic for 'drawn out'.

actress of my partner's acquaintance once called her 'head condom'. (Putting it on, she turned to Jo and said: 'Don't want to fuck up the barnet.') The woman two rows behind me, meanwhile, subjects her companion to a monologue about how good she is at disciplining her niece and nephew. There's nothing in the opposite direction but an occasional grunt of acknowledgement. Turning round I realise that they're actually seven rows behind me; the woman's got one of those voices that carries, rather like penguins using different wavelengths to communicate over the general hubbub. When she finally gets off it's hard to tell if the hissing sound is the door or her companion's sigh of relief.

This ride is a mere half an hour, delivering me into Dunbeath at ten to seven. There's even less here than in Helmsdale, though as with there, the hills and sea lend this village an air of bigness its buildings don't deserve. Also as in Helmsdale, there's a sweeping feel to the place, the same essential layout: a huge dip of the road down into it, then a crossing high above a river, a few houses, then a climb back out into open country. The only difference here is that there's no pub in the middle, just a bar/restaurant at the top of the 'up' hill. From the outside it looks like the uncared-for clubhouse of a non-league football club, but inside it's warm and welcoming, with about 60 different whiskies behind its small bar. I've learned my lesson there, though, so have a pint of the Trade Winds bitter. The owner (inevitably a Sassenach, of the Geordie strain) asks if I want to eat – everyone else is, after all – but I stick to the beer and the incredible view over the bay. I feel pleasantly sad, wallowing in the melancholy of this being the last night of the trip.

Reading about Dunbeath only heightens the mood: it was

here, in 1942, that the Duke of Kent died when his RAF plane hit a hillside. He was the second of Queen Mary's sons that she had to bury, and there would be another (King George VI) before she finally hung up her own tiara.

There's something about sitting here, gazing out over the sea, that doesn't feel quite right. As I walk back down into the village, still with a while to go before the Wick bus arrives, the answer comes to me. I take out my phone and call Jo. The daylight's really beginning to go now, and the display burns brightly in the gloom, throwing out the single word 'Home'. We fill each other in on our news; I hear how Barney has been, tell Jo that I should be home in a couple of days. Then I tell her I've just been looking at the sea for half an hour.

'Bet you loved that.'

'I did actually.'

'Are you feeling okay?'

I explain. (Not that Jo needs it – her thinking is 40-odd years ahead of mine.) It's the insignificance. That feeling I got in Bristol, the comfort to be derived from feeling small. *That's* what the sea can do for you. I always thought its sameness was boring, those millions of acres of water spread out before you, each one exactly like all the others. But that's the whole point, isn't it? The immensity of it, the vastness; something so huge you can't help but be bullied by it and made to feel tiny. No matter what you do, or how much you achieve, or how big and clever you think you are, if you bring those feelings to the sea they'll just dissolve in it. Nothing matters here – certainly not you. From now on I'll be glad you're never more than 72 miles from the sea in Britain. As I finish the call, and wander up the other hill in a darkness that's almost total, I think of Dylan Thomas. I always used to love his lines about how you shouldn't 'go gentle into that good night', how you should 'rage, rage against the dying of the light'. Live life to the last drop and all that. But that was before I saw rage – and its cousin fear – as a bad thing. How can it be good to die angry? Surely the best life is the one that accepts it has to end.

The bus appears, the very untrendy coach they call the X97. Whoever it was who said if you find yourself on a bus after the age of 26 you're a failure got it wrong. If you find yourself on a bus after the age of 26 and you're not okay with it, *then* you're a failure. The sea and buses, good for both the soul and the ego. They whip you into shape.

I get on board, and take out my money. 'Single to Wick, please.'

9

In which we reach the end, and learn that it's a beginning

'I have breakfasted with you, and shall sup with my Lord Jesus Christ.' The last words of Robert the Bruce. I, on the other hand, have breakfasted with a very interesting B&B owner in Wick, and shall sup on the Inverness to London sleeper.

Last night's drive to this, my penultimate destination, was a 40-minuter on the A99, the A9 having headed west to Thurso. For much of the trip I couldn't tell the land from the sea, or the sky from either of them. Very appropriate, then, that one of the places we passed was called Blackness. Another was Thrumster, a name that might have to be given to one of Barney's toy cars when I get back home. Apart from the villages, or rather scattered collections of houses, the only time I could see what was happening was when we passed a bonfire in a field near a place called Lybster. Even then I could only see the flames, not what was being burned, or who was burning it. All very *Wicker Man*.

We arrived at 8.44 p.m. My room had a 'Jack and Jill' bathroom, namely one shared with another room on the other side of it. Each of us had a door leading directly into it, which could be locked from the inside. Not an arrangement I'd necessarily be keen to repeat, but still, another first. The occupant of the other room was a Jack rather than a Jill, by the sounds of things, unless she does something standing up that women normally don't. He was long gone by the time I hit the breakfast room for the trip's final fry-up, leaving only me and the proprietor. We fall into a chat about the project (unsurprisingly many of his guests are Lejoggers), as well as about Wick and this part of Scotland in general. I didn't know how battle-scarred it was: the first German bombing raids during World War II were aimed not at Britain's capital but at its north, as part of Hitler's efforts to keep the Royal Navy out of Scapa Flow so he could capture Norway. The first Luftwaffe raid on Britain was in October 1939, killing 16 sailors in the Firth of Forth. The first British civilian to die in the war was an Orkney man on 16 March 1940, while on 1 July 15 people were killed right here in Wick. Scotland also saw the last air battle of the conflict, off the Aberdeenshire coast on 21 April 1945, just a few days before the ceasefire was agreed.

Yet despite all this, the story I hear from the proprietor is one of union, not division. 'There was a prisoner-of-war camp near here, in Watten,' he says. 'It was so remote that whenever any Germans escaped, within a few minutes they were praying to get recaptured. After the war lots of them stayed in Britain. They'd been accepted by the locals and they liked it here. Lots of them married local girls.' Another little chip comes loose from our bombastic national myth.

The last morning of the trip is a peach, the sun gods blessing my last perusal of a town. Handy, this, because Wick doesn't have too much cheer of its own. One of its chippies has closed, and even a church is up for sale – £100K, in case you're interested. The particulars are listed in usual estate agent's style: 'the building incorporates a spire . . . seating at ground level . . . as the property is currently empty, early entry can be given'. Wick also has surely the world's only shop specialising in 'TV, videos and fishing tackle'. A newsagent displays a sign saying that 'as a mark of respect to the 96 Liverpool supporters who died in the Hillsborough disaster . . . and the following weeks of blatant lies the *Sun* newspaper printed, the *Sun* will no longer be available'. The local newspaper reveals that the major sport round here is shinty, while a sign outside the Camps bar says that it was Wick's first to reopen when prohibition came to an end in 1947. *What?* Here, in the land of the hard stuff? But it's true. An Act of 1913 gave Scotland's communities the chance to vote for temperance, and Wick was one that said yes, bringing down the shutters on its pubs and bars in 1922. If you knew the right people, however, and the right knock to give on the door, you could still find a dram. One illegal 'shebeen' operated right behind the police station. Twenty-five years to the day after the law came into force it was repealed.

Wick might not be the most inspiring place, but it does offer something no other place on the planet can compete with: the chance to stand in the world's shortest street, as recognised by the *Guinness Book of Records*. This is Ebenezer Place, all six feet nine inches of it. The only thing it contains is the door to the No 1 Bistro, part of Mackays Hotel. The hotel occupies a triangular site, and when it was built in the 1880s the council deemed this, the thin end, to be a street, and ordered the owner to put a name on it. There's no one around, so after a couple of tries I am now able to say, for the rest of my life, that I once jumped the entire length of a street in one go.

And then 9.40 a.m. draws near. Part of me doesn't want it to, but I force myself to go and wait at the bus stop near the bridge in the middle of town. I take out my collection of tickets, all carefully numbered with the journeys they relate to. Forty-five buses have brought me from Land's End to here. These little pieces of paper, which people always throw away, often as they leave the bus itself, have carried me across Britain. They've shown me the country of my birth, the humdrum little heroes.

The X77 arrives. It's a white coach with blue-and-orange fittings, and has seen at least a couple of decades' service. It's also empty, this being only its second stop. I get on and ask the driver – a Londoner, naturally – for a single to John O'Groats. He sells me one for £3, and I pocket the ticket safely along with all the others. I take a seat on the front row, on the left, praying that he won't ask me why I'm going there. I don't want this to be anything other than a normal bus journey. And, bless him, he doesn't. It's just a day at the office for him, the forty-sixth and final bus ride for me. The countryside's totally flat now, and as the bus bumps along the narrow and dilapidated A99 (its edges are crumbling away at points), the project feels like it's coming to a suitably remote end. Over to our right the North Sea glints in the sunlight. With no hills to hold it back, the wind howls around us like a demonic Highland pipe. One of my lasting memories of the project will be of Britain's wind turbines; I see my final six now, though only five are whirring. The last one must be turned off. It looks like a sulking child.

We pass a cyclist going in the other direction – a Jogler starting his odyssey? I remember that walker on the first morning near Land's End, just about to finish his. Then there are some cows in a field, two of them engaged in an attempt to add to the numbers. The 16-mile route is lined with bungalows, a few farm buildings and not much else. We're far removed from the madness of Britain's property market now; until recently, when a house fell down the owners would just build a new one, leaving the other as shelter for sheep. The last village we pass through is Keiss, a handful of old houses with a few handfuls of modern ones placed around them. The driver pauses for 30 seconds to let anyone who's been waiting for him appear from their house. No one does. I'm still the only passenger. Then, although the map tells me there's a place called Auckengill, there doesn't seem to be anything there. Freswick is nothing more than a derelict stone barn. My final ride is going to be a solitary one.

There is almost no other traffic on the road now. Despite this an old man drives his Hyundai slightly slower than I could push it, and we're forced to overtake him. That simply doesn't feel right, so it's good when moments later an Audi overtakes us, rebalancing the highway karma. Although we're heading due north, the coastline has stretched out a bit to the east, putting several fields between us and the sea for the final few minutes of the journey.

I'm starting to feel nervous now. The thin sliver of blue ahead on the horizon gets a little wider, the white flecks on it more recognisable as waves. Then there's the sign: 'John O'Groats – A Welcome at the End of the Road'. A minute later we pull into a car park. Arranged around it are a few small whitewashed buildings, very similar to those at Land's End. The bus pulls to a halt at the far side of the car park, where there is a shelter. A normal plastic bus shelter, with normal Perspex windows, just like the thousands I've passed during the last 11 days. It is 10.09 a.m. This is it.

'Here you go,' says the driver. 'John O'Groats.'

'Thanks,' I say, collecting my rucksack and standing up. I want to make these the only words that pass between us. But I can't. Something inside me needs to mark the moment, so I tell him what I've done, and how he's my forty-sixth and final bus. He offers his congratulations, and we chat briefly about Lejog, then about why he moved up here; for the peace, he says. When he goes back to London he can only stand it for five minutes and has to get straight back up here.

I step down and he pulls away, leaving me utterly alone. As it turns out there won't be anyone else here for 15 minutes. Slightly to the south, in the fields the other side of the car park, are several luxury holiday chalets, a recent attempt to rescue John O'Groats from the reputation that earned it a Carbuncle Award from the same organisation that took such a dislike to Cumbernauld. As part of the same effort the hotel a few yards to the west is closed for renovation. It occupies the site of the house owned by Jan de Groot, the fifteenth-century Dutchman who gave this place its name. He built an eight-sided table for himself and his seven sons so that no one would sit at its head and gain precedence. The café next to the hotel has been modernised too – it's a minimalist steel-and-glass thing free from logos. It's only as I'm leaving with my takeaway tea that I notice a familiar symbol on the small cardboard stands occupying each table: the green wavy-haired Starbucks mermaid. The woman behind the counter confirms that the café is operated by the company. Apparently even global giants can do 'subtle'. They need to: the other buildings are gift shops and clothes shops and a tourist information place, all very modest with nothing too tacky and nothing too loud.

Unlike at Land's End, the ground here slopes right down to

294

the sea. There isn't a beach, but there is a tiny stone harbour. I walk out along the thin concrete jetty that forms the right-hand side, a waist-high wall protecting me from a damp tumble. Right at the end is a pole with an orange wind sock, which flutters towards the east. To the west, a couple of miles out to sea, beyond a small fishing boat that has just left the harbour to start work, is the uninhabited island of Stroma. In the distance you can dimly make out the Orkneys. I survey the coastline stretching away to my right and left, around which Gnaeus Julius Agricola (the Roman general who conquered much of Britain) once sent ships to establish that we really are an island. It's obvious as you look to the left that John O'Groats isn't, after all, the mainland's most northerly point: that honour belongs to Dunnet Head, about 10 miles to the west.[1] Halfway between here and there is the Castle of Mey, a particular favourite of the Queen Mother. She loathed what the Forestry Commission did to the land round there, marking them out – as she did anyone who incurred her wrath – with her custom of 'lowering glasses'. 'Let's lower our glasses to so-and-so,' she'd say, and everyone would have to hold their drinks below table level.

So this is it: the end. I stand here, waiting for the feelings to arrive. They do, but none of them are very dramatic. None of them are The Answer or The Revelation. That's the beauty of getting older: you come to learn that travel isn't about destinations, it's about anticipation and memory. Looking back is when you do your learning. Right at this moment I

---

1. John O'Groats gets the fame and the travellers because it's one end of the longest line between two inhabited places on the mainland. The other, of course, being Land's End.

feel like John Hillaby completing his walk here: there's no big sense of drama, just a gentle feeling that 'the mosaic of my own country and its people had become a sensible pattern'. And like that guy from County Durham who cycled Lejog, and who had such a hard time heading away from home again when he stopped off there. He does complete the trip, but on arriving at John O'Groats feels none of the 'elation of a conqueror, or a cup winner; instead I only felt a mild sense of achievement, a pleasant satisfaction, a feeling that is still with me two months on as I write this journal'.

But the person I think about more than anyone else is T. S. Eliot. 'In my end is my beginning,' he wrote in *The Four Quartets*. John O'Groats isn't giving me anything other than a desire to carry on travelling. To East Coker, for a start, the village in Somerset that Eliot visited before writing that poem (hence its title – each of the quartets is named after the place that inspired it). I've been meaning to go there for years. Of course I won't find anything when I get there, other than the satisfaction of ticking something else off life's list. As I just have with Lejog.

'We shall not cease from exploration,' writes Eliot in one of the other quartets. Too true. It's time to move along again.

Twenty-four hours later, I'm standing at Liverpool Street train station in London. On the departures board, next to the train I'm taking back home to Suffolk, are four words. At first sight they made me groan in despair. Now they're just making me laugh.

As I look at them I think back on the journey down here from John O'Groats. The first stage was a taxi back to Wick. It felt strange, after 11 days of sharing my vehicles with other people; I kept waiting for the driver to slow down and pull into bus stops. But he didn't – it was foot down the whole way. Only after a few miles did it really sink in that I could direct him wherever I wanted, that once again I was master of my own itinerary. No more being dictated to by restrictive routes and tie-you-up timetables. I would let you know what the driver and I spoke about, but he was a late dose of *Local Hero*, a Scotsman whose accent would have needed industrial machinery to disentangle it. All I could pick up, as I stared at the back of his intimidatingly sinewed neck and shoulders (approximate width: eight feet), was that his daughter had just gone down to London to start university. I wouldn't fancy being the boyfriend who caused her any heartache.

Then from Wick it was an afternoon train to Inverness. The line veers further inland than the main road I'd taken northwards, so it allowed views of more of the Highlands, including, at one point, a castle undergoing massive renovation. The scaffolding was covered with blue-and-white netting arranged to form a 50-foot version of the Scottish flag. We also passed near a place called Arabella, the first time I'd heard that name since a toddler went runabout in Ilkley. At Inverness there was a wait for the sleeper service to London. It was the perfect amount of time, I realised with delight, to nip over to that Jamaican restaurant for dinner. Having ordered my beef patties and steamed callaloo (a green Caribbean vegetable), I read the framed newspaper articles on the wall. The owner was originally from Montego Bay, and after working in Scottish hotels and restaurants wanted to stay and open his own place. I'm glad he did – the grub was top-notch, as pleasing as the swagger with which he placed it on the table, adding a cheery '*Look* at that, man'. He seemed a good boss too, patiently steering a slightly hapless local lad through his paces in the on-display kitchen. Scotland seems a strange place for someone from Jamaica's sun-baked northern coast to end up. Apparently, however, there are strong connections between here and the island. Its Scottish population is descended from the 1,200 prisoners of war sent there by Oliver Cromwell in 1656.[2] Jamaica has an Inverness, an Aberdeen, a Glasgow and two Cullodens.

After dinner it was back to the railway station. On the way I passed a young woman carrying a cello case, who reacted to a text she received with: 'You little fucking mo-fo.' My private train berth awaited. I've always wanted to say that: it was the first time I'd ever taken the sleeper, and while I was a touch disappointed that neither Hercule Poirot nor any mysterious European princesses were on board, it was still an exciting experience. Having dumped my rucksack on the bed, I proceeded to the lounge car, procured a large brandy and worked out the trip's statistics. All in all, the 46 buses that took me from Land's End to John O'Groats clocked up a combined total of 1,106.53 miles. For the pleasure of those rides I was charged the grand sum of £190.65. This works out at a shade over 17 pence per mile. You can't grumble at that in Austerity Britain. While the pen was to hand I also filled in the membership form Adrian Cole had given me in Bristol. I shall soon be a fully paid-up Lejogger. I'm not sure which of the many awards I might be eligible for, but all will no doubt become clear.

When I returned to my berth the train's clackety-clack soon had me asleep. Some time later, however, I awoke suddenly.

2. The father of hip American musician Gil Scott-Heron was Scottish-Jamaican. In the 1950s he became the first black footballer to play for Celtic.

Peering round the window blind, I struggled to work out where we were. It was a city, but minutes passed before there was any clue as to which one. I always love this feeling of not knowing your location. Not that you get it that often, of course; perhaps that's why it's so special. Discovering we were in Preston, I settled back down, thinking about the last 11 days and how they've changed the way I'll see my home country. From now on I'm never going to be bored by the sea that surrounds it, or forget just how much of a myth 'crowded Britain' is, or read H. V. Morton with quite the same reverence.

But above all I'm never going to take for granted what a calm place Britain is. That feeling from Worcester will never leave me; the sense of this country having had its revolution and its empire, and being content to age peacefully. Birmingham's in there too, that moment of coming to terms with the place I ran from in my youth. W. H. Auden's words return to me: 'The world's great rage, the travel of young men.' No doubt if I'd done Land's End to John O'Groats in my twenties I'd have seen it differently, but the 41-year-old me has found it a very soothing process, a lesson in being at ease with yourself. The phrase 'Broken Britain' gets thrown around a lot these days – the image of the country as angry and violent and dangerous. But it's nonsense. Okay, we might wind each other up – as Ken Dodd says, the oldest joke in the world is that 'the people in one village think the people in the next village are barmy' – but compare us to other countries and it's amazing how amicably we deal with it all. If there's one quality Britain has that's stood out more than any other on this trip, it's compassion. Not the overly sentimental sort, rather a quiet awareness of other people and their problems, a recognition of their need for space, and occasionally, when it's needed, the willingness to help. A fellow passenger on one of my buses was a teenager, travelling on his own, who spent much of the journey loudly quoting lines from *Thomas the Tank Engine* in an American accent, as though they were part of an action movie. At times the monologue became aggressive, though never threatening. The driver kept a subtle eye on him, as he'd promised the lad's mother he would when she put him on the bus (clearly he was a regular passenger). The two women in front of me exchanged a single glance at his behaviour, but no annoyance. And that was it. There were no extreme reactions. Maybe that's an aspect of Britain that used to bore me. Now I see it as our greatest strength.

I also think about Adrian, travelling the length of the country with his son, and wonder which journeys I'll go on with Barney. Lejog is the longest slice you can cut through the cake of Britain, but it's not the only one. I quite fancy the Coast to Coast route devised by legendary fell walker Alfred Wainwright. It takes you 182 miles from St Bees in Cumbria to Robin Hood's Bay in North Yorkshire. Wainwright suggested you should dip your boots in the Irish Sea at the beginning and the North Sea at the end. How old does Barney have to be before I put the idea to him? What will Britain be like by then? What will it be like by the time he's the age I am now? I think of the country as it was in 1971, the year of my birth. Back then women still weren't allowed to work on the Stock Exchange and Spam was something you put in your sandwiches.[3] Who can possibly imagine what it'll be like in 2050? Change can come so quickly. I'd reached my twenties,

---

3. It had also, the previous year, been a Monty Python sketch. It's because computer enthusiasts tend to be Python fans that the word gained its modern meaning.

and was just getting used to the idea that the sci-fi fantasies of my childhood were never going to happen, and the world was going to carry on much as it always had, when wham, along came the internet. The man generally acknowledged as its father is an Englishman; perhaps Tim Berners-Lee will go down as the last great British inventor, before we finally give in and hand over to China. Not that his name is universally known. When he appeared in the opening ceremony of the 2012 Olympics, one American TV commentator told her viewers: 'If you haven't heard of him, we haven't either.' Her colleague suggested, without irony, that viewers should Google him.

That's all for the future, though. For now I'm here, at Liverpool Street station, looking up at those four words on the departure board. The phrase they form is so common in modern Britain that it's almost the country's motto. But for me, this morning, it has a very personal resonance. Weekend engineering work is taking place on a section of the line out to Suffolk. So next to the listing for my train it says, very simply: 'Rail replacement bus service'.

Acknowledgements

Thanks to Adrian Cole, Caroline Taggart, Pete Brown and Jo Caulfield for the fascinating chats about Britishness in its various aspects. Also to Harry Scoble, Nigel Wilcockson, Gemma Wain, Imogen Lowe and Amelia Harvell at Random House, and to Special Agent Charlie Viney.

Thanks to First Great Western and Scotrail for help with all things train (as opposed to bus), and to Harry Mount and Travis Elborough for the facts about Scarborough and Baedeker's respectively. Though doubtless being them they would each have known facts about the other subject too.

But as ever, the biggest thanks go to Jo and Barney.

Index